GUILDFORD  COLLEGE

The Advertising Kit

A Complete Guide for Small Businesses

Je

D1638025

LEXINGTON BOOKS
Lanham • Boulder • New York • Oxford

LEXINGTON BOOKS

Published in the United States of America
by Lexington Books
4720 Boston Way, Lanham, Maryland 20706

12 Hid's Copse Road
Cumnor Hill, Oxford OX2 9JJ, England

British Library Cataloguing in Publication Information Available

The hardcover edition of this book was previously catalogued by the Library of Congress
as follows:

Smith, Jeanette.
    The advertising kit : a complete guide for small businesses / Jeanette Smith.
        p.   cm.
    ISBN 0-02-929515-7
    1. Advertising. 2. Small business. I. Title.
HF5823.S619   1994
659.1—dc20   93-40134
                                                                   CIP

ISBN 0-7391-0428-4 (pbk. : alk. paper)

Printed in the United States of America

For George Arnold
a pro's pro

Contents

Preface

"I've tried it, *but* it doesn't work! "I want to advertise, *but* we can't afford it!" "Yes, we must advertise, *but* I don't know which medium to use—they all tell me theirs is the best!" There are so many "buts!"

To borrow a phrase from Lily Tomlin, "Just remember, we're all in this alone." This is an owner's manual to help you do it alone, and provide you with the know-how to make informed choices, tap into your specific market with cost-effective, money-smart advertising, and construct advertising messages that work. It's written for small business people who know they can't afford an advertising agency, and are afraid that do-it-yourself is impossible, too. It shows you that do-it-yourself can produce great advertising.

After it's helped you decide what kind of message, layout, and illustration will reach *your* consumers, it walks you through the procedures so you can do it yourself. But it also tells you how to find little or no-cost "semi-pros" when you want a little help.

The book is structured so that, with your busy schedule, you needn't read every chapter. You should, however, pay close attention to the first eight chapters, but then you can skip to only the one or two chapters which, by that time, you'll know have purpose and meaning in your customized advertising plan that precisely fits your unique needs.

A couple of chapter extras you may want to read in addition to the first eight:

• Publicity—covered in Chapter 17—is an extra, beyond advertising, that can pay off in big, big dividends. Publicity is not free advertising, but it's advertising that money cannot buy. And it, like co-op, can stretch your message far beyond what your advertising budget says your business can bear.

• You thought you couldn't afford an advertising agency? With this book, you can afford *nine* professionals! Right here—in Chapter 18—is advice, counsel, and tips from nine prominent advertising professionals. Each offers highly useful information, a how-to, or some form of instruction or guidance to accomplish a desired advertising result.

The Advertising Kit is meant to be marked up. If you're not tempted to circle or underline or highlight some of the contents, it will have missed the mark. Make notes in the margins and use sticky notes to flag sections you expect to return to from time to time. Reach for it over and over again when you need a clever idea for attracting new customers or when you need straightforward, no-nonsense advice on writing and placing an ad.

The glossary at the back of the book not only defines terms used in the book but also explains the jargon used so casually by media reps, who may try to intimidate you with their smooth sales pitches full of the lingo of their trade.

Ray Bradbury said that we've got to jump off cliffs all the time and build our wings on the way down! *The Advertising Kit* is here to help you build your wings.

1

Business Advertising: A Portrait

What Is Advertising? What Can It Accomplish? And How Does It Work?

"**D**oing business without advertising is like winking at a girl in the dark," said the late British author Steuart Henderson Britt. "You know what you're doing, but nobody else does." He was absolutely right. If *you* are winking in the dark, turn on the light, or recognize that you're wasting a lot of winks. (Think of those winks as dollars.)

When you turn on the light, you may be terribly confused. You may wonder what your ads should say and where you should place them: in the newspaper or on radio (and if on radio, on what kind of radio station). Or should you advertise mainly through direct mail or use some other medium?

And even with the lights on, you still can't see how advertising will bring in new business and yield added profits. You want to know the amount to spend on advertising, how much you can—and should—afford.

Successful businesspeople must know not only the *what, why,* and *how* of advertising but the *when* and *where* to advertise and to *who(m)* to direct the ad message. And that's not all of it. They must be wholly familiar with exactly what are the present and would-be customers' *motivations*—what makes them *want* or *need* the product or service. Or, if the advertising is meant to promote the business itself, what kind of message builds a company's image and name recognition, promotes goodwill, and produces feelings of trust and integrity?

Even with the Lights On, the Advertising World Is Confusing

The abundant technology and the diversification of media that exist today dictate a wholly different advertising approach from just a few years ago. There are television channels now that didn't exist until recently and new, highly specialized cable television stations that precisely pinpoint the interests of viewers. Radio has far greater diversification and more types of programming. Balloon and blimp advertising seem to be making a comeback and are beckoning to large and small businesses. There are media that no one previously dreamed of, such as electronic billboards with moving messages that can be purchased a day at a time. Digital broadcasting via personal computers and interactive television let consumers communicate directly with sellers or vote or play games.

As this communications explosion continues, changes in technology are guaranteed. And as they do, the number of advertising messages, on average, that every person in the United States is exposed to continues to grow past its present rate of almost 1,400 each day— 500,000 a year.

So What Is Advertising?

Ask twenty-five people what advertising is, and you'll probably get twenty-five different answers. Even advertising professionals differ in their definitions.

For most people, businesspeople included, advertising is a mystery. They have a pretty good idea what they want it to accomplish, but they don't understand the advertising process well enough to attain their goals.

There is no concise, simple definition of advertising. It is meant to inform, promote, motivate, persuade, modify behaviors, and, most important, influence the thinking and purchasing actions of its audience. Many years ago newspaper editor Arthur Brisbane said, "A good advertisement must do five things and do them all. If it fails in one, it fails in all. It must make people see it, read [listen/watch] it, understand it, believe it, want it."

To gain an understanding of what advertising is, it may help to describe what it is not. It is *not* a cure-all for dwindling sales or an outmoded product or increased competition. It is *not* an exact science with established rules that produces systematic, predictable results. It is *not* art per se, although it produces pictures and words that appear on television screens, in newspaper and magazine pages, in direct mail pieces, or on outdoor boards. There is, however, a science and an art to planning and producing sales messages, and that's what this book is all about: to guide you in the science and the art of effective, moneymaking advertising.

Have no worry that you do not have sales abilities that will transfer to do-it-yourself advertising ventures. No matter what your job description, or whether you're the business's owner or a staffer, realize that you do have selling skills. Your success in business comes from your ability to persuade, to convince, to *sell* someone on your point of view, your abilities, your skills—on your product or your service.

Selling? Persuasion? In advertising they are synonymous. Advertising is meant to *persuade* or *sell*—to influence readers, listeners, and viewers through nonpersonal paid presentations of information by identified entities on the merits of a product, a service, or a company.

If you still are bothered by the thought that you must be a salesperson in order to do a good advertising job, think of yourself as a *persuader*. And remember Ralph Waldo Emerson's saying, "Skill to do comes of doing." The more you *do* it, the better you'll become at it.

Most definitions of advertising don't differentiate between advertising and selling, between selling and persuasion, or among advertising, public relations, and publicity.

Advertising, PR, and Publicity Work Together

Advertising, public relations, and publicity often are confused and the words used interchangeably, but they are not strictly synonymous.

Advertising is public relations. But public relations is much more. It's the way your customers are treated, the way your telephone is answered. It's your sponsorship of an event that raises money or contributes learning, or anything that provides a public perception of who and what your company is.

Publicity is public relations but also news of your company, and it may be the same news you plan to use in advertising. But if a publicity release is used by media, it will be because it contains news of interest to a number of readers or listeners, not because it is meant to persuade consumers or to sell something. It will be treated as *news* and used in the *news* sections of print media and on *news* programs on broadcast stations. In credible media, there will be no charge for the space or time in which the news is carried. Publicity is thus advertising that money cannot buy.

Together, advertising and publicity can be a legitimate and effective solution to a large problem among small businesses: making buyers aware of the seller.

Benefits from the Do-It-Yourself Technique

Throughout this book you will be guided in ways to do all that will best benefit and profit your company, and in chapter 18 advertising professionals offer advice and counsel, without their costly fees.

One of the best arguments for do-it-yourself is that you can't afford not to do it yourself, and that is in terms of both money and knowledge. First, it is a rare small business that can afford the services of qualified professionals. But there is an equally important reason to take on the job yourself: You, and perhaps *only* you, have access to information about your company, product or service, customers, and financial status that will make your advertising program focused and productive. Much of the information may be in your head and not accessible to anyone else. If you must assign the job to a junior or senior staffer, even that person undoubtedly knows more and is more personally involved than any outsider ever can be and can direct a *better* advertising program on the company's behalf.

There's another plus that may heighten the beneficial effects from do-it-yourself: the news media may find your efforts and accomplishments newsworthy and give you publicity you could never acquire otherwise. It happened to a young, small sign company.

AdCraft Graphics and Mastercraft Signs in Mabank, Texas merged to form a company capable of designing and constructing signs of all sizes and shapes. An all-news cable channel offered to tape a cable spot as an extra value in combination with the commercial time chief operating officer Jim Paullus had purchased to announce and describe the company's new proficiency. (*Extra value* is a term used by media when extra services, extra time, or space, an unpaid tagline is added to a public service announcement or a special event commercial, without cost to the advertiser.) Because the newly formed company had no funds for video production, Paullus wrote the script himself and with the manager of a construction enterprise acted as spokesman for the newly merged company.

Two area newspapers, one a daily and the other a semiweekly, sent reporters and photographers and ultimately published Sunday feature stories about the merger. The publicity was advertising that no amount of money could have purchased. Paullus later remarked that one person who contacted him as a result of reading the story mentioned that he felt the newly formed company must have a very high degree of dependability because the information about the company was in a news story instead of in an ad. None of the publicity would have happened if an advertising agency had handled the cable spots.

What Can Advertising Accomplish?

Advertising enables you to reach more prospects more practically and more productively than through any other means now available, including personal selling. If you are looking for more customers or business, you can be certain that a portion of your market has not been reached, regardless of your product or the vigor of your competition. Advertising can help you to reach those potential customers.

The consumers in your particular business niche have limited dollars available, so you must be prepared and willing to fight for your share of both the customers and their dollars. "There is no way for the American economic system to function without advertising," says John O'Toole, chairman of the board of Foote, Cone & Belding, the world's eighth largest advertising agency. He explains, "There is no other way to communicate enough information about enough products to enough people with enough speed."

Among the many reasons to advertise are the following:

- To attract new customers. This may be the dominant reason for ongoing advertising when you consider that more than 20 percent of all families move each year. Twenty percent is a big gouge in your customer base; multiply that by five years, and you have a real problem.
- To reattract former customers.
- To promote the same product or service to a new audience.
- To build—or rebuild—the business's image and reputation and the public's remembrance of the business's name, product, or service.
- To fend off the competition, fighting for as big a share of your market as they can get.
- To make the public aware of a new identity because of a corporate merger or acquisition.
- To introduce a new product or a new service. People can't buy what they don't know about, no matter how much they respect and admire your company or like your other products or services.
- To establish differences between your product or your service and that of your competitors.
- To offer a "special": special prices, special features, or special hours or days.
- To add distributors or open new territories.

What Is a Realistic Return on Your Advertising Dollars?

At this point you have a general picture of advertising and what it can accomplish. Now you undoubtedly would like a realistic estimate of the return you can expect from the advertising dollars you spend.

Those who know and understand advertising say it is an investment, not an expense. Nevertheless, every businessperson wants one question answered: "If I invest so many dollars, what can I expect at the other end?" A better question may be, "How can I tell if I'm spending my advertising dollars effectively?" The return on an advertising investment can be measured in a variety of ways: traffic, awareness, image, and goods sold.

It is important to recognize that most advertising doesn't actually sell a product or a service (unless an order form is included), and it's not meant to do so. Rather, advertising is impersonal selling. It is intended to persuade, to convince, and to bring a buyer to the point of sale. In most cases, the sale still has to be made, one on one. Thus, traffic—the number of people who respond to an ad and visit your business—is a measure of advertising.

In order to purchase your product or service, customers must be aware that you offer what they need. Awareness is measured in the ongoing assessment of consumer attitudes.

Image has to do with the way consumers *think* about your company, product, or service. All advertising promotes an image—either a good one or a bad one. Everything you and your organization do, everything you say in the name of your business, says something about your image. If you're a high fashion retailer, for instance, a cluttered ad with a lot of reverse type will present the wrong image. If you're a discount store selling the same category of goods as the high fashion retailer, the ad should make your business look inexpensive. Like awareness, a measurement of whether you've achieved the image you desire comes through assessment of consumers' attitudes, which you will be exploring in chapter 3.

Ultimately the cash register tells you how well your advertising is working through the amount of goods sold.

Steps to Successful Advertising

One of the major reasons so many small businesses fail is that their operators lack the know-how to generate effective advertising. This book will teach you the basic steps to make an advertising program the effective money-making machine is *should* be.

1. *Look at where your company is now.* First, take a long, close look at your own company—both a close-up image and the full-figure portrait that the public perceives. Try to separate your judgmental evaluation tendencies about something as personal as your business from your ability to assess the facts objectively. Far too many companies act as if they have only strengths, no weaknesses. It's a natural tendency but amounts to putting on rose-colored, blinder-style bifocals.

2. *Know the customer.* The biggest problem on the part of small business advertisers is lack of awareness that 80 percent of the work must be done before construction of the advertising message is ever begun or the time or space for it is purchased. Part of the advance work is learning about the consumer. Advertising and sales have a common characteristic, and successful salespersons do exactly what is demanded of successful advertisers: learn all there is to know about the product or service and try to learn as much as possible about prospects before ever mentioning the product or service. In this way, they can tailor the sales message to the prospects' strongest needs and desires.

3. *Know the competition.* You may feel you have enough to do without keeping an eye on the competition, or you may feel you can't get enough information about them. The second reaction is better than the first but only if you use the information to your best interests. Too many small businesses keep a close watch on successful competitors and then mimic their words and actions because they feel the competition knows more than they do about achieving success. That can be a highly destructive strategy. (Later you'll see how even the big brains at Sears thought that way and how it botched their progress for years.)

It is important to know and understand the competition and use the information to improve your product or service, locate and establish your place on the success ladder, and then, like a good salesperson, tell prospects the benefits and advantages they receive from your product or service over that of the competition.

4. *Set an affordable advertising budget.* To avoid impulsively spending dollars your company can't afford in the heat of enthusiasm for the advertising program or a particular medium, allocate a specified amount before giving thought to construction of the message or the media in which it will be presented. A bottom-line figure also helps you avoid unwisely matching competitors' advertising expenditures because you may feel they may know more about media purchases than you do.

5. *Devise an advertising plan based on your company's goals and objectives and the findings from your research.* Setting goals and objectives to achieve the advertising results *you* want for *your* company is as important as setting a budget. Goals and objectives are the foundation of the plan. The plan is set to achieve public acceptance

of your product or service and devise the specific actions the public must take for you to accomplish your objectives.

6. *Thoroughly investigate a variety of media to establish which will reach your audience and produce the greatest returns in terms of audience reached, traffic produced, and sales created.* Building the right media mix to achieve your company's advertising goals requires an understanding of the information you must acquire from media representatives, which questions you must ask to gain that information, knowledge of how to compare costs and make audience comparisons among media, and when and how to negotiate better advertising rates.

Adverbabble . . . or Greek?

Advertising has its own jargon: *psychographics, demographics, geographics, positioning, audience share, advertorials, infomercials, documercials, market share,* and a great many more. Rest assured you don't have to learn to speak this Greek; just become familiar with the meaning of the words and phrases so that you can understand what media salespeople are talking about. (A glossary in the back of this book provides definitions of advertising jargon you may come up against.) Nevertheless, there are three words in the lingo of advertising you should get to know rather well: *demographics, geographics,* and *psychographics.* They are the principal avenues to getting to know your likely customers.

The demographics of your customers, consumers, or clients encompasses much more than merely how old they are, whether they're male or female, and their income bracket. It also includes their level of education, marital status, family makeup (single or two parent, dual working parents, number and ages of children, etc.), and employment status and occupation.

Geographics refers to place of residence or work. It includes climate and whether the location is urban, suburban, or rural. Geographics is important when you want to target people in a specific location. The thinking is that people with similar characteristics tend to live near each other. For example, people with similar food tastes tend to cluster in specific areas, as do people whose incomes fall within similar brackets. Another instance is retirement areas or communities where people over a certain age and with similar incomes reside.

Psychographic data give details that let you design your advertising message as if you were talking to friends with whom you are well acquainted. It includes the life-styles they maintain; their attitudes, values, and beliefs; motives that trigger their buying actions; and the extent to which they use your product or service—or would like to use it.

The Public's Perception of Advertising

People have become increasingly wary of advertising claims, and their disapproving views are inclined to transfer to all advertising, including yours.

There is sound research to support the public's attitude. As far back as 1978 a survey done by Market Facts, Inc., for *Advertising Age* showed that 43 percent of respondents not involved in advertising deemed it as having the lowest ethical standards. In a 1983 Gallup poll, which compared twenty-five occupational groups in terms of honest and ethical standards, advertising was rated twentyfourth. Only used car salesmen were rated lower. These disapproving viewpoints are inclined to transfer to all advertising, including yours, and through it to your company. Integrity and ethics are standards you will want to portray in your advertising because, as one advertising professional advises, "In the future what a company stands for will be as important as what it sells."

Now that you have a clear picture of what advertising is, what it can accomplish, and how it works, let's get on with the business of developing your advertising plan.

2

Start with the Inside Information

Look At Your Own Company. Then Set an Advertising Budget Your Business Can Afford

Look at Where Your Company is Now

Before you investigate your potential consumers and your competition, take a long, close look at your own company:

- Is the business's name easy to remember, pronounce, and spell?
- Does the name depict the kind of service or company it is?
- Does the company have a distinctive, easily remembered, easily recognized logo?
- Is the logo used consistently on all company printed materials, in addition to advertising?
- Is the company location included in all advertising (not only the full address and zip code but an identifying landmark, such as, "At the corner of Sixth and Main Streets")?
- Is the telephone number easy to locate and always included?
- Would an 800 telephone number bring in more business?

- What is the public's notion of the company? friendly? professional? aloof? helpful? other?

After you've answered these questions, you will be able to identify both your strengths and your weaknesses. By recognizing your weaknesses, you can avoid including them in the plan and set advertising goals that will surmount them.

Some of the monoliths in business—Sears is an example—at times have not recognized their weaknesses and consequently suffered severe problems. As a result of Sears's inadequacy and the competition's adeptness, KMart built itself into the number two retailer in the country behind Wal-Mart.

To get a true picture, call on others to help. Ask both upper- and lower-level insiders to rate the company, and ask outsiders, customers as well as noncustomers. The results not only will show your company's strengths and weaknesses; they will subtly tell you the company's image. And knowing your company's image is as important as avoiding weaknesses. If you find that public perception of what your company is or what it stands for is incorrect—or correct but negative—no matter how clever or sizable an advertising program you conduct, it will not be as effective as it should be.

When you've tallied the answers, which amounts to a rating of your company, put the information aside. Later, after you have gathered information about your competition and customers, call together the people within your company in whom you have faith about their ability to recognize and measure the result(s) fairly and honestly. That's when you can truly assess where the company is now and where you want it to be in the future. That's when you can develop a successful, customized advertising plan.

Set an Advertising Dollar Allotment

One of the most important—and most difficult—decisions is the right amount to invest. You as entrepreneur or chief operating officer or manager of your company know better than anybody what you can afford. No book, nor any individual, can tell you specifically where to advertise, what to advertise, when to advertise, and how much to spend on advertising.

As an investment, the dollar amount you allocate for advertising should depend solely on what your company can afford. Investing usually calls for an ongoing pay-out, and a specified allotment is called for in order to avoid over- or underspending.

Set the Allotment Now

There are strong arguments for setting an advertising dollar amount at this point, before you've devised an advertising plan and, most important, before you've talked to media salespeople. Setting the figure at this point saves you from becoming a sitting duck for impulse spending, which is easy when you are faced by a seasoned salesperson and hear a high-impact sales pitch that often promises the moon plus a few stars if you will only buy space or time in the particular advertising medium this person is peddling.

There's another strong reason for setting the figure now. You have not yet checked out your competition and therefore won't be influenced by how much they are spending on advertising. Being aware of what successful competitors are doing may tend to influence you to buy the media they use and spend similar amounts because you feel they probably know more about all this than you do. But where they advertise and the amounts they spend may not be right for your enterprise. Further, it's not the amount of dollars spent that is as important as how and where they are spent in order to reach the right consumers and to achieve your goals and objectives.

To avoid both of these hazards, set a bottom-line advertising amount *now*. The way it's spread around—the medium you choose to spent it with—can only be a guesstimate at this point, but that total figure is based entirely on what the company can afford.

Ways to Set an Advertising Budget

There are a number of different methods for devising an advertising budget and how the dollars will be divided, and each has some weakness. The method that was popular during the 1970s and 1980s was based on a percentage of annual gross income—from 4 percent to 10 percent, with the average allowance between 4 and 6 percent. The weakness is that some businesses have larger sales incomes than others. For instance, the size of most real estate sales is much higher than in any other business. Even a

1 percent allocation for this type of business can amount to a whopping advertising figure.

Probably the most popular means for calculating a figure is one in which past sales are used. But when sales decrease and a stronger advertising program is needed, there is no provision for it.

A similar method is contingent on estimates of future revenues. You predict the upcoming year's total revenues and then subtract all expenses (other than advertising) and your projected profit. Whatever is left is spent on advertising. Unfortunately, there is no money available for advertising until sales are actually made.

One of the more logical and reasonable methods is based on specifying the advertising program's goals and objectives and figuring how much it will cost to accomplish them. This is an excellent method for devising an advertising allotment for a small business, but it requires a degree of training and background before it can be accomplished satisfactorily. Later, when you've set your plan based on your goals and objectives, you may wish to consider this means as the way to divide the funds within the affordable, bottom-line dollar amount.

Probably the easiest way to figure your total advertising dollar amount is to assign all net profits to be plowed back into advertising. Last year's net profits amount is this year's advertising amount. The weakness is you can't plan ahead because you don't know what profits there will be. And if profits are low that's when you need more advertising to boost them.

Then there's the way so often used in large corporations. For want of a better name, call it prophesying. It relies on the experience, knowledge, opinions, and prophecies of respected high-level management figures. There is no reason you cannot use this method *if* your experience and knowledge qualify you to make such estimates. There are numerous corporate executives who say this technique works as well as the most sophisticated, mathematically formulated methods.

You must choose the method that best suits your company and your style of operation. Be prepared for adjustments both after you've done all your research and formulated the best possible plan for your purposes and throughout the span of your advertising program.

All you want now, however, is to determine that overall, total, affordable advertising dollar amount.

How Total Ad Dollars Are Earmarked

Budgets call for explicit, detailed assignments of dollar amounts, and as a businessperson you may be uncomfortable assigning only a bottom-line figure. So that you will have a better understanding of how your total advertising dollar amount eventually will be divided and so that you will be more comfortable at this point working only with a total figure, let's look at how the total amount will be distributed.

A good rule of thumb for a small business is the 80–20 percent—or even 85–15 percent—method. At least 80 to 85 percent is designated for the purpose of buying media—newspaper, radio, direct mail, or whatever mix you choose. (The choice can be made only after you've done all your research.) The remaining 15 to 20 percent is assigned to production costs.

Large companies and corporations that use large amounts of television or any other media that require costly production methods, usually use a different percentage spread: 60 percent for media and 40 percent for production. (There are ways you'll learn later, in chapter 11, whereby you too may be able to use television and keep production costs much lower.)

Stretch Your Advertising Dollars

Before you set an advertising dollar allotment, there are ways you should consider to stretch those dollars. The first three ways won't have much impact on the bottom-line figure you want to arrive at now. The fourth method, however, could decrease the dollar amount you must pay and increase actual advertising considerably. We will look at it in some detail.

1. Repeating advertisements saves money by saving production expenses and thereby allows more money for media purchases. Studies show that ads do not lose their effectiveness when repeated a number of times and that a fourth insertion of the same ad attracts approximately the same number of readers as the first one. Service-oriented businesses profit the most from repeating ads because what they sell doesn't change often. Grocery stores and supermarkets, however, must change ads each time they offer different products.

2. Use ads that run in newspapers or other print media as direct mail pieces. Very little revision is necessary to convert an advertisement for mailing. Sometimes a reproduction of the original ad can be used as a self-mailer when printed on heavier paper or as an enclosure in a letter, announcement, billing, or other message. There are no second charges for layout, art, or other preparation.
3. Alternate media so that you use either different publications or different broadcast stations—using the same message—or change from broadcast to print and vice versa.
4. The most cost-effective way to stretch advertising dollars is with co-op advertising.

Co-op advertising is a method by which a manufacturer or vendor partially or totally refunds advertising expenditures to a retailer. (Co-op is short for cooperative.)

Co-op is a win-win arrangement for both parties in the partnership. It expands your advertising dollars and provides additional product visibility for vendors and manufacturers. It also allows them to take advantage of your ability to buy time or space at a much lower local rate than they must pay as national advertisers.

Co-op is an arrangement whereby a manufacturer or a vendor agrees to refund advertising costs in part or in full. An example is when each new car comes from the factory it has a manufacturer's allowance for advertising for use by the dealer. The amount may be from $100 up to $400 or $500 on more expensive cars. This allows the dealer to promote the brand with greater frequency in support of the manufacturer's overall campaign.

Another example is the arrangement some very large footware manufacturers (such as Nike) have with local retailers. The co-op allowance is based on the volume of footware products the store purchases from the manufacturer, and the only restriction is that the co-op funded advertising must prominently display the brand name in the ads. The more these retailers purchase, the more dollars they receive.

In recent years some of the larger footware distributors (such as Nike) have begun to work closely with large distributors (such as Foot Locker) to provide them with advertising materials or to work hand in hand with them in preparing the materials. The reason—

manufacturers want more control over the quality and content of advertising messages.

The most common cost sharing is on a fifty-fifty basis. For every dollar you spend, there is another dollar to expand your advertising program. Cost sharing can range from 25 percent to 100 percent of your advertising space or time costs.

Co-op funds also may provide the extra advertising dollars that qualify your program for media volume discounts, thereby stretching your ad dollars even further. When, for example, the amount of space you are able to buy is doubled, the larger amount can be enough to entitle you to discounts offered by both print and broadcast media to encourage quantity purchases.

In spite of these huge benefits, it is estimated that billions of co-op advertising dollars go unused each year. The reasons? Many operators of small businesses don't understand how co-op works or think it is far too complex to be worthwhile. Certainly there are conditions imposed by the distribution or manufacturing side of the partnership. Restrictions on which medium may be used are common; in most cases, newspapers are the preferred medium. There also are rules set by individual manufacturers that include proof of performance—confirmation that a print ad or a broadcast commercial actually ran and that its contents were as agreed on.

Specially prepared advertising material, logos, graphics, and precise wording sometimes are required. But when such conditions are called for, the manufacturer usually provides the professional layouts, scripts, or recordings, with space or time to include your company's name and relevant information. This is an added enticement for many small businesses because it can amount to a sizeable savings in production costs. Even with the more limiting restrictions, you are the beneficiary of advertising you would not otherwise be able to afford.

If you have adequate funds to afford production costs, the best co-op programs are the ones that let you design your own ads so they conform to your objectives. But always get prior approval in writing of all co-op advertising—of the medium in which it will run, the dollar amount it will cost, and the copy that is to be used—especially that which is conceived and designed by you.

There is extra work involved in using co-op advertising. You must document the advertising, for example, but that means merely alerting your print media sales representative before the ad runs, so that tear sheets—pages on which the ads ran in newspapers or magazines—can be sent to your co-op partner. If co-op funding is provided for broadcast spots, you must make arrangements in advance for an extra copy, or sometimes two, of the billing—a statement of total charges by the station—and for scripts of live spots to go to the co-op backer.

Many co-op agreements state that the manufacturer will pay for a certain percentage of the space or time—say, 50 percent—as long as the manufacturer's or vendor's product receives at least half of the space or time. But this leaves 50 percent of the space strictly for your own advertising message. If you are fortunate enough to have this arrangement, keep the two sections separated in the ad so that there will be no confusion on your co-op partner's part about which and what are his half and which and what are your half of the advertisement.

If you want more information about co-op, your media rep may have all the information you need, including a list of possibilities within your field. If the information isn't available locally, contact either of the following for such information:

Co-op News
45 South Park Street
P.O. Box 633
Hanover, NY 03755–0633
603/643–2667

Newspaper Advertising Co-op Network
1180 Avenue of the Americas
New York, NY 10036
212/704–4566

Organizations representing television cooperatives and cable cooperatives are listed in chapter 11.

Put It ALL on Paper, in Detail

At this time you won't actually be dividing and assigning that overall advertising dollar amount, but it isn't too early to set up a system for keeping track of advertising expenditures. Putting the figures on paper lets you assess both before and after the way the money is spent, helps you check that the priorities it shows are in fact the priorities you want, and gives you a history that lets you look back over months and then years to see where the advertising and the apportioning worked and where one or the other requires adjustments. Without such records, you must reinvent the wheel each time you make a new assignment of advertising dollars.

The word *paper* is used loosely. You probably will enter the figures into your computer and may print them out on paper. If you do not use a computer, it doesn't matter the kind or type of accounting ledger you use, with one exception: a looseleaf notebook with ledger paper provides the flexibility of adding or removing pages.

When you set an apportionment pattern there must be space to enter the months of the year and list the separate advertising media you think you will use. This is another reason for using a flexible format; later (in chapter 7) you will make media buying decisions after you've called in media salespersons to acquire facts about each medium. The bottom-line dollar amount will not change, because it's the amount you can afford, determined objectively without outside pressures. But the places where you put those dollars and the manner in which you spread them around may change repeatedly throughout the lifetime of your advertising program.

A simple way is to list the twelve months across the top of each page and specify the media you think you will use (for instance, newspapers, radio, direct mail, Yellow Pages) down the left side of the page. Later, when you've made your media purchases, you will set up supporting pages that show each medium by name or station call number; size of the ad in column inches or length of the spot in seconds; the dates and, in the case of broadcast media, the times of day or night it ran.

Most businesses set plans, including budgets and dollar allotments, a year in advance. But the realities of business, including the extent of the effects of advertising on profitability and of economic upturns and downturns, seldom can be foreseen, so when unpredicted events happen, there may be a call for adjustments.

If you are working on paper, use pencil instead of pen—for obvious reasons. You can count on the fact there will be revisions as you go along. Later, sticky notes can be used to give you a quick tally of the most effective ads and the most cost-effective ones. Then your history can be evaluated and adjustments for the future can be made in minutes.

Close Monitoring

You will be wise to monitor your advertising closely and continually. Then, if a decisive new trend, serious changes in buyers' attitudes, or an unexpected economic disruption shows up to alter your plan, your penciled records allow you to move fast. Even a substantial change in media or postal rates can call for almost instant dollar reapportioning. Be ready, with a good eraser and a sharp pencil, to make advantageous revisions.

Monitoring alerts you to positive results from specific advertising methods or media placements, which then allow you to restudy your apportioning methods and shift or allocate more money to the more productive advertising. Conditions change constantly, and every business must chart its course by trial and error. Keep alert for changes that bring opportunities, because business is never so good that it can't get better.

Start a Copycat File

Although copycatting has nothing to do with the assessment of your company or setting dollar allotments for advertising, it is something that should be started *now*.

Start immediately to collect samples of advertising that makes an impression of one kind or another on you. As you read newspapers or magazines, or receive direct mail pieces, collect the ads that you strongly react to, either positively or negatively, and save them in a file. As you gather them, try to assess why a particular advertisement jumped out at you from a page full of advertising clutter. What is it about a direct mail piece that makes you want to respond? What draws your attention: the layout? the benefit? the message? the graphic? Make notes right then, while the reaction is fresh, because later circumstances may be different and the immediate feeling will have declined or died.

Pay particular attention to print ads in the size(s) you anticipate you may use. This file will become your idea bank, not to be copied but used to stimulate your creative juices. Each time you have an advertising message to write or an ad to construct, find a message or a layout from your file that is similar to one you wish to portray.

Some people call this the copycat method. For this purpose, let's call it OPB—using Other People's Brains. Often it amounts to using the brains of the most creative and experienced advertising professionals in the country—the ones you can't afford to hire.

Don't copy the words, graphics, or layouts—just the ideas. Use them to stimulate your own ideas. Hitchhike on their creators' knowledge, training, and experience to help you build advertising messages that attract readers and get your message through to them. Don't infringe on copyrights or plagiarize. Just use the idea.

There is additional information in other chapters about available collections of successful ads. For instance, chapters 10 and 11, about radio and television advertising, contain information about tapes and videos that present the best TV and radio commercials, how and where to order them, and the costs.

3

Targeting Your Customers

Customers Are the Yeast
That Raises the Dough

The linchpin of your advertising success is knowing exactly who are your prospects. You must know who you are trying to talk to—demographically and psychographically and perhaps even geographically—in order to separate them from that immeasurable throng of consumers called the "mass market." Herb Kelleher says, "The business of business is people." He ought to know what he's talking about; he's the guiding figure of one of the country's most successful airlines, Southwest Airlines.

This chapter helps you pinpoint your target—who you want to talk to, to get your message to, the person most likely to buy your product or service. The next chapter sets out ways and means to locate that person. You will learn how to single out from that mass market your likely future customers and to get to know their wants, needs, and buying motives. Otherwise, you'll waste your advertising money on people who will never buy from you.

A 1991 survey helped Greyhound Lines, Inc. determine who was riding their buses. That survey of passengers and potential passengers reported in *The Dallas Morning News*, told the company that:

- 58 percent of its passengers were female.
- 31 percent were married.

- 13 percent were unemployed.
- 16 percent were retired.
- 62 percent were white, 24 percent were black, and 10 percent were Hispanic.
- 22 percent were older than 55 years, 24 percent were 18 to 24 years, and 21 percent were 25 to 34 years.
- about 54 percent did not own cars considered reliable enough for a trip.

In conducting such a demographic profile, Greyhound was digging for would-be riders. Also behind Greyhound's desire to identify riders undoubtedly is a wish to accomplish two advertising objectives:

1. Select media that reach people in the categories pinpointed by the survey.
2. Craft advertising messages that not only catch the attention of these people but speak to their interests, wants, and needs and stimulate action by them.

A large part of identifying customers is identifying their buying motives, their wants and needs. With all its megabucks and sophisticated marketing know-how, Ford Motor Company acknowledged as recently as 1991 a lack of understanding of the wants and needs of its customers. "There's a gap between what the customer wants and what management thinks the customer wants. And what we're trying to do is close the gap," says Toby Hynes, director of Ford's marketing research. If a company the size of Ford Motor Company, with access to the foremost marketing and advertising minds in the world, recognizes that it doesn't know enough about its customers, it stands to reason that other businesses also desperately need to know more about their customers. Small business or megacorporation, the main paths to generating a correct consumer profile is psychographics.

Targeting

Choose Effective Media

The mass market—a spectrum of individuals whose characteristics are as varied and broad as their numbers—as a target market is inert and all but dead. To reach your customers, it is essential to target *only your customers'* wants, needs, and interests.

Advertising methods have been forced to fit a totally changed marketplace and economy. Now messages must be aimed at dual-income families, working women, and people whose savvy is highly sophisticated and who are exceedingly skeptical of advertising claims. If you don't know your desired customers and don't direct your advertising message accordingly, your message won't reach people who are likely to buy.

Consumer research pays off in another way; not only can you construct a message that appeals to a person's specific interests, you are able to pinpoint media that the individual reads, watches, or listens to. When you do this, you don't squander advertising dollars in media that do not reach your target. Instead, you lower costs by purchasing media with relatively smaller circulation numbers but whose smaller numbers are precisely the people you want your message to reach.

Although there still are mass media—television, newspapers, and general magazines that appeal to the broad range of interests of the general public—there is a spiraling expansion of media so narrow in the appeal of their subject matter that they are of interest to only the most explicit segments of a market. For instance, some radio stations—even some cable stations—count their audiences not only by age segments but also by specific areas of interest. There are rock, country, and classical music radio stations, as well as talk and all-news stations. Cable television pinpoints audience interests to an even greater degree: all sports, all music, all news (even all business news), weather stations, and programming for Christians, for science fiction buffs, and movie junkies.

The same is true of publications whose audiences are so vertical in nature that, as an example, among publications for motorcyclists, one magazine is strictly geared to professional women who enjoy the sport of motorcycling. There is a tabloid newspaper for nonprofit organizations and one about the use of computers and computerization for real estate professionals. Other publications zero in on hobbyists and low-end professional video camera users. Some publications and broadcast stations direct their content to specific ethnic groups.

Let's say you want to reach real estate people. You individualize your message to be of interest to this market segment and place that message in a publication structured to the interests of the real estate segment of the business community, or you reach them through a direct mail message by means of a database list of realtors. The realtor segment can be refined even further, by kinds of property sold and other characteristics, to meet your specified appeal even better. Knowledge of your target consumers is the means to choosing the media that reach them.

When you can reach a concentration of any desired target group, you increase the odds of attracting more customers and sales. That's why it is smart to choose only publications or broadcast stations that focus their news or programming to your special interest group.

On the other hand, if you have an auto repair shop, it doesn't matter as much how widely diversified are the life-styles and interests of the people who live or work near your business. What is important is that almost every one has a car. In this case, you localize or regionalize your message so the people receiving it know the benefits of doing business with your neighborhood shop. You send that message to them through local media or a mailing list that pinpoints a specific geographic area, say, within a radius of three to five miles of your shop. Of course, if you repair only BMWs, you will save money if you locate and send your message only to people who own or drive BMWs.

Target the Precious Few

Entrepreneurs and top management often have a problem accepting this targeting technique when they see the seemingly meager numbers turned up by the research. Small numbers may make you think you don't have enough prospects to make your effort worthwhile and tempt you to revert to mass market thinking. Resist the temptation. It can sound even more tempting when, later, you get around to talking to media salespeople, and they quote you numbers in hundreds of thousands of their viewers, listeners, or readers. But these high audience figures may produce only meager numbers of people who have the right characteristics to respond to your message.

It bears repeating: The tighter and more focused the segment is, the greater are the returns in terms of customers and their dollars. When you're presenting your message to those who really want or need your product or service, through a medium that they choose to listen to or read, the odds are high that they will buy what you're selling.

It takes courage to identify and stay within a clearly defined target segment, but it pays off in the end.

Ethnic Groups

This country is a melting pot, but each ethnic group has characteristics that distinguish it from every other one. For several reasons, you need to know which ethnic groups are strong present or potential consumers. You may think of them as a "minority market" and therefore relatively unimportant in numbers. Statistics show, however, that minorities soon will outnumber the rest of the population in the largest metropolitan areas in the United States, and they may outnumber the general population within the first few decades of the next century.

If your research of potential consumers indicates a substantial ethnic base, dig out the figures. You could be tapping into one of the best-kept secrets in advertising. African-Americans, Hispanics, and Asian-Americans collectively spend over $250 billion a year on retail purchases. As these groups increase in numbers, they also are increasing in urbanization, affluence, and education.

Black Americans, for example, spend $30 billion annually in the travel industry. They buy 34 percent of all hair products sold in the United States, and they represent 19 percent of the toiletries and cosmetics market, according to the Direct Marketing Association.

Predictions indicate that Hispanics will surpass African-Americans as the nation's largest minority population by the end of this decade. Advertising spent on the Hispanic market is double the amount spent in 1986 but is still only $515 million, a fraction of the 1991 $118 billion U.S. advertising budget. This market is largely untapped. For example, the average Hispanic household gets only 20 or 30 coupons and 20 catalogs a year, while the non-Hispanic household is flooded with 2,600 coupons a year and up to 20 catalogs a week. Publishers are slowly recognizing this imbalance. *The New York Times* announced in July 1993 it would tap into this market, first with a Spanish-language weekly aimed at Latino residents in a relatively small area in California. *The Times* is dipping its toe in the waters, and there is little doubt others will quickly follow, probably jumping in with big splashes.

Asian-Americans are responsible for more than 32 percent of all $40,000-plus income households. Metropolitan Life, in learning that Asians are concerned about their families and are good insurance prospects, also learned that they need to be spoken to in their native language(s).

The power of delivering communication to Hispanics in Spanish also must not be underestimated. It is confirmed by the number and popularity of Spanish-language television stations.

Statistics usually are easy to find, but it's not always easy to detect the thinking of specific ethnic groups. If you watch the business section of your newspaper, you may learn what business giants are doing as a result of their costly research that warrants looking into as an avenue for your company to follow. For example, when in mid-1993 GTE Telephone Operations rolled out its first major Spanish-language product advertising campaign (with a $3 million plus annual advertising budget), it was a tip for other businesses with a Latino consumer base to sit up and take notice. The news story and the campaign pointed to three tips that might be useful to small businesses:

1. Even industry giants don't spend those kinds of bucks without sound data confirming that the investment will pay off.
2. The campaign would be conducted in Texas, Florida, and California, which means that any company located in those states whose consumer profile includes Hispanics should aim its message to them.
3. The news divulged something about Latinos that a non-Latino operated company might not realize but might apply to its own situation. The director of consumer product promotion for the telephone company said research showed that a large number of GTE's customer households speak Spanish but that many don't have telephone service because they come from Mexico, where there is often difficulty in obtaining phone service; they assume the same situation exists in this country. That could tip you to check whether they assume the same about your product or service, and if it's true, you can give them the correct message in their own language.

A word of caution if you decide it's important to deliver your advertising message in Spanish. There is multiculturalism in many Latino families and some words have multiple meanings for the millions of people in this country who claim Spanish as their native tongue. Anna Macias, a reporter for *The Dallas Morning News,* says she spent a college semester living with a family in Washington, D.C. The father was Cuban, the mother was Puerto Rican, and the children's nanny was Salvadoran. Macias is a Mexican who later married a Chilean. If you're not an expert in Spanish, get help writing your advertising copy because each culture may have different meanings for some words. "There are at least four words for ice cream, six ways to describe beans, and three names for a light bulb," says Macias.

Macias tells how she almost offended her Washington hosts when she said, "*Se fundio un foco*" or "a light bulb burned out." It didn't mean anything bad, but it sounded obscene, she says. "Their light bulbs are *bombillos.* But in South America, I lived in the dark until I learned how to say *ampolleta*—the other word for light bulb."

Language

Children certainly aren't classified as an ethnic group, but in advertising they are a distinctive pod that requires marketing understanding beyond any so far developed. If you number children among those you want to reach with your advertising message, it will pay you to learn to communicate with them. "Oh, I have kids of my own. That's no problem," you say. Not so, says the author of three books on marketing to children, James McNeal: "What we don't understand about children is how they think—how they process and retrieve information. When we listen to them as toddlers, or first-graders, or tweens, they use words which we use incorrectly because we don't know their exact meaning."

Then McNeal asks the big question: since we don't know how to speak to them in their language, should every word and symbol of marketing communications targeted to children be tested? His answer: for the most part, yes, at least until there is substantial evidence of effective dialogue between children and advertiser.

If you think the advice to pretest sounds like an added expense you can't afford, perhaps you can put it in the context that not to pretest can be far more costly. That can mean all your untested advertising and the dollars spent on it are squandered.

The 65-Plus Market

Another group that should not be overlooked when you identify your potential consumers is those who are 65 years and older. Although incomes among subgroups vary widely, in general, those over 65 have more assets than those in younger age classifications.

Finding Your Target

It's not enough to define your target audience as, say, retirees. Not everyone in that demographic group behaves alike as consumers. Some drive Mercedes, some drive Dodge vans in which they sometimes go camping, and still others drive Ford trucks. Some have only social security income, while others have comfortable pension funds and are interested in investments. The tighter and more clearly defined your target group is, the more likely your returns will escalate in numbers of customers and dollars at the same time that the costs of reaching that target group are reduced.

Psychographics is the indispensable means by which you are able to describe how present and potential consumers feel, think, believe, and behave. It's the only way you'll get to know them well.

The Ways Data Are Gathered

Data about current and future customers can be purchased from research companies, but that probably costs more than the budget allows. One of the best ways to know what customers are thinking, believing, doing—and buying—is to *listen* to them every opportunity you have, in your store or in your office, and pay attention to what your staff tells you about consumer reactions.

Personal interviews are the most time-consuming and least productive in terms of numbers of responses, but they may be the easiest to initiate. Rarely a day will go by when you won't have the opportunity to ask several people who already are customers the questions you've previously defined. The same is true of friends, both personal and business. And there are opportunities from time to time to question absolute strangers, on a one-on-one basis. The latter group are the most likely to give you totally candid answers. Also try to climb inside your would-be consumers' heads by reading what they read and by watching and hearing what they watch and hear. Try to walk the aisles of your business in their shoes and shop the way they shop.

There are a number of other do-it-yourself ways to gather the information you need:

- By circulating questionnaires in store, by mail, or other impersonal distribution methods.
- Through in-person questioning.
- With telephone surveys.
- Through focus group sessions.
- Through "devices."

A device isn't really a method for gathering data. It's listed with methods because it is a means to get people to respond to questionnaires.

One frequently used device is to conduct a contest that requires entrants to fill out entry forms, which require the additional information you desire. If a questionnaire is delivered by mail, it might include a coupon or some other device to stimulate action, which can be cashed in when the questionnaire is filled in and returned. Adding questions on warranty cards is another frequently used device.

If you think you might use the device method, begin immediately to note questionnaires you receive and start a copycat file of ideas you could adapt to encourage recipients to send or bring in information. Questions are the basis of all data-gathering methods listed above, and roughly the same questions can be asked regardless of which technique you use. Unless yours is a brand new business or you don't have regular contact with your customers or clients, you probably already know some of the information that will help you draw your consumer profile. So before you start constructing a questionnaire or go looking for consumer data, sit down and circle the appropriate word in the form that follows:

A profile of my present and future customer is a (married, single) (man, woman, teen) (age by segment—e.g., 10–17, 18–24,

25–35, 36–50, etc.) with a (high, low, moderate) income, and a (high school, college, professional) education.

(He/She) prefers a (detailed, straightforward, simple explanation; easy-reading, humorous, lighthearted, compassionate) appeal in my advertising, but also (will/will not) want (facts, statistics, technical data).

Because he/she is a working (husband, father, wife, mother, single parent), he/she wants a product that can be used (easily, quickly, without preparation)—or a service that (is located nearby, can be summoned by phone, will send a representative). Or, time isn't a major concern, so he/she enjoys using a product that requires (some, a medium amount of) preparation.

He/she lives in a (large metropolitan area, medium-size city, small town, rural area).

He/she drives a car that is (less than 3 years old, 3–6 years old, over 6 years old), or travels to work and shopping by (car, bus, rail, subway).

He/she (does, does not) buy (my product/service, a competitor's product/service, or any similar product/service), and uses it (daily, weekly, monthly, other).

The circled information tells you how much you already know about your present and would-be customers and therefore do not need in any questionnaire you ultimately assemble to conduct personal interview surveys or to reach people by less personal means such as sending a questionnaire through the mail.

Start with Your Own Files and Industry

The more information you can gather from available resources, the less you must gather by questioning individuals. Begin with your own company records, which may have a fund of data: names, addresses, records of purchases, returns or complaints, frequency of purchases, and the length of time the individual has been or was a customer. It's less costly to reactivate a former customer than it is to locate new ones, and you may find that as many as 80 percent of your customers haven't been around to buy recently.

A good portion of the information you require may be available from trade or industry associations or magazines. Either resource may have gathered the information as a service for its members or its advertisers.

If you have an 800 or 900 telephone number, your telephone bill may give you a totally customized list of consumers because the telephone company must capture and list callers' numbers in order to bill you. Using a cross-reference directory, you can locate each caller's name and address and add them to your ever-growing list of people who are interested enough in your product, your service, the incentive you offer, or whatever else your advertising message offers, to make the call. That kind of list—of those who had to take action by calling you—is better than just about any list available at any price. And it's free.

Perhaps your business is located in a state that offers caller identification services; the caller's number is displayed as the call is connected. All you need to do is copy the number. Then, through the same channels used to identify 800 and 900 callers, you can acquire callers' names and addresses.

Don't Forget the Library

A college library or the reference department of your public library are invaluable resource centers. Don't be reluctant to ask for help from reference librarians. They appear to enjoy assisting in any kind of research, and their training gives them extensive knowledge about where and how to locate appropriate data.

Don't underestimate the value for your purposes of the information the Census Bureau gathers. And if your library is a designated government depository, you have access to an abundance of data. (To locate the closest government depository, call any U.S. Government Office and ask where the nearest depository is located.) The 1990 census, the most enormous information-gathering effort ever undertaken in the United States, contains demographic and economic detail for every state, county, metropolitan statistical area (MSA), and place in the United States—for the nation's largest metro areas, right down to zip codes. There are data about:

- population
- detailed age breakdowns

- income and income distribution
- race and ethnicity
- employment by occupation and by industry
- educational attainment
- housing by units, owners versus renters, vacant
- housing value and rent breakdowns
- breakdown of commuting methods

Many libraries carry copies of *CACI Marketing Systems*, a book that lists demographic information. Some of the data, listed by zip codes and census tracks, include:

- income by family, household, per capita
- average family size
- education for those age 25 and over
- home values
- occupations
- race
- travel time to work, including time spent waiting for public transportation

Standard Rate & Data Service publications, which appear monthly, contain rates for and data about business publications, newspapers, spot television, and other media. They include listings of media organized by types; business, grocery, insurance, and travel are examples of the hundreds of categories included. There are roundups of data organized by states and counties that give estimates of population, gross household income, and household expenditures. Expenditures are separated into categories: food, drug, general merchandise, automotive, service stations, furnishings. The numbers of black and Spanish who live in each county also are reported.

Other Sources of Data

Look in the Yellow Pages directory under Information Brokers. Depending on the size of your area, firms may be listed that can do comprehensive business research and are capable of analyzing government databases to specification. They conduct searches of newspapers, magazines, reports, and software—all for a price, of course.

If your requirements are moderate, your budget may be able to afford these services.

Chambers of commerce also have statistics and other valuable information about people in specific areas, as well as about businesses in their area.

Conducting Surveys

How to Conduct a Free or Low-Cost Survey

Few businesspeople have the time or inclination to conduct their own surveys, but hiring professionals is costly. Nevertheless, there is a method that costs little, although it requires preparation and instruction: hire or enlist college students or older high school students.

When students are enlisted, it is wise to find an instructor of a business, marketing, or advertising class to assist with the project. Often instructors are enthusiastic about an opportunity for their students to learn survey techniques and their benefits. Also, the survey itself elicits more objective answers because students can introduce themselves and say they are taking the survey as an assignment for their class. Such a method appears to those being surveyed to be a teaching/learning process and does not seem to be purely commercial in nature; therefore, the numbers and nature of responses are better.

Work out in advance with the teacher or instructor how the students will present themselves if they are to query people in person, or if by telephone what they should say, how many contacts they must make, and how they will be compensated for their work. (Compensation sometimes is in the form of class credit by their instructors, or it may be in a monetary form from you.)

You also must prepare the survey forms (one for each respondent), listing as few questions as feasible. If possible, use index cards; they are easier to handle when tabulating them. If it is to be a person-to-person survey, decide where it will produce the best results—at a mall, at some other neutral location, or house to house.

Personal Interviews

Personal interview questioning is an excellent means of locating information. Typically interviewees will respond to a friendly, sincere individual and in most cases be happy to give the questioner information, *if you let them talk*. People who are not trained interviewers often have difficulty waiting for answers to their questions. A pause following an answer becomes an uncomfortable moment for both participants. But an interviewer who waits following the answer to a question may find that the person being questioned volunteers additional information in an effort to fill the silence with words. The best policy is, let them talk—and then wait for all of the answer. If you use students or any other untrained interviewer to gather information, be sure they understand the need for this strategy.

Surveying by Telephone

The telephone has been the most popular means of conducting personal interviews but is fast becoming the least productive. A few years back, before telemarketing became the most used—and perhaps most offensive—means for reaching people, a telephone survey was plausible. Today the public is so resistant to intrusions into their private lives that dialing a number and asking the adult who answers if she will give ten, twenty, or thirty minutes to answer questions is not likely to yield many participants. In areas where telemarketing is frequently used, public response can be outright hostile. If the name of your company can be identified in any way with the telephoned questionnaire, it may be wise to find another means of reaching individuals to avoid adverse public reactions for your business.

If, however, you think that telephone calls are a viable means to get the information you require, determine how the random selection of interviewees will be made. The best way to determine the selection method is to try for a return of .5 percent to 1 percent of the population in your locality and then apply the number to the listings in your telephone book. Selection of every third, fifth, or tenth name listed in the local telephone book is the usual method. If you use a metropolitan telephone book, every tenth name probably will provide more than an adequate count. If yours is a small town, you likely will select every third name to call. Count on the survey's requiring several weeks to complete.

Now let's put together a basic questionnaire with which you can query people in person or by other means.

The Questionnaire

Only you know exactly the information you require, but here is a generic questionnaire to which you can add or delete specific categories to customize it to apply to your business and your customers.

Age:_____ teen, _____ 20–25, _____ 26–35, _____ 36–49,
_____ 50–65, _____ 66–older

Sex:_____ Geographic location:_____

Income level:_____ Education level:_____

Marital status:_____ Size of family:_____

Occupation:____white collar, _____ homemaker,
_____ blue collar

Ethnic background: _____ black, _____ Hispanic, _____white,
_____Japanese, _____Chinese, _____ Korean, _____other*

Purchase criteria: _____ price oriented _____ style oriented

Residence: _____ owns _____ rents _____ house _____ apartment

_____ Owns vehicle. _____Type of vehicle

_____ Uses public transportation

_____ Average distance traveled to reach your business location: _____ 1/2 mile or less _____ 2 miles or less _____ 2–10 miles _____10 miles or more

_____Has _____ has not previously purchased your product/service

Purchase(s) made by: _____ cash _____ check _____ store credit card _____ other credit card _____ billing

Frequency of purchase: _____ daily _____ weekly
_____ monthly _____yearly _____other _____

*(If ethnic background is important, don't merely list Asian. Break out divisions, because each group is distinct.]

Reason for interest: _____ recommendation, _____ newspaper ad, _____ radio spot, _____ direct mail, _____ other (kind) _____

(If media provide the introduction to your product or service, find out which medium is most frequently read or listened to: Which: newspaper _____; radio station _____; individual program _____; cable channel _____.

Time of day/evening/night most frequently spent listening to preferred medium: 6–8 A.M. _____; 8–noon _____; early afternoon _____; 3–6 P.M. _____; news hours _____; 7–11 P.M. _____; midnight and later _____.

A Word of Caution

Every industry has a language of its own. Retailers may need translation more than others. They tend to speak of bugs and dogs, for instance. An outsider listening might think they're speaking of cars when they speak of "fords" when they're really referring to a hot item that sells consistently.

Don't use jargon in your questions, no matter how well you believe the terminology is understood. If you find it absolutely necessary to use a term that is unfamiliar to the general public or one that has several meanings, be sure to define it.

The manner in which you phrase questions is important. You are looking for forthright answers, so word the questions accordingly. Keep in mind a KISS aphorism: Keep It Simple, Straightforward.

Don't expect your respondents to do much writing. Allow them to check off answers that apply to them or write short answers.

This survey process may seem too time-consuming. Certainly it does require time, but much of the information is knowledge that each salesperson must gather from every prospect prior to every sale. True, a survey may be a bit more involved than just sitting across from a potential customer, chatting to learn about this person's life-style, family, type of job, likes, dislikes, and needs so that the sales message can be aimed directly at that individual's wants and needs learned from the conversation. But unlike personal sales, prospect data are gathered just once. Then you are able to use the data for every media purchase and every advertising message to influence many, many prospects.

Focus Groups

Focus sessions are a means to get immediate feedback, a way to assess perceptions, and a method that permits you to observe the process without affecting the way questions are answered.

You might say that a focus group is a microcosm of your market—a group of eight to twelve people brought together in a room to express attitudes about your product, service, or company. It's often called attitudinal research, and in many respects it's more valuable than traditional surveying methods because you're able not only to find out what people think but why. You also can use focus sessions to gather information about how the public positions your company, product, or service. (Positioning in marketing means the place consumers perceive a product, service, or company to be among its competition or the place you as an advertiser attempt to place your product, service, or company in the minds of the public.)

If there are negative public perceptions—which could range from an unfriendly or uncaring image to a belief that you supply far fewer goods and services than is fact—you will want your advertising to reverse these negatives in order to reestablish your position further up the scale among your competitors. You also will wish to develop better rapport with customers and dispense better information about what you do offer.

Focus groups do not provide you with the numbers that let you determine, for instance, that 21 percent of a segment of the population could use the product, but 11 percent believe—or perceive—it is not as effective as that of your competition, or it is overpriced. As with groups of jurors, those who take part in focus group sessions can be swayed by a strong, opinionated participant. In other words, focus sessions do not provide facts, but they do give you a sense of public reaction.

Benefits from Focus Group Research: An Example

America West Airlines isn't exactly a small business—it's the nation's ninth-largest airline—but after a Chapter 11 bankruptcy, they needed to know how to reach potential customers with an effective message. They used focus group interviews in four cities, and that focus research yielded information that even the smallest business can produce. America West shrewdly took what they learned and used it to distance themselves from their larger rivals.

They conducted more sessions (thirty) in cities across the country than are ordinarily necessary or productive, apparently because they didn't quite believe the results. "We kept hearing the same things, maybe in different words or spoken in different accents: 'Just treat me like a human being,' 'Treat me like you really want my business,'" Warren Rucker, America West's advertising director, said. "When you hear what people are saying, you scratch your head and say, 'It's so basic, so elementary. Shouldn't respect be taken for granted when you fly?' But being treated with indifference, almost arrogance, was such a persistent theme."

The advertising strategy the airline used was to sell an attitude instead of larger seats or better food. In their print ads they say, "Respect. It's basic. Something you have every right to expect when you fly. Yet on some airlines, this expectation often leads to disappointment." Actually, the financially strapped America West is unable to compete on amenities, so they used what they learned in focus group sessions. They pitched something they can afford, that money can't buy. It's hard to think of any other research method that could produce the same information, which gave America West the opportunity to address the real, hitherto unrecognized, interests of their customers.

The Mechanics of Focus Group Sessions

Focus groups are most fruitful when made up of no more than eight to twelve people, plus a moderator. It's important that the people are chosen at random but represent individuals who are in a position to purchase or use the product or service. For instance, if yours is a computer store or service, it wouldn't be productive to include people who have no interest in computers or are intimidated by them. But because computers are used and purchased by both men and women, be sure to include both sexes and a range of ages.

To elicit the most honest data, use an experienced moderator and hold the session at a neutral location such as a school or a library's conference room. If your company is linked to the focus group, it is likely to influence participants to give answers they think you want to hear—or if they hold some sort of a grudge, to say things that are not true for the benefit of others present.

Companies that specialize in conducting focus sessions have specially designed facilities with one-way mirrors that let you watch without being watched. These facilities and services are expensive; one session can cost between $2,500 and $3,000. The services and facilities are available from some of the organizations that are listed in Yellow Page directories under Market Research and Analysis.

There is a less expensive way, though: make it a college or university project. Talk to the dean of the MBA program or an instructor in marketing or advertising. More than likely, the suggestion that a trained student act as facilitator of a focus session will be viewed as an opportunity not otherwise available. If the session is held at the college, perhaps other students can observe, and their comments may be a valuable contribution.

The Do-It-Yourself Focus Session

Choices of a moderator and the questions to ask are the most important aspects in setting up a focus session.

If you moderate the session, give no hint of your association with the company, product, or service, and act and speak in as objective a manner as possible. If you have someone else do it, choose a person who can be professional and in command without being overbearing and who has the ability to get people to talk freely yet keep their conversation from wandering off the question or the subject at hand.

Questions must be carefully prepared and worded to give no hint of a desired response or reaction. You want honest, truthful reactions. And you want questions constructed to call for more than yes or no answers.

Make provisions for taping the session. In a study of the playback, you'll likely hear comments you missed during the session or get a better, more objective understanding of answers.

File the tape along with the names of participants and their identities and any other preparatory data. This information may be useful six months or a year later in organizing another session—if the first is successful—or in reassessing the information in the light of new developments.

The Last Step: Gathering and Compiling the Data

You either have all the information you can locate about your present or would-be customers or you think you have it all. (Holes in the blanket won't show until you spread it out and get it organized.) At this point, it's time to decide what stands out about the target as individuals. From your information, write what you believe is a definition of your market segment. Be specific and exact.

Go back to the first questionnaire in this chapter to learn how much you already knew about your consumers. Write a similar kind of profile as you know it now, based on the information you already knew plus the data you've gathered and compiled. When you've finished, you may find you have more than a profile. You have a full figure portrait. As such, it becomes more personal, someone you know well enough that when you get around to making media choices and writing advertising messages, you'll know exactly who it is you're talking to and which media avenue to take to reach them.

There's a practice you undoubtedly follow every day in your business: *Find out what your customers want—and give it to them.* That also is the formula you will follow for a successful advertising program, with one addition. In advertising you not only give them what they want, you tell them about it. Carry that one thought with you as you build your advertising program.

4

Sneak Peek

Shortcuts to Locating Customers and Everything You Ever Wanted to Know About Them

A well-known president and chief executive officer of a Southwest-based advertising agency says that just about any list of people is now available because of computer technology. Without cracking a smile, George Arnold of EvansGroup gives an example: "If you want a list of lefthanded Irishmen with handlebar moustaches, who live west of the Mississippi, in manufactured housing, and you know where to call, the reply will be, 'I can get you that list.'" Or, "Want to send junk mail to short fat guys with glasses?" asks *The Wall Street Journal*. That list is available too.

The consumer database industry, which continues to explode in the numbers of companies and kinds of data that now are on the market, has lists to fit your requirements. A person's name, address, height, weight, eating habits, even use of corrective lenses, as well as other pertinent identifying information, may be stored by any grouping desired, including geographic location, vital statistics, or personal classifications, right down to those for left-handed Irishmen.

Databases

A database is a gathering of names from a number of different records into a single computer-stored catalog with at least one factor in common. The creation of databases came about because of the needs by businesses of all sizes of economical lists that pinpoint selected groups. In the beginning, only lucrative big businesses could afford the high costs of the lists, but the savings in production and mailing costs from reaching only specifically targeted individuals made them worth the high costs. Today the technology has been refined and expanded to a point that charges for abbreviated database lists are affordable for just about any size business.

There are advantages to using lists that pinpoint your target group:

- You save the cost of materials and postage of blanket mailings that reach people who have no interest in your product or service.
- A single source saves the time required to search numbers of lists.
- Carrier routing can be used to take advantage of lower postal rates.
- It avoids duplication of names. (Before database lists, several identical mailings commonly went to many of the same people.)

Database companies get their information from a variety of sources, including the U.S. Census, product warranty registration cards, and telephone surveys. Most drivers do not realize that the personal information on their licenses, such as height and weight will turn up in data banks across the country. (This is the case in twenty-six states.) Credit reports also are a source, and checkout scanners, which track and report shoppers' daily purchasing habits, provide a profusion of useful information. For instance, "high ticket" buyers are tabbed by purchases of so-called fancy foods, such as premium beers, frozen yogurts, and refrigerated pastas.

There is a profusion of database companies that can provide precise lists of persons to whom you can target your message(s). If that message is what the targeted individuals want to hear, your company will attain the increased share of audience and share of market that brings in the added revenue you are seeking. (In advertising lingo, *share of audience* refers to people. *Share of market* denotes the dollars spent on a particular brand within a competitive field of brands.)

Just as advertising has changed its focus from mass marketing to niche marketing, the development of databases has become the driving force to reach the best individual prospects. The conviction is that large and small advertisers and marketers must locate the wanters and the want-nots—it's as important to know and understand the want-nots in order to avoid them as it is to find the wanters.

Another reason to track down individuals who are known to want or need your product or service comes from a survey reported by Michael J. Anthony Applied Training Service. The survey shows that for every 100 merchandise items that shoppers plan to buy, they make 30 unanticipated purchases. In Texas talk, that's gravy for the biscuits.

Cherry Picking by Computer

An individual customer may be listed on the databases of fifty different companies. But with current capabilities to assemble various data pods, advertisers can learn individuals' purchasing inclinations, price preferences, company and brand loyalties, seasonal activities and "power purchase" periods, and financial stability projections. They can learn how individuals or families live and where they live—their life-styles, habits, hobbies, values, even their personality types and intelligence levels.

Keeping track of customers' preferences and purchases is becoming increasingly affordable as the techniques for accessing and maintaining have become more available and costs have plunged. Much of the information is available on line to consumers with personal computers who subscribe to a service. Some subscription services are advertised regularly on television. No longer is this a choice only for corporate giants; now the need for database information is basic to small businesses' advertising and marketing plans.

Once you've acquired the names, addresses, and whatever other data are attached to them, they become your business's database. The consumers in your database provide the dollars that run your business. It's important to have your own continuously updated data factory: consumers move, change their wants and interests, and switch their brand or company loyalties.

The Mother of All Databases: The U.S. Census

After the no-cost list you were able to build from information about your present and previous customers, the next least costly list—the U.S. census—is a database that is accessible to everyone. It's one that you should turn to for all kinds of data. The 1990 U.S. Census was the most successful one in thirty years, *American Demographics* publisher Peter Francese told the Advertising Research Foundation. "Throughout this decade, the census' demographic and geographic information will be the mother of all databases." When you examine what it offers, you'll agree.

The Census Data

There are three basic categories of information you can draw from, according to your company's needs:

1. *Population.* Social characteristics: education (enrollment and attainment); place of birth, citizenship, and year of entry in United States; ancestry; language spoken at home; migration (residence in 1985); disability; fertility; veteran status. Sex, race, age, marital status, and Hispanic origin also are included.
2. *Economic characteristics.* Labor force; occupation, industry, and class of worker; place of work and journey to work; work experience in 1989; income in 1989; year last worked.
3. *Housing.* Year moved into residence; number of rooms and number of bedrooms; plumbing and kitchen facilities; telephone in unit; vehicles available; heating fuel; source of water and method of sewage disposal; year structure was built and number of units in structure; tenure (owned or rented); value of home or monthly rent and shelter costs, including utilities, and if it is congregate housing, whether meals are included in the rent; vacancy characteristics; farm residence.

Locating Census Information

The 1990 census data products, released between 1991 and 1993, are available in both traditional and new formats. The conventional printed reports and computer tape files are the most widely used, the most convenient, and the most readily available. But the Census Bureau also offers data on microfiche, on CD-ROM laser discs, and through its online information service, CENDATA. It provides more data on tape and other machine-readable products than in printed form.

For the first time, the entire land area of the United States and its possessions was block-numbered, which means that the census provides statistical data for 7 million census blocks. The cost and storage of block data of this magnitude would be prohibitive if the data were published in printed reports, so they are available only on microfiche.

There are a number of booklets, some of which are free and some are sold. One that highlights key information about 1990 census information and illustrates a variety of ways the data can be used is free: *Census ABCs—Applications in Business and Community*.

The Census Bureau's Customer Services is the principal source for general information and for a list, with telephone numbers, of Census Bureau specialists. Also, it sells most of the machine-readable data products, microfiche, and maps (such as county block maps, county subdivision outline maps, and census tract maps). The 1990 census printed reports are sold by the Superintendent of Documents.

Customer Services
U.S. Bureau of the Census
Washington, DC 20233,
Phone: 301/763–4100
Fax: 301/763–4794

Regional Offices

Atlanta, GA	404/347–2274
Boston, MA	617/565–7078
Charlotte, NC	704/371–6144
Chicago, IL	312/353–0980
Dallas, TX	214/767–7105
Denver, CO	303/969–7750
Detroit, MI	313/354–4654
Kansas City, KS	913/236–3711
Los Angeles, CA	818/904–6339
New York, NY	212/264–4730

Philadelphia, PA   215/597–8313
Seattle, WA   206/728–5314

Superintendent of Documents
U.S. Government Printing Office
Washington, DC 20402
Phone: 202/783–3238

Now there is a company that does the digging for you and lets you turn your computer into a census database for a state, a region, or the entire country. Prices for the PC software range from $195 to $395 for individual states to $2,000 for the entire United States. For information about the software contact:

UPCLOSE Publishing
P.O. Box 1147
El Granada, CA 94018
Phone: 800/352–5673
Fax: 415/712–1190

Ready-Made Lists

If you are unable to build a consumer list from your own files, from telephone bills, or from census data, the least time-consuming and probably the most cost-effective means is to purchase a list from one of a number of database research companies. They can be found under Mailing Lists and Mailing Service Companies in the Yellow Pages. Most large mailing service companies own certain databases/lists or can put you in touch with a list broker.

List Costs

The more precise the descriptive requirements you request, the more expensive the list will be. If, for example, you're looking for those left-handed Irishmen, the list may cost you $1.00 a name, because you are asking for five of what advertising professionals call "screeners": (1) left-handed, (2) Irish, (3) handlebar moustaches, (4) west of Mississippi, (5) manufactured housing. However, if you can live with a list that calls only for left-handed and west of the Mississippi, it may only cost you 20 cents a name.

The price of lists becomes far more affordable when you factor in production and postage savings gained from eliminating uninterested people—once you have access to lists that target only your profiled potential consumers.

Magazines and Newspapers

Magazines previously offered demographic and geographic buys, but now one advertiser's program, which came up with its own target list, has expanded availability. It focuses on zip codes. Buick introduced the change when it targeted its ads in seven major magazines to run in issues going to 4,940 of the country's more than 40,000 zip codes. This intensely vertical targeting permits an advertiser to enclose in the magazines a personally addressed card to the subscriber. A business that wants to reach beyond a city or county can choose a zoned edition of a magazine and call for delivery of personally addressed cards to subscribers, chosen by zip codes, who match the business's profiled target.

Newspapers now can pinpoint precise target groups, such as dog owners, and have a distribution force that physically passes every household in their market every day.

Newspapers have just begun to create the necessary database services, and for some it's still in the early stage. Most newspaper executives, however, consider the technology an inevitable and important part of the industry, so it's worth checking the database information your newspaper can offer you. Keep in mind that a newspaper has the ability to put your message right alongside your reader's coffee cup any morning you designate.

There has been an explosion of the kinds of database information available, and database companies are becoming highly specialized. There are data about brands such as aerosol hairsprays that tell exactly how many cans of what brand and in what sizes are shipped within a specified area, and what size cans of what brands are selling in a company's targeted market area.

5

Check the Competition
What You Don't Know Can't Help You

The chairman and CEO of RJR Nabisco, Inc. made a point that transfers well to small business advertising: "We need to adopt that legendary Noah Principle. No more prizes for predicting rain. Prizes only for building arks." Professional researchers like to say that advertisers are divided into two groups: the winners and those who end up saying, "You mean I should have researched more than just who's buying my product? I should have found out what my competition is up to?"

The last part of the investigative process that must precede purchase of media and construction of your advertising message consists of taking a hard look at what your competition is doing. No longer, particularly in the intensely competitive 1990s, is it enough to count on intuition or to guess about consumers, about the competition's strategies, or what your advertising program should be. Millions of advertising dollars are wasted that way by otherwise sophisticated and intelligent businesspeople. Then they complain that advertising doesn't work.

When you've finished this last probe, you can add the information to the other facts you've collected, sort it all out, and build a profitable advertising plan. The plan will get you the big prize: the people who want and need your product and the kind of action that substantially boosts revenue. From here on, then, there are no more prizes for merely predicting rain.

Why Bother to Check Out the Competition?

If you don't know what your competitors are doing, you will know less than your customers know. How will you know if your price is right—whether you're underpricing, or overpricing, or merely meeting existing market prices? How will you know the ways your product or service is better or different, so that you can play up benefits and differences in your advertising messages to catch the eyes of those potential consumers you've already pinpointed? And if, quite unexpectedly, your customers respond to a competitor's buying appeals, how do you know so you can react quickly and adjust your advertising appeals to overcome the problem? Competitors' problems can be object lessons for you.

Victor Kiam in his book *Going for It!* admits he knew very little about electric razors and that he even shaved with a blade razor. But when he considered buying an electric razor company, he asked retailers what they thought. They told him that Norelco dominated the market but that they thought Remington had the best product. Kiam didn't just take their word. He bought a Remington and tried it every morning, comparing it with his blade model. Then he bought all the other major electric brands and tried them versus Remington and the blade razor. When he was sure that Remington was the best, he bought the company. In other words, he checked out the field—all the competitors in it. That is your assignment now.

There are services that can track your competitors' media plans and expenditures, but nobody else can do your fact-finding job better than you, regardless of how much money you can allocate to hiring others to do it for you. You are the authority about your company and the kind of business it is. If you assign a staffer or hire an outsider to gather information about the competition in your field, they will have to pick your brains to learn what you know before they can do as good a job finding and evaluating—even recognizing—the information that is worthwhile.

What Differentiates Competitors?

There is a single element that makes each top-level competitor different from others: each provides different benefits, thereby attracting and holding consumers who want and need certain unique benefits. Consequently each competitor comes to serve a segment of the market in a way that gives the company a distinct advantage over other contenders. However, there are always uncommitted prospects between each competitor's market segment where a strong competitive campaign will find—and attract—uncommitted would-be consumers.

You want to establish and maintain your own undisputed segment of the market that competitors will have difficulty invading. But because most consumers are willing to try new products, services, and suppliers, you want to hunt new prospects among fringe prospects not yet loyal to a competitor.

Your challenge is to define your competitors' market segments so that you don't waste time, money, and effort attempting to invade their undisputed territories and to identify the areas between competitors' segments of the market where there is little or no competitive advantage. It's far, far easier to attract buyers who have no allegiance to one of your competitors.

Key Information About Competitors

You may think you're prepared to duke it out with the competition, but you can't pick up the gloves until you know who the competition is, where it is, and what it's up to.

Even though Victor Kiam checked every one of his competitors, and it's true that the more information you're able to gather the better, it's not necessary to check every competitor—only those with the greatest impact on your business or whose advertising has the overall greatest effect on the entire market. Check out the competitors who are in your neighborhood or offer the same product or service at the same price to the same type of customers.

Your competitors' advertising philosophies and tactics are a little like body language: they often tell more about the subjects' thinking than the subjects wish to be revealed. Gather as much information as possible about:

- The media used and the frequency.
- The degree of targeting used.
- The quantity and estimated cost of advertising.
- The kinds of messages: sales appeals, image builders, or primarily product/service oriented or company oriented.
- The product or service benefits they feature most often and the advantages they boast about.
- Any theme and what it is intended to convey.
- The advertising message that would be the most intimidating to each of your major competitors and how each would respond.

Assess each competitor's strengths and shortcomings as you see them and as others see them. Get your employees', your friends', and your customers' perceptions of the competition (but question customers in a subtle manner).

The competition's weaknesses offer your greatest opportunity for success. If you don't know their shortcomings, how can you attack those weaknesses and cash in on them? And if you don't know their strengths, how can you avoid trying to mimic their strong points that don't fit your operation, as happened when Sears tried to build on KMart's success?

Compare the competition's pricing with yours. Do they give discounts? Do they offer coupons, premiums, or contests?

What place in the market does each competitor hold? Does each appear to be satisfied with market position, or are there indications they will spend larger amounts in advertising to strengthen market position?

Among competitors, are there indications or evidence of present or planned retaliation to restrict others' growth? What form would such reprisal(s) take?

What are the points their salespeople emphasize to customers?

Finding Information About Competitors

An excellent way to be sure you're digging out the right information is to call on your own employees. Discuss with them the information you plan to seek and ask them what other facts you should be looking for. By involving them, not only will you get information, you will get *participation,* which breeds enthusiasm and support.

As you did when you were tracking consumer data, go to the library. Start your search with the business reference librarian at a large public or college library. Most libraries keep all manner of general business magazines, small business publications, and national and local newspapers' business sections. There are trade publications—you may already subscribe to one or more—that keep readers up to the minute on developments within specific fields. Most libraries keep such information on microfiche or stored on computer.

Almost every industry or trade field has its own organization, which can be a gold mine of free data. Inside information often is passed along through newsletters, annual reports, and even in speeches reported in industry trade journals. And don't forget, or underestimate, the information available from the Small Business Administration.

Continue to Keep Track of the Competition

Monitoring should become a habit. It's just as important to monitor your competition's actions continually as it is to carry on an ongoing monitoring program of your customers' actions and reactions and to check the effectiveness of your advertising and that ad dollars are being wisely allocated. Never forget that your competition is always right . . . right behind you.

6

The Plan

Combine Your Goals and Your Budget to Develop a Plan

Humorist Evan Ezar says a plan is something either abandoned or unfinished. For many businesspeople this droll statement is a sad truth; they are too busy to follow the blueprint so painstakingly crafted when they started the business or when economic trouble showed up and a loan officer demanded one.

Nothing can really happen until you answer the questions, "Where are we going? What are we trying to accomplish?" The same questions must be answered about your advertising expectations.

George Arnold, president and chief executive officer of Evans Group, a leading advertising agency, offers a financial reason for having clear objectives: "As much as 90 percent of the advertising dollars spent by small businesses is wasted, because it is misdirected." But don't be concerned. When you've followed the procedures outlined in this chapter and throughout the rest of the book, you will know what advertising works for you and—more important—what doesn't.

Goals and Objectives

There is no way—except by extraordinary luck—that you can devise and carry out a successful advertising plan without first setting advertising goals and objectives. Most successful entrepreneurs and managers agree that well-circulated and well-understood goals accomplish highly desirable results. They

- motivate management and employees.
- lead employees and customers to action.
- guide managerial efforts effectively.
- cut down or eliminate unproductive tasks.
- set courses of action.
- eliminate any goals or objectives at cross-purposes with major purposes of the organization.
- establish priorities.

The words *goals* and *objectives* are not synonymous, although they often are used—and confused—synonymously. A goal is a statement of broad direction or interest that is general and timeless and not concerned with a particular achievement within a specified time period. A goal must be attainable. An objective is a planned accomplishment that can be verified within a given time and under specifiable conditions, which, if attained, advances the system toward a corresponding goal. An objective must be measurable.

Any one of the following are considered advertising goals; not one could be considered an objective.

- To increase sales.
- To stay in touch with customers in order to increase repeat business.
- To get in touch with prospects who are not customers in order to bring in added business.
- To tell customers and prospects who we are, what we do, and why they should do business with us instead of with our competitors.
- To improve the company's image.
- To broaden the company's visibility.
- To increase company name recall.

Objectives must be practical and specific. Ask yourself:

- What is our organization really capable of achieving?
- What is happening among our competitors?

- Should we take a restrained or an optimistic view?
- If we take a restrained attitude, how will it affect our present and potential customers? If our objectives are too optimistic, will it negatively affect our personnel because they do not believe the objectives are attainable?

Make objectives practical, achievable, and specific, but design them to require some stretching on the part of those within the business. The heart of an objective is specificity. A well-written objective should include four components:

who: a specific statement as to the individuals who will perform the objective

what: the specific accomplishment when the objective has been achieved

when: the specific point in time when the objective is to be achieved

how well: the specific criteria of success to be obtained

There is a deep, deep hole into which inexperienced writers of objectives often tumble: they fail to state their objectives in measurable terms. They use words such as, *to know, understand, appreciate, grasp the significance of, enjoy,* or *believe.* But how can you measure understanding? appreciation? belief? Usually you can't.

Objectives are more easily measured when stated concretely—for example, *to construct, identify, maintain, increase, decrease, reduce, improve, eliminate, differentiate, solve, compare, list,* or *locate.*

Let us say that your goal is "to increase sales of our product/service." The objectives might be as follows: I/assigned staffer will:

1. Gather specified data and pertinent information about potential customers by December 1.
2. Write an accurate portrait profile that will provide sufficient information to construct advertising messages that will attract profiled potential customers' interest and generate their action.
3. Target these profiled individuals in highly vertical media directed to their interests.
4. Produce a 10 percent increase in sales,
5. by the end of the current fiscal year,
6. and thereby increase our profits by 15 percent.

There can be short-term and long-term advertising goals and objectives. Ultimately, it's best to have both. Choices are made to fit the company's overall goals and objectives or to fit the time frame of a specific advertising dollar allotment.

The Plan

At this point you have your road map—your goals and objectives that tell you where your company's advertising is going and what it is trying to accomplish—and you have a bottom-line advertising dollar allotment. Now it's time to crunch the two into a strategy and spell out the advertising plan on paper. Why on paper, when the elements already are etched on your brain? For two reasons:

1. To circulate among your staff. There is a strong reason behind this: the more you involve those who work with and for you, the more support and enthusiasm you will receive from them.
2. For the future, to have something to look back on and to assess. But like your allocation of advertising dollars, don't set your plan in concrete. No matter how matchless is the final strategy you devise, it will require ongoing monitoring and changes from time to time.

Every business that advertises needs an advertising plan, and it should be as specific and achievable as possible. As with goals and objectives, a plan can be designed for the short or long term or any time frame in between. Begin by setting your advertising plan for a year, a kind of midterm compromise. Later, as you monitor the plan, you undoubtedly will want to develop both shorter- and longer-term plans that better fit the company's overall business plan, that conform to short, intensive advertising campaigns, or that accommodate adjustments or changes in media purchases.

Base your entire plan on your answers to the following questions:

1. What impression and effect do you want your company and/or your product or service to make on the public?
2. What specific actions must be taken by the public if your company is to achieve its stated goal and its objectives?

3. What time frame must be built into the plan to accomplish your goal?

Your plan—whether it's for your entire company or only for your advertising program—is essential to get you to your destination. "If you don't know where you're going," Yogi Berra used to say, "you could wind up someplace else." A tailored plan sets the most direct route to keeping it all within your budget's constrictions and to increasing revenues.

There's a far easier way: conduct a mental "which" hunt. Which ads work? Which don't? Which media reach our prospects? Which don't? And then to think, "Oh well, next year will be better," and just leave it at that. Don't take the easy way out!

The strongest justification for the mental effort and time required to construct your advertising plan is that a customized plan makes it possible to follow your own course rather than follow the leader in your efforts to make your company a "non-prophet" organization.

Image

Part of the advertising plan is knowing the image you want to convey. In early 1991, *Advertising Age* reported that "the KGB is considering an image makeover." A major American advertising agency had approached the Department of Societal Relations of the Soviet Committee for State Security, better known as the KGB, with proposals for an image campaign, according to the deputy director of the KGB's press center. Then he added, "How the committee will proceed is still absolutely unclear."

The point is that perhaps your thinking runs only toward advertising to sell your product or service, and you haven't really thought about setting up the plan to include an image buildup or makeover. You aren't alone. Most businesspeople, retailers in particular, feel that any advertising that isn't aimed directly to sell products or services is wasted. Not so. Establishing a strong positive image or working for an image makeover may be the key to selling your product or your service.

Advertising can restore a tarnished image. In 1989, the manner in which Exxon handled the *Valdez* oil spill turned its image from excellent to about as poor as any company could have. Exxon could not control the publicity it received, but it could have steered the public's perception of the company—its image. Unfortunately, Exxon didn't use the advertising avenues open to it for that purpose and has never completely rebuilt its good image.

Denny's did jump on the advertising bus to reverse public opinion after a couple of its franchises created a nationwide stir about not offering the same service and consideration to blacks as to whites. The company mounted a high-visibility television campaign with the company head and a number of workers offering apologies, pledging no discrimination, and affirming appreciation of the public's patronage.

Image does count. What the public thinks about your company shows up on the profit—or loss—side of the ledger. *The Wall Street Journal* sums it all up in a headline over one of its own advertising messages: "How Much Do People Need To Know About Your Company Before They're Willing To Give You A Chance?"

There is no advertising rule that says only a product or only a service may be advertised. Every ad you place for a product or service is also an image ad for your company. There are innumerable instances where advertising of a national product is built strictly on the product itself, and the public knows nothing about the company behind the product or service. On the other hand, undoubtedly you can think of numerous instances in your own experience when you have purchased something purely on the strength of the good name of the company that sells it. When you need new tires, for instance, you may not know which brand is best for your needs. Each major brand touts its product as the best, so you buy from a local company you trust or whose excellent reputation is well known.

The image your advertising projects is prevalent throughout all of your advertising, and as recognizable as the company image your people project in the way they answer telephones or deal with consumers. Establishing a friendly, caring attitude in your advertising and building remembrance for your company's good name and reputation may account for service or product sales you'll never be able to attribute directly to an advertising program by the company.

Slogans

You may want your advertising plan to include the times and ways a slogan will be used throughout your advertising program. A memorable slogan can create continuity, (it may be the single element besides your logo that is carried throughout your advertising), create remembrance, and increase the public's belief in good company traits. Over time and with repeated use, it will become as recognizable as your logo.

Devise a company slogan that describes how you want the public to perceive your company. Then use it in every ad and with every public display of your product or service, even on packages and direct mail pieces. Here are some slogans to stir your creative juices:

Signs of excellence (sign company)
Thegoaheadandgetitstore (appliance rental store)
The bucks *start* here (bank)
We really can sell a car for less. And we will.
You should be in our shoes (shoe company)
We stay in touch with you every step of the way (real estate company)
Dish it out . . . we can take it (paper plate product)
A new way of seeing things (photo film)
It's hard to stop a Trane (plumbing company)
A touch does so much (hair product)
Like 3 soaps in one
Just plane smart (airline)
We know how much it means to be the very best (food product)
It's your store (supermarket)
The Super Ones (channel 11—television)
It's our nature to help (gardening store)

As you collect slogan ideas, remember that the best ones say something about the company or product or service or something about what it does.

If you have trouble coming up with a slogan, turn the problem into an opportunity. Conduct separate contests among your employees and among your customers or clients. Both groups know what they think is great about your company or product or service, and someone may come up with a winner. As a result, you also attract positive attention from the public (even some publicity, if you alert the press), and you learn what is important to other people about your company.

The Public's Actions

Detailing specific actions that must be taken by the public in order for your company to achieve its stated goal and objectives sounds difficult. It isn't. It's already there, in the objectives to accomplish your goal, to be summarized in your plan.

As an example, take the goal mentioned earlier—"to increase sales of our product/service"—and the objectives written to achieve it. Pick the objective that specifies what you want the public to do. In this case it is "to produce a 10 percent increase in sales." The difficult part is already done: the research that told you the kinds of information to use to reach that segment of the public open to your messages and the lines of communication—the media—that will reach them with your messages, so that they will make enough purchases to produce that 10 percent increase.

Build Time into Your Program

Give your ads a chance. Give them time. Advertisers tend to change advertising messages or themes too soon and too often, and understandably. The advertiser sees the ad or hears the spot so often before and during its run that he or she soon tires of it. It's unlikely, however, that the people you want your message to reach are exposed to it more than a few times.

Include in your advertising plan an estimate of how long each message will run. Don't be concerned that you will repeat a message too often over too long a period because, like your dollar allocations, you will be reevaluating your plan on a regular basis, and changes can be made whenever there is tangible evidence that a change is really needed.

Repetition can be highly profitable. BMW used its "ultimate driving machine" slogan to build and maintain its hugely successful upscale position all through the 1980s. For fourteen years Pepperidge Farm used as its slogan, "Pepperidge Farm remembers."

Your regular evaluations won't tell you how long an ad is productive after it has ceased running, but a study by Information Resources, Inc.'s Behavior-Scan service makes a strong point for running advertising for extended periods of time. Among the findings from the ten-year study are that advertising produces long-term sales growth even two years after a campaign ends. (Note that the report states "after a *campaign* ends." This finding does not apply to single or occasional ad placements.) Leonard Lodish, chairman of the marketing department at the University of Pennsylvania's Wharton School who wrote the study, says, "These gains come not from new users but because people buy more or buy more often as they become established customers."

Downturns and Upturns

As a businessperson, you undoubtedly are concerned about constructing a plan that provides for economic surges and downfalls. *The Wall Street Journal* gives excellent advice: "The way to minimize a downturn and take maximum advantage of the upturn is to maintain a strong communications link with your buying public."

Should you advertise even in recessionary times, a genuine test of the power of advertising? *The Wall Street Journal* makes some strong, accurate statements and supports them with highly regarded studies:

> When times turn bad, they're made worse by hesitation, halfway measures and panicky decisions. Such as the decision to reduce or eliminate advertising. The fact is, companies that maintain or increase their advertising spending during recessions get ahead. A less crowded field allows messages to be seen more clearly, and that increased visibility results in higher sales both during and after a recession.

One study *The Journal* cites is by the American Business Press ("How Advertising in Recession Periods Affects Sales"), which found that companies that did not cut advertising during such times had the highest growth in sales and net income, and companies that cut advertising during the recessionary period had the lowest sales and net income increases.

A study by McGraw-Hill confirmed the long-range advantage of keeping a strong advertising presence. It found that companies that cut advertising in 1981/82 increased sales by only 19 percent between 1980 and 1985, while companies that continued to advertise in 1981/82 enjoyed a 275 percent sales increase.

The facts are clear: set your advertising plan according to your goals, regardless of the state of the economy, and strengthen your resolve to stand firm during recessionary times.

Forecasting

Forecasting or predicting is important for a number of reasons. Perhaps the most important was pinned down by Hank Ketcham in a "Dennis the Menace" cartoon. Dennis, wearing a heavy jacket and standing in the snow in front of a "liminaid" stand, offers a profound observation: "You gotta expect seasonal slumps, Joey." The same is true for your advertising plan. You gotta *plan* for them.

Internal traffic and sales records will provide the best basis for your projections. Eventually you will be able to evaluate how well your media choices and message content achieve the goals and objectives you developed. For the time being, be satisfied with guesstimates, but do include them to establish their importance as part of the advertising plan, and to give you something to compare, in your future evaluations.

Testing the Plan

Except for one segment, testing strategies, your advertising plan is complete. Testing is measuring accomplishments and is gauged by your success in achieving your goals. To test your plan you must devise questions appropriate to your individual situation—for example:

- What were the sales figures of our product/service before we set our program in action, and what are the figures now?
- What were initial estimates for the change or success? To what degree have we achieved those estimates?
- How have those appointed to carry out various functions succeeded in achieving those functions?
- How has our advertising plan succeeded in staying in touch with present customers to increase repeat business? getting in

touch with prospects who are not customers to get new business? reaching customers and prospects with our message about who we are, what we do, and why they should do business with us instead of with our competitors?
- Are we accomplishing our ongoing goal to make more money? to what degree?
- Is additional help needed from within the company? from outside? Will they do the job in total or in part?
- Has the program stayed within the confines of the dollar allotment originally set? If not, why not?
- Have the selected media produced the results anticipated or they pledged?
- Are additional funds needed to extend the program into more or other media?
- Did we meet our time frame?

Perhaps there are bigger questions than those just listed:

- How will you recognize success?
- What is the level of acceptable performance?
- How good a job must be done before you will feel that you achieved the objective(s)?

Regardless of whether you are testing the plan or an individual ad, testing should be ongoing and continuous. Keep a file of your ads, with test results attached. By keeping records of the numbers of telephone or coupon responses, inquiries as well as sales, that were directly attributed to each ad, you can make comparisons to each future advertisement. This gives you another measure of how well your advertising program is meeting the goals and objectives in your plan.

Building In Testing

The easiest—but not recommended—way to test the effectiveness of your advertising is the unanticipated way one businessman did it. Acclaimed business speaker Joe Griffith tells it this way: "A reporter asked a businessman if [his] advertising paid. 'Yes, why only the other day, we advertised for a night watchman, and that night the safe was robbed.'"

"There is absolutely no trick to finding out if advertising works," says Ira C. Herbert, president, Coca-Cola America. "Simply stop advertising!"

Obviously there are many other ways to test the results of your advertising efforts. The way advertising professionals measure success is expensive; they gauge the selling power of each ad: whether it is remembered and whether those who saw it changed their attitudes.

Psychologist Daniel Starch, well known for his research studies, fixed the ultimate worth of an ad upon five factors. The ad must be:

- seen
- read
- believed
- remembered
- acted upon

An inexpensive way to gather *individualized* results is merely to ask people you meet inside and outside your business a question designed to show how many and to what degree these five factors were employed in a specific ad. It won't be scientific, but it certainly will give you a no-cost glimpse of how you're doing.

The Easiest Ad Test

The easiest, most uncomplicated, most efficient way to test an ad is to pretest it. If you're wondering whether one layout or another is better or whether the headline wording and body text in one ad is better than a different wording, run both for a very short test schedule and compare the results.

Pretesting layouts is not to test the ad's beauty; it's to test its pull power. For example, a layout using one graphic as opposed to the same layout using another graphic or a difference in size or placement of the graphic might mean differences in attracting reader attention.

Few cities have more than one newspaper, but if yours is a two-newspaper town, make a coupon part of each ad and run the two ads simultaneously. If you key the coupons in one ad differently from the other—place different numbers or letters somewhere on each coupon—you can tell which ad had the greater pull power. If you don't wish to use keyed coupons, responses can be checked merely by asking each customer, "In which paper did you see the ad?"

If your town is a one-newspaper town, you can test the two ads by running first one and then the other over identical periods of time but in different weeks. Try to make the separate time periods as nearly identical as possible. Don't, for instance, run one ad during a normal week and the other on the same day during a holiday period.

You can check which day of the week brings the greatest number of responses by running the ad on each day of the week. This requires a seven-week test period to provide at least a week's period between runs to separate responses. This also requires some means of identification from the customer or by coupon to identify the day on which the ad appeared.

Testing Image-Building

Testing public reaction and response is relatively easy. If you keep in close contact and communicate with your customers, you'll know their reaction. And response tests out at the cash register.

Image is more difficult to test. Professionals call image-building ads "attitude advertising." It's the advertising you conduct to heighten the good attitude the public has about your business—its services, policies, reliability, honesty, and integrity. Such image builders are used to strengthen reputation and may call for separate ads, but if you are following the advice presented in this book, you know that attitude advertising also is a part of every ad.

This type of ad is difficult to measure because there rarely are the immediate response factors of telephone calls, coupon returns, or sales by which to judge it. This kind of ad builds results over time, and its effects are recognized when people express or subtly indicate preferences for your product, service, or company. The best test is to compare public attitudes against the goals you set for attaining improved opinions and increasing recognition.

7

Choosing Media

Build the Right Media Mix

Dow Jones News/Retrieval, in a self-promotion ad, shouts that "The flood has arrived. May we interest you in an ark?" In chapter 3 we quoted RJR Nabisco's chairman/CEO: "No more prizes for predicting rain. Prizes only for building arks."

It's time! The flood is upon you! And the plan you just finished is the ark that will carry you through a literal flood of media people wanting to help you get your advertising message out. Because the media portion of your allocation of advertising dollars is the largest and most significant share of it (up to 80 percent—the remainder is for production), where your ad messages are placed is one of the most important decisions in the entire advertising planning process.

Hazards

This chapter's task is to make you aware of the perils that await purchasers of advertising space or time and to set forth the means and methods to ensure that you make the best, most effective, most financially productive media buys to fit your goals, objectives, advertising plan, and advertising expense allotment.

At this point your job is to assess each medium's effectiveness in relation to your purposes before you spend a penny. Not only must you know how to handle overly zealous, sometime unscrupulous media salespeople, you should also be aware of new concepts and trends regarding media purchases. This knowledge can make you less vulnerable to a wide range of sales pitches.

For example, salespersons outside media may attempt to get you to spend your advertising dollars in other ways. They may claim that there is a dominant new trend to decrease advertising spending in traditional media. In support of the argument, they may cite a consultant's or economist's declaration that retailers are "focusing on getting customers to spend more rather than on getting more customers, [by] shifting spending to in-store merchandising, such as signage, and away from image advertising."

Such an argument can sound reasonable, particularly if the trend seems to indicate that everyone is doing it. Your research, however, which subsequently gave you the information to produce your advertising plan, is the only information that is right for your business, regardless of trends.

The Bombardment Becomes Heavier

It's likely that media salespeople have been bombarding you ever since your business opened its doors. Once word gets out that you have an advertising plan and money allocated for media purchase, the dam breaks, and the flood is on.

It can be a difficult time. "Real Life Adventures" cartoonists Wise and Aldrich put it into perspective for many small business would-be advertisers: "It is less frightening to walk into a gang of toughs than a gang of [media] salespeople who work on commission." It is important to be prepared and to be informed so that you govern decision making when you come face to face with media salespeople.

Now you'll find that media choices seem never to end. The list of merely the more traditional media types seems unlimited: newspapers, radio, magazines, television, direct mail, Yellow Pages, billboards, transit, and point of purchase ads (POPA).

As if there aren't enough conventional media, new ones are being added ceaselessly, it seems—some that appear almost on the fringe of absurdity. Have you heard about the sales throng that's out in force trying to peddle sales messages mounted on the backs of public toilet doors? Their level of creativity is expressed in the name of one of the companies specializing in these kinds of ads: Privy Promotions.

You've probably heard about place-based media because they've been around for awhile, and although they fall within the so-called creative category, some make sense. They follow users to schools, doctors' waiting rooms, and supermarkets. For instance, there are ads on the backs of supermarket purchase tapes, but the most popular place-based advertising is mounted on the basket you push around at the supermarket, to pitch products that the store wants you to purchase. Have you heard about ads on t-shirts on live models in New York City? And the latest is advertising on eggs you buy in grocery stores and on hot dogs.

You need a sturdy ark to rise above these kinds of creative advertising selling frenzies. It's your responsibility to your company to challenge every media form and demand that it demonstrate and prove its value. "Audience measurement is a key issue," states Betsy Frank, whose job as a senior vice president of a large international advertising agency includes new media. "It's too expensive for a company marketing a new medium to merely have a 'neat' idea. The medium has to show us how the opportunity fits in, what it provides that other opportunities don't, and the exclusivity of the medium."

Comparing Media

The numbers of media salespersons are countless, and they are determined to sell their products, regardless of whether the product fits an individual advertiser's needs.

The watchword in today's economy is "prove it." Not only must you be wary; you must be informed and prepared. It is your responsibility to challenge every media form in which your research indicates you may wish to advertise. It's your obligation to insist that they prove their value for your specific requirements. Before you make your final buying decision, consider the advantages and disadvantages of each:

	Advantages	Disadvantages
Newspapers	Short lead time Low cost per thousand Flexibility Extensive coverage of market	Competition from other ads, news stories

Magazines	Long life of ad
	Multiple readership
	Market selectivity
	Good reproduction of photo-
	   graphs
	Availability of color
		Long lead time
		Lack of flexibility
		Waste circulation
		Higher cost per thousand than
		   newspapers

Radio	Fast results
	Short lead time
	Flexibility
	Relatively inexpensive
	Market selectivity
	Substantial audience loyalty
		Short message life
		Limited to one sense
		Fragmentation of audience
		   (many stations compete for
		   listeners

Television	Fast results Impact Extensive reach Scheduling flexibility	High cost of airtime High cost of producing commercials
Direct mail	Most persuasive medium Can reach specific target groups	High cost per thousand "Junk-mail" problem

The good news is that in any given period there are good buys, and rates can be negotiated.

It's also good news that media sales managers are stressing how buyers should be treated. "The buyer is king," states Time Inc.'s vice president of sales. "The buyer is judge and jury. The customer is always right." The subhead on an *Advertising Age* special section spotlighting "Media Buying and Planning" says, "When sellers go acourtin' nowadays, they better treat buyers like royalty. Media sellers not heeding this advice: Off with their heads!" And it's not just the national media catering to big buyers that are recognizing this. The change extends all the way to local media and to small businesses.

How to Deal with Media Reps to Achieve Your Ends

The two most important things to remember and insist on is that you will be making the decisions, and you will retain control of the entire investigative and purchasing procedure.

You already know from your research what your objectives are and who you want to reach through advertising. You have a strong profile of your potential buyers. And you have a set number of dollars to spend plus a plan that will build the traffic and draw the people. You also are well aware that certain types of media will not reach your targets. A couple of obvious examples:

- if your target audience is predominantly retired people, your message on a rock radio station will never be heard by your intended targets.
- if your "constituency" is under age 25, an ad in a publication such as *Modern Maturity* will be money thrown away.

It's just common sense to fish where there are fish and to use the right bait to hook the kind of fish you want.

You Want Answers

There may be a number of things you're not sure of. What about radio? What about magazines? What about newspapers? Or television?

These media supposedly reach "everybody." The big question for you is whether they reach your audience. And if they do, will your limited advertising dollars permit using the specific medium you'd like to use, such as super-high-cost television? Or does the size of your dollar allocation for advertising demand using an alternate medium? There are so many questions, major ones, that must be fully answered, or your efforts and money will be washed away in the flood.

Media salespeople can, and should, do the analytical work for you as part of their sales job. Actually, they undoubtedly already have a large part of the information on file.

This is a time to be *objective,* to put out of your mind anything and everything you think you know about who reads newspapers, who watches television or listens to radio, and where, when, or why. Even if you had a handle on the information a year or so back, circumstances have changed so radically that the information may be obsolete today.

And this is NOT the time to let your opinions enter the picture. This is the time for Facts. And objective assessments. So, let the media sales people do the work for you! Call them in! However, call in only representatives from media you think may offer audiences that match your consumer profile and meet your reach and frequency requirements. And remember that you must retain control of the meetings with the salespersons whom you ask to bring you the information you need. Don't let them intimidate you. They have a product to sell, and they are just as willing to work hard to sell it as you are to work for success in your business. You are asking them only to do what is part of their selling job.

You are a very important person to media salespeople; your advertising dollars—no matter how many or how few—are their bread, peanut butter, and the jelly that goes with it.

Call salespeople in one at a time. Give each person the narrowly defined profile of your target consumer in written form. Title it a Fact Sheet. Never give them copies of your advertising plan or any of your other research information. Then ask each person only two questions:

1. "Why should I use your medium?" Let them know that this question is not, "Why should I use your newspaper [or your station, or your outdoor billboard]?" The question is: "Why should I use the *medium* of newspapers, or radio, or television, or outdoor boards?" You tell the person: "Here's the information about who my target is. Now you tell me why I should use your medium to reach this target. Convince me that your entire medium is the right one to reach the people I want to reach."

2. "How does your entire medium compare in cost to other media?" In a nutshell, you are asking a representative of one medium to tell you how the medium stacks up in terms of cost against all the other media available to you. You are not asking for a comparison of the individual newspaper with its direct competitors—other newspapers.

Those are the only two questions you will ask. At this time, no other information is significant or needed. When each person has answered the two questions, and only the two questions, send this person away! Even if the salesperson leaves to get the information, ask that it just be dropped off, and send him away again.

There isn't a good salesperson around who won't persistently try to switch the conversation from *your* boundaries to presenting specific information about his individual station or newspaper (or whatever medium is represented). But remember that you must remain in control.

You don't want—and shouldn't permit—any sales pitches or other information to be presented until after you've had time to gather, compare, and assess all the data from all the people you've asked in response to the two questions. (This is a protective measure. It circumvents a salesperson's grabbing an opportunity ahead of your assessment, to offer that "bargain" you just can't refuse.)

The answers to the two questions will provide you with a basis of comparison. Each medium has a different perspective and different figures, and each salesperson within that medium has different data that pertain specifically to the individual medium.

A Basis for Comparison

You are looking for data that will allow you to determine the one, two, or possibly three least costly ways to reach your target on the basis of cost per thousand impressions (CPM), a formula to measure the cost-effectiveness of your proposed media buy(s).

Radio and television are computed in time—seconds and minutes; print is figured in terms of space—lines and column inches. Under these confines, comparisons would be impossible. So the single common denominator for all media is called **cost per thousand** impressions, figured against your specific, narrowly defined target audience. CPM gives a reading on the cost of reaching your audience. Professional media buyers use CPM to evaluate costs of advertising among various media.

As an example, you are considering buying time for radio commercials. CPM works to estimate a single station buy to tell you the cost per thousand listeners who will, according to the station's surveys, hear your spot. CPM is calculated by multiplying the advertising cost times 1,000 and dividing by the total audience in that specific 15-minute segment in which your spot runs.

Let's say the airtime for running your spot is $500, and let's assume that the station's data show 45,000 people matching the age of your target audience are listening in the time period you're considering selecting. Here is the formula:

$$\text{CPM} = \frac{\$500}{45\text{M}} = \$11.11.$$

The figure is cost per thousand impressions for a single spot that costs $500. Typically, though, you would measure CPM over a complete schedule, not just for one radio spot. One spot—or one ad anywhere—is pretty much a waste of time and money (and there are facts to back it up a little further in this chapter). But if you're running several spots over a week's period, then you can figure your CPM based on the total cost of the schedule and the cumulative audience measured in quarter-hour increments for each quarter-hour time period in which your particular commercial ran over the period.

In this case, you can use the CPM formula as a comparison guide between radio stations. It is dependable, however, only when used to compare costs between stations when both reach the same target audiences.

It works the same way for a newspaper. Again, you have $500, but this time the paper reaches 68,000 readers who match your consumer profile. The cost then is $7.35 per thousand.

Additional Information Sources

Detailed national surveys are available, and there may be local or regional spin-offs of data by research firms that show specific comparative information about audience reading, listening, or viewing habits.

When the media reps bring you the requested information, undoubtedly a large portion of it will have come from one of the sources listed below. Although you can expect media reps to do the work for you, sometimes you may wish to do a little checking of your own. These are the best-known national surveyors:

- Audit Bureau of Circulations (ABC): newspapers, magazines, business publications, miscellaneous publications.
- Nielsen Station Index (NSI): radio and television in 220 markets.
- Daniel Starch and Associates: periodicals.
- Standard Rate & Data Service (SRDS): lists the rates and audience composition of virtually every available advertising medium.

Call Only the Right Ones Back

From your assessment of the data gathered from those first two questions asked of media salespersons, you now know which overall medium is best to reach your specific target, to achieve your objective, and to fit your allocated ad dollars. Now it's time to find out which individual medium within an overall category will be your choice. If, for instance, you've decided that radio is your best channel of communication, you will call in radio salespersons from stations that seem to reach listeners who match your consumer profile, to provide you with specific answers to specific questions. Ask each representative these questions:

- How many listeners does your station claim, substantiated and qualified by Nielsen?
- Who tunes in your station, demographically? by the quarter hour?
- Geographically, where are your listeners located?
- How many individuals in this age bracket, of this gender, in this income or level of education category, can you deliver in each time period?

The answers come from data each station has on file. Each can run up a computer-generated chart that shows precisely how many people, by gender, within specified age brackets, and by districts within the boundaries of each station's market, fit your requirements. Ask the same questions of each radio station representative.

If you plan to question print media reps, here are some questions you will want answered:

- Does your publication serve a special interest group—for instance, is it a journal for lawyers? Or is there regular special editorial content within the publication especially for real estate people (or whoever makes up your target audience)? How often and how extensive is that special content included? What are the numbers reached?
- Are you providing circulation or readership figures? (Circulation figures always are smaller than readership numbers, and they are a truer, more consistent, count.)
- Does the publication have a paid circulation, or is it free to readers?

- When were your circulation figures last updated?
- What is your percentage of editorial content to advertising matter? Most daily newspapers keep their editorial-advertising ratio to about fifty-fifty, and seldom is it over 60 percent advertising. The point of this question is that you don't want your ad lost in pages and pages of other companies' advertising.
- Is your editorial content of interest to my target audience?
- What arrangements can I make to have your editorial department include news stories about my company when we have something that has news value?
- Does your publication have special merchandising assistance such as naming our company or including our log in appropriate pieces of your publication's marketing materials, or do you offer free layout assistance? Are there other regular services or assistance you offer?

You can be sure that all salespersons have the answers to your questions pertaining to their individual medium. But getting the answers may be quite difficult: in the majority of cases, their medium is not the right place for your advertising messages, so they don't want you to have data that permit you to make that determination. Stand firm and demand this information. If they don't provide it, you will know those outlets are not right for your program.

Assess the Information

Because the information you are receiving confirms your belief that advertising is the way to go, your enthusiasm probably is at warp speed. It may be truly difficult to hit the pause button, take a deep breath, sit back and objectively assess information a sales rep has given you.

Make yourself a promise: you will not agree to any media purchase until after you have interviewed all individual media reps on your list, have all their information in hand, and have sent them away again to give yourself a cool-down period. There is a sound reason for this: when you have each representative's data before you, you may be astonished to notice that each medium seems to be number one among its competitors!

The information is presented in a manner to make it appear that this station, this newspaper, this magazine, is best in its field and the best for your purposes. (Later you can use the same technique for your advertising messages: choose areas where you excel and word the messages so that your target consumers will regard your product or services or company as the best among its competitors.)

This is where CPM comes in. With CPM you can determine how many people each medium reaches in your specific target audience—a verifiable means of comparison.

Tips for Media Buying

Following are some reminders and information to keep in mind as you talk to media salespeople:

- Ask for a break-out of subscription and single-copy sales figures. The latter—mainly newsstand sales—are not as reliable as the former because they fluctuate, sometimes radically, according to days of the week, holidays, even the weather.
- Every publication is proud of its special standing in a specific area, and some "firsts" are impressive. But be sure they have meaning with regard to your audience or your purchase.
- Be careful when a broadcast representative quotes frequency numbers to you. It may sound like a too-good-to-pass-up bargain when you're offered 100 spots to run at the station's choice of times in place of a single commercial to run at your choice of time, say during drive time, when people are on their way to and from work. You can bet the amount 99 more drive-time spots would cost you that the 100 offered will be aired in the low single-digit hours of the morning when every one of your prospects is fast asleep . . . unless, of course, you're pitching a sleeping aid to nonsleepers.
- Check rebates. If you run a greater number of ads or spots than the contract originally called for, which perhaps puts you into a discount price category, you are entitled to that discount. Or, if the audience quoted by the medium is not reached, a substantial number of media give credits to their advertisers. Check that you receive the discount or the credits.

How Many Media, How Many Messages, Are Enough?

There are million-dollar questions here. It is generally accepted that two or three media provide deep enough penetration for most small businesses. And generally the cost factor places more than that number beyond what most small business ad budgets will bear. Actually, one or two media may be quite enough, and possibly all your advertising dollar allotment will bear.

How can you decide between using two newspapers or one newspaper and one radio station? The answer doesn't come from you. It lies in the media habits of your target audience. For example, if you're selling a product that's bought mostly by teenage girls and young women, putting that advertisement in a newspaper would be a waste of money because the readership level of newspapers by teenage and young women is low. Nor would you put your message on an all-news, all-talk radio station because that's not the kind of radio they listen to. You would choose media that catch their eyes and ears, such as a regional edition of *Seventeen* magazine or a rock station that's skewed toward young females.

If one medium ultimately is considered enough, the job of determining which single medium to choose requires a little more effort to be sure it is the best and most productive in terms of your goals and the most effective in relation to numbers of dollars to be spent.

A bigger question—and a much more difficult one to answer—is, How many advertising messages are enough? No one has come up with a solid answer to this question. There is no formula that will give you an ideal-numbers answer. There are far too many variables, such as ad size or commercial length, the type of service, product, or company you have, and the times (in terms of hours for broadcast and days for newspapers and direct mail—or of seasons) when your advertisement runs.

Nor are there any statistics that show how often a consumer must see an advertising message for a particular product or service before buying that product or service. Yet all advertising professionals acknowledge that the rate of exposure is a critical factor in designing a media plan. Seeing an ad once is rarely enough to spur a customer to make a purchase. Many years of research show that it almost always takes at least three appearances of the same message even to catch a consumer's attention. The first one registers subliminally, the second gets noted, and the third typically is the first time the consumer consciously receives the message.

There is an exception, however, which specifically involves retail advertising in newspapers and Yellow Pages. A customer with a need for a car battery—it went dead yesterday—consciously goes to the newspaper, usually to the sports pages, to look for good buys in batteries. The same is true of such items as water heaters that on average fail at eight- or 10-year intervals. If a buyer is looking for a particular kind of dress to wear to a wedding, your women's wear clothing store ad might register with her first time out. In other words, when there is a burning need for a product or service, one appearance of your ad is sufficient. But it is a fact that consumers who are not predisposed to buy on the spot require multiple exposures to the same message in order to get the message.

There's more than adequate research showing that the value of repetition is cumulative, which means that far too often advertising is pulled or replaced just as it's beginning to work. The Advertising Research Foundation and The Association of Business Publishers have produced data that show that low levels of advertising yield minimal sales gains, while higher frequency triggers   gains of up to 600 percent.

The advice? It's the same for your company as for General Motors: let your advertising work for you. You're going to be tired of it long before it registers with the consumers it is targeted to reach actually see it, before they understand it, and it causes them to take action.

Rate Negotiation

Rate negotiation is a way of life. Published rates are viewed as an asking price, and most print buyers say that, despite their public stance, even newspaper publishers accept negotiation of price and other elements as a normal aspect of doing business.

Negotiation can be for lower prices, bigger ads, or more repetition. The best approach is to figure out exactly what you want. The common denominator in all negotiation is dollars per unit, so every negotiated extra really equates to a lower price. A bigger ad for the same dollars is really a lower price per unit; more insertions for the same dollars is really more units per dollar. However you negotiate it, it means that you're paying less per column inch or less per radio unit or less per television unit.

A Beta Research Study by *Advertising Age* turned up vital information that substantiates that rate cards are not etched in marble and are more readily negotiable than ever before. As *Ad Age* put it, advertisers are asking for and getting more bang for their ad buck: "Many media sellers outwardly deny—but privately concede—negotiation has become a way of life. Fully 44 percent of buyers say only 20 percent to 59 percent of all media buys are made at published or stated rates. Only 5.4 percent of those polled say all media buys are made at published prices." Rate negotiation, though, is not as widespread in newspapers as it is in broadcast or magazines. And it is a common practice in the television and radio industries where formal rate cards don't exist and prices are determined by supply and demand.

A small business isn't in as good a position to negotiate as large corporations, unless the medium is hungry for business. However, regardless of the amount of space or time you plan to purchase, you have nothing to lose by seeking lower rates, more space or time, or whatever other favorable negotiation you can manage. Times are never so good that there aren't some sellers who are willing to negotiate.

The essential point to remember is that no matter how great a rate cut you can negotiate, buying something on sale doesn't save money. Actually, it costs money. It just costs less money than it would have at the original price. So don't blow the budget out of the water just because you are able to negotiate a fantastic rate. Your job is to assess each medium's effectiveness in relation to your purposes before you spend a penny.

Media-Buying Services

If you feel you can't cope with media salespeople, your knowledge is too weak, or you are too busy, consider media-buying services. These services typically work on a commission basis, usually between 7 and 12 percent of the media buy. Their rates depend on the scope of the negotiations they must carry on with media. For instance, negotiating time with television and radio stations is far more complex than buying space in newspapers and magazines. One reason is that there is only so much time available, but print media can expand their space as needed to accommodate an increase in advertising.

As a small business with limited advertising dollars to spend in any one medium, the commission rate you will be charged will be at the high end of the scale because big businesses' big buys produce larger profits; hence, commission rates can be lower.

There Is a Way to Run with the Big Dogs

Relatively small businesses may be able to buy national publications to advertise a (sort of) local service or product. If substantial benefit would come from an ad for your product, your service, or your image appearing in, say, *The Wall Street Journal* or *USA Today,* there is a way you can achieve the benefit without actually going national.

Many nationally circulated publications have regional editions. *The Wall Street Journal* has seventeen advertising regions. *USA Today* offers twenty-six regions. This means that you can choose a single region in which your ad will appear. The cost is considerably less than publication nationally, but it still may be a budget buster for most businesses.

8

Writing Advertising Messages

The Message Is the Same.
Only the Format Changes

There are media people who will create and prepare your ads or commercials for you, and media salespersons will try to use that to snare your ad dollars. Nevertheless, having any medium create your ads can be a big mistake. The reason, as the saying goes, is that when you get something for free, you get exactly what you pay for.

The do-it-yourself technique works best because you know your product or service, your company, and your customers better than anyone else. By employing only a few tricks of the copywriting trade, you can turn out ad messages that will achieve your advertising objectives. There's a large personal payoff here too. The practice of writing has immeasurable value because it causes ideas to take shape. There is nothing so clarifying as writing things down, and the practice of writing your own advertising messages will increase your ability to think and communicate clearly.

If you use sales skills as part of your regular work, you're ahead in this copywriting exercise because you can turn that knowledge and ability to your advantage. But if you are reluctant to count sales skills among your assets, think of them as persuasion techniques, something you practice every day, regardless of the nature of your work.

The very heart of an advertising message is persuasion—persuading someone to buy something, to believe something, to do something. That's also at the heart of selling.

This chapter is about message content. It tells you what it takes to be a copywriter; about the elements of good copy; what goes in the message; technicalities involved in constructing the message; and whether to use humor. Remember that although advertising formats are different in each medium, the heart of your message is basically the same regardless of the medium. Assemble the ingredients you wish all of your advertising messages to contain, regardless of the medium in which they are placed.

Why People Buy

There are a lot of salespeople who live by Sinclair Lewis's declaration that people will buy anything that is one to a customer. Certainly scarcity is an important factor in buying decisions. Scarcity implies value and attractiveness. A limited time factor also stimulates buying. But mostly people buy to solve problems, to gain benefits, or because there is a unique quality that sets a product or service apart from that of its competitors.

The fact is that people read or listen to whatever has interest value to them. They are anxious to know about your product, service, or company if you connect it to their desires and needs or to their problems.

One of your most serious challenges is to give readers or listeners good reasons to spend their money. People have become cautious about spending and need a reason to buy. If, for instance, you're selling costly items such as real estate or recreation vehicles, you might offer insurance as an incentive; if anyone in the household loses a job, the payments are covered for a specified time. A worthwhile coupon is another possibility. Incentives that are applicable to your product or service dictate the kind or type of buying incentive to use.

Elements of Good Copy

Good advertising copy should inform, attract the eye or ear of the targeted individual, and be specific about the benefits of the product or service. It should be believable, sincere, and honest; be easy to read and easy to understand; and include components that will be remembered: an easily recognized logo and perhaps a graphic and a slogan that establishes identity and remembrance.

An ad, says an advertising veteran, is the answer to four questions:

1. What have I to sell?
2. Why should you buy it?
3. Where can you buy it?
4. What is the price? (If you omit price, consumers often assume the price is too high.)

Two vital ingredients in good advertising copy are enthusiasm and a caring, helpful attitude. Enthusiasm ranks right at the top of the list in producing a customer-catching advertising message. If you're not enthusiastic about your product or service or about your company, how can you expect to build others' interest in it? Reflect your enthusiasm in your writing. Enthusiasm, however, does not mean exaggerating, boasting, or writing in vague superlatives.

A helpful, caring attitude is an important characteristic in successful selling. Apply that thinking, and include it in your advertising message.

Health care facilities are no strangers to sermonizing about how caring and helpful they are, but one in Portland, Maine, got off the soapbox and provided tips on overcoming insomnia under a headline that said: "A lot of ads are boring, but this one could put you to sleep." The topic touches home with almost every reader—who hasn't experienced insomnia at some point?—but it also gives readers a feeling that the caregivers would be helpful in surmounting any health care problem. A major omission in the ad, however, was address and telephone number. Nowhere was the reader told how to contact the facility after reading a last part of the copy: "Now, close your eyes, sweet dreams, and remember, these pointers have been brought to you by [name of the facility]."

Message Guidelines

Warmly Greet Your Consumers

Advertising is saying, in a friendly, helpful way, "Hello. I have an important message for you." Friendliness helps express the caring attitude.

Beer ads have a corner on warm, friendly messages. They usually do it with a photo showing friends enjoying each others' company. One Moosehead billboard took a slightly different approach. It uses a lovely photograph of a lake at sunset with a small boat to set a relaxed, friendly scene. Superimposed over the photo are only seven words: MOOSEHEAD. MY TIME. MY FRIENDS. MY BEER.

A shoe store selling a well-known brand of women's shows uses a headline, "If pain persists, take two of these." A pair of the shoes is the only graphic, and the copy block describes the merits—benefits, if you will—from wearing this particular brand. The reader can identify with the message and feels a comfortable reaction.

Integrity

Readers may not think of integrity and honesty on the part of the advertiser as a benefit, but it's extremely important to them, so in every possible way, maximize the reader's or listener's belief in your business's integrity and honesty—and dependability.

The public has come to distrust just about everyone and every statement or claim, so the biggest element you have going for your company, your product, or your service is the public's belief and trust in it. Don't jeopardize the trust you already may have earned, and do all that you can to keep building it. Always write honest, truthful, sincere advertising messages.

There's No "I" in "Customer"

Give consumers the information about your product, your service, your company—or whatever else you are advertising—from their standpoint, not yours.

It's said there are two kinds of advertising people: "I" people and "you" people. Your copy should be "you" directed. What it all comes down to is reader interest; people want to know how a product or service will benefit them, how it will solve their problems, enhance their prestige, help them, save their money, time, or effort, please them, serve them, or entertain them.

They have little or no interest in what the product, the service, or your company means to you. There's no letter *I* in the word *customer*. It does have the letter *U*—spelled "you"—though.

It's natural to want to brag about your company or product from your perspective: We're the biggest, the best, the foremost. Instead, brag about it from the consumer's point of interest: (You can) count on us for friendly service, fast delivery, guaranteed dependability."

An example of an "I/we" people ad was for a bank. The headline ran the length of the space in mega-size type, with text running a line between each line of headline copy. The self-congratulatory headline literally shouted, "MONEY TALKS, AND IT SAYS WE'RE ONE OF AMERICA'S 100 SAFEST BANKS. AGAIN." It broke the "I" rule, but the copy establishes integrity like few other companies are able to—by quoting a leading financial magazine's "short list of the nation's 'supersafe' banks." In this case, the back patting is justified because it establishes a superiority the public wants.

Words Are Triggers

Words *are* the advertising message, whether it's in written or spoken form. Words are your tools, your triggers. Choose them to trigger emotions, trust, and beliefs that you want your reader or listener to feel and react to in a positive manner. Remember to choose words that drive your message home with the least amount of mental effort by your readers.

Be Sure There's Something In the Message

Be sure the message is not an empty pinata—fun to swat but with nothing worthwhile inside when it's swatted open. Your message must inform.

People want information. Many advertisers don't yet recognize this essential fact, but there is increasing evidence that substantive, informative advertising demanded by today's consumers is being used with much greater results by more and more advertisers.

Benefits Are the Meat of the Copy

Benefits are what every reader or listener looks for in advertising copy. There's always their unspoken question to be answered: "What's in it for me?"

Because this is such an important aspect, pull out the list of consumer benefits you made in chapter 3. Then gather your staff to help rank them in the order of their importance *to users*. You won't use them all in a single message (that would drag the copy out and invite readers to flip on past your message), but some media formats permit the use of more benefits than in other forms, so keep your prioritized list on file to save time whenever you write an advertising message.

A moving company loaded its print publication ad copy with benefits. The headline said, "A moving story that has a great beginning, a snappy delivery, and a happy ending." What reader, faced with the dread of moving day, wouldn't respond well to the oblique reference to a promise that the experience can be pleasant? The body copy offers more benefits, including an offer of a free copy of a "fact-filled reference [that] contains everything from packing tips to parental advice from child psychologists." It continues with assurances that the movers will provide prompt, reliable service and reminds the reader that there is an end-of-the-rainbow finish: a happy home.

Connect with the Reader or Listener

One of the most important things your advertising copy must do for the reader or listener is create interest. Otherwise readers merely flip past your ad or broadcast spot or mentally turn it off.

Advertising professional John Lyons calls newspaper and magazine readers "flippers." He says a flipper is "to printed media what a zapper is to electronic media. A zapper mutes or tunes out TV programming—and commercials—via remote control."

Your job then, is to grab interest because even the best trigger words can work for you only if potential buyers actually read or listen to your message. And only you know what will trigger your consumers' interest and the words that will "flipper-proof" your advertising message.

Newspapers are renowned for excellent self-advertising. The *Minneapolis Star Tribune* was out to capture readers who like to fish, so it used two graphics: an actual-size comparison of the human brain and a fish brain. The small copy block at the bottom of the page was in recognition of the need for speed reading by busy individuals. The headline read, "You Wouldn't Think You'd Need Our Fishing Tips." The copy was not only short but amusing enough to be appealing:

Despite man's much superior intellect, fish have always been elusive prey. Which is why you should include the *Star Tribune* in your tackle box. Every Sunday and Wednesday in the Outdoors section, we'll provide information to help you be more successful. Of course, we can't guarantee results, but it beats relying on dumb luck.

Avoid Bad Taste

"Bad taste" covers a multitude of advertising sins—for example, sustaining an ethnic stereotype; using fear or intimidation to get people to buy; attempting to make a potential buyer feel guilty; indicating a reader or listener is wrong; any show of a lack of sensitivity, tact, or feeling; crude language even if it is in current use. Perhaps one of the best examples of bad taste advertising showed up in New York City in one of those offbeat "creative" advertising mediums, sidewalk stencils. Stenciled on the pavement was this message:

FROM HERE,

IT LOOKS LIKE

YOU COULD USE SOME

NEW UNDERWEAR.

(The name of the lingerie company followed.)

Some professional advertising people maintain that it is better to be noticed than ignored, that a touch of bad taste won't hurt. No, no, no! A message that has even a slight touch of tastelessness adds up to only one result: the potential buyer turns against the product, the service, the company. Messages in poor taste can so outrage readers or listeners that they will go out of the way not to buy the product or service. More than that, they will go out of the way to tell others not to buy it.

Comparing your product, service, or company with that of a competitor can provide useful information for a consumer if it's done in an informative manner. But bashing the competition rarely, if ever, convinces anyone of your superiority, and it can send recipients of the message running in the opposite direction.

Telling Is Not Selling

Telling is not selling. It's not even persuading. People won't read your message if it doesn't give them information they want or need. But they won't buy merely from a recitation of information.

You have your prioritized list of benefits and the substantial reasons readers or listeners will be interested. Now it's time to tell them what to do. Now it's time to sell.

Hard Sell or Soft Sell?

There are two selling approaches: hard sell, using aggressive, high-pressure selling tactics, and soft sell, which employs subtle, unaggressive methods. The type of business, product, or image you have or wish to portray determines the approach you take. Soft sell is used most often to sell image. Hard sell is like a barker at the state fair who stands at the entrance to a tent show and loudly shouts his sales pitch to attract passersby. It's used when there is serious competition and a sharp need for sales but little necessity for product identification.

One 30-second television commercial uses hard sell with humor in a hammy way that gets its point across without "barking" too imprudently. It's not a new concept to use a television evangelist as a spokesperson, but this one does it better than most others: "How many among you have used unskilled mechanics to change thy oil—to lay unworthy hands upon thy suffering brakes?" A congregation of cars flaps its hoods and honks its horns in response. The salvation comes when the evangelist says that Precision Tune can "cure all thy automotive ills." Obviously, this kind of sell will not work for a bank or an accounting firm that wishes to build and maintain an image of dignity, honor, character, and integrity. But it's not as blatant as used car companies are inclined to use, and the touch of buffoonery tends to soften the hard sell.

Writing the Message

To begin to write an ad message, speak to an imaginary customer and use a tape recorder to record your words. (Think of it as renting space in the mind of your consumer.) Actually sit down with a friend or business associate, and mentally place that person in the position of the reader or listener you wish to persuade. Then talk about your product, or your service, or your company—whichever is the focus of your advertising message. Tell your listener the main one or two, and at the most three, points your research showed are his or her prime interests, and present them in the order of their importance.

Transcribe your talk onto paper, being sure to preserve the conversational tone. These transcribed words become the first draft of your copy. Now you can edit—tightening, shortening, and honing to the bone—your final message.

Always remember that the words you write are not fixed. You are typing or handwriting them, not engraving them. And even after they're set in type and ready to be printed, they still can be changed. You can test-run your ad, and after it has run, pull it and make changes as many times as necessary, until it presents the money-making message you mean it to be.

You won't actually write your final copy until you know exactly the amount of time or space in which you intend to run it so that it can be constructed to fit the format of the individual medium in which it will run.

Long or Short?

The word *ad* is part of the term *ad rem*, which means, "to the point, pertinent." Advertising copy definitely should be to the point and pertinent. It can be long or short, depending on the amount of space or time purchased, and how much information the reader needs in order to make a decision.

Educator and former adman Maurice I. Mandell asks, "How much should copywriters write?" and then gives a useful answer:

> There is little question that [copywriters] have to capture and hold their audiences; and the longer they have to hold them, the more likely they are to lose them.
>
> Yet the rule, "the shorter the copy the better," is not necessarily sound either. There are advertisements that contain *very* lengthy copy and still get high readership. Perhaps a sounder rule is that copy should be as long as is necessary to tell the story, but without unnecessary verbiage.

In other words, long, boring copy won't persuade. It won't even be read.

Use Short Words, Short Sentences, and Short Paragraphs

The simpler and more concise and succinct (not terse) that the message is, the more readily it will be understood and remembered. The headline of the moving company ad already referred to is almost as long as the text beneath it. There are two paragraphs containing a total of five sentences, each honed to a fine point.

Read ads with an eye toward writing them. Newspaper stories are also good to study the use of short words, short sentences, and short paragraphs without sounding disjointed, jerky, and uneven.

An excellent illustration of these three tenets is a two-column, seven-inch ad for a ranch that appeared in *The New York Times*. The headline—"The Best Place to Begin the Rest of Your Life Is . . . "—is intriguing enough to make you want to read on to the copy—short, sweet, and full of benefits:

- a three hour drive from New York or Boston . . .
- an hour from the Albany and Hartford airports . . .
- minutes to [a number of sightseeing highlights] . . .
- surrounded by the most breathtaking landscape in the world . . .
- the best gift you'll ever give yourself.

The ranch name with an 800 number follows the body copy. And following that is a repeat of the headline, which is the business's slogan.

Use Adjectives Sparingly

You can weaken copy with an abundance of adjectives. The right adjective in the right place is fine, but those who are new to the writing business sometimes feel that every noun must have its adjective.

When you do use an adjective, use an explicit one. *Very* means little. The reader wants to know more about the product, or the service, or the company than that it is very strong, very honest, very dependable. In what way is it strong, honest, and dependable?

When you do use an adjective, try to make it one that triggers an emotion, a feeling, a sensation, a sentiment. An example given by the late United Press International reporter Frederick Othman illustrates: "If you're using brown as a color word, instead of describing it as dark brown, call it chocolate-colored. That," said Othman, "suggests food and any word connoting food adds interest value."

Avoid Participles

Nouns and verbs are mandates for action and give copy strength. Participles—verbs that function as adjectives, as in: a *skyrocketing* cost or a *solved* problem—can go a long way toward weakening your writing. The reason is that when participles are used, verbs are not, and without verbs, the writing is feeble, dull, and lifeless.

Write It Right

"One morning I shot an elephant in my pajamas. How he got in my pajamas, I'll never know." With characteristic humor, Groucho Marx vividly made the point about how swiftly meaning can change when words or phrases are wrongly juxtaposed. It can be funny, as Marx's example is, but this is not the kind of humor you want to present.

One sure way to weaken your copy is to use the passive voice. Passive voice and passive verbs are weak. Instead choose strong, active verbs to make your writing clearer, shorter, and more exciting. *Was* or any of the "to be" verbs are a big clue to passive:

> *Weak:* You've been told you will have to trade in your car for a newer model.

> *Better:* You *know* it's time to buy a newer car!

Similes, which compare things and use *like* or *as* to show the comparison, are an excellent way to make your ad copy more effective than a car horn in New York City. You might tell a consumer that "it's an investment as ready to take off running as a retriever after a tossed ball." Or, the motor is so quiet it runs "like a butterfly sipping nectar."

No one remembers everything that's said or written, but they remember everything they feel, so remember Frederick Othman's example about using *brown* as a color word—to use *chocolate-colored*. That comes very close to being a simile.

How's Your Grammar?

Check every detail in your ad for accuracy, even grammar. A set of "unrules" you may wish to keep handy as a checklist and grammar reference guide was published in *California Publisher:*

1. Don't use no double negative.
2. Make each pronoun agree with their antecedent.
3. Join clauses good, like a conjunction should.
4. About them sentence fragments.
5. When dangling, watch your participles.
6. Verbs has to agree with their subjects.
7. Just between you and I, case is important too.
8. Don't write run-on sentences they are hard to read.
9. Don't use commas, which aren't necessary.
10. Try to not ever split infinitives.
11. Its important to use your apostrophe's correctly.
12. Proofread your writing to see if you any words out.
13. Correct spelling is esential.

A Few Words About Humor

Some advertisers say humor sells. Others think that there is nothing worse than humor that isn't funny. And some advertisers say that when humor is used, people are inclined to remember the wit and forget the product. There is research, however, that indicates tongue-in-cheek ads outscore other types because funny ads or commercials are memorable and persuasive. Humor also tends to accomplish what today's overly busy people keep demanding: to "lighten up."

A message that uses humor well is almost all headlines:

COME.

SIT.

STAY.

GOOD DOG.

The copy below the headline is a mere three lines ending with an all-caps logo with address and telephone number, and it's only then that your funny bone gets tickled. The ad is for a Chicago hot dog eatery:

Chicago Dog House has Vienna Beef Hot Dogs smothered in your choice of toppings. And with our fast service, you won't have to beg for your food.

There are freelance copywriters who specialize in humor, but charges for their services usually are high. Take heart, though. Bob Hope's joke writer, Gene Perret, says that "everyone can learn to use humor effectively." Your local library has how-to books and articles on the subject. Study a few of them, and learn the skill. Humor used in your advertising copy could yield extra dollars for you.

If you use humor, make sure that it fits the situation. Don't kid about funeral services or death benefits in insurance policies. In other words, don't offend. And don't, even humorously, criticize your reader's judgment or taste.

Call attention to what you sell, not to yourself as the writer. Many for-hire humor writers want readers to think about how clever the words in the ad are rather than about how and where they can buy the product. This attitude not only decreases the likelihood of a sale but may create dislike for the product.

You have nothing to lose in attempting humor. The worst that can happen is you'll recognize it doesn't quite come off or isn't right for this particular advertising message, so you toss the copy and start over in a more straightforward manner. If you have doubts, read the copy to associates or friends, and watch their reactions.

If you have the gift of being able to make your readers or listeners laugh or smile, by all means use it. If humor is a struggle, it undoubtedly is better to avoid the attempt.

Writing the Close

Before you even sat down to write the message, you knew the purpose of the ad and what you wanted the would-be customer to do: buy your product; redeem a coupon; become a client of your accounting firm; list property with your real estate firm; have a car fixed at your repair shop. Just as in person-to-person sales pitches, every advertisement for a product or a service must ask for an order. So before you sign off the copy, ask that reader or listener to do whatever it is you've been leading up to.

Perhaps you're not asking for a sale. Perhaps you want another kind of response: for example, make a request for literature, send in a form giving pertinent information, or accept a free gift. But whatever it is, you must give the details about how to do it and tell the consumer to do it now. You must ask for action.

If you're asking the person to buy, provide a form that makes it easy to order with a place for the reader's name, address, and telephone number and with adequate space to write the information.

If you are calling for payment, provide the methods of payment you accept. If payment includes personal checks, state how the check should be made out.

Include on the order form the mailing address where the order form and payment may be mailed. Don't make readers look elsewhere in your ad for your company's name and mailing address. Also provide a telephone number, with information about whether you accept telephone orders, but also so readers can obtain additional information. Or perhaps your ad triggers a reminder of something else the reader wants to order. If the telephone number is handy, the customer may call to make the purchase or set up the appointment, which would go unmade if he or she needed to look up the number.

Make it as easy for readers to respond as you can. Anything that makes responding complicated or difficult may be the single reason that discourages a potential customer from acting.

Check Your Copycat File

If you're still not sure of the direction you want to take, pull out your collection of ads that have impressed you, piqued your interest, or stimulated your desire to buy or do business with the advertiser. Read through the ones that seem to be heading in the direction you wish your advertising to go. Don't read with an eye to copying them; read to get ideas.

In 1969, Milwaukee newspaper promotion director Newell G. Meyer presented valuable information at a meeting of the International Newspaper Promotion Association (INPA) that included two checklists. They are reprinted here as checklists for your copycat ideas and because they are excellent questions to ask at an advertising evaluation meeting of staffers.

A Summary of Some of the Kinds of Self-Interrogation That Can Lead to Ideas

• *Adapt?* What else is like this? What other idea does this suggest? Does the past offer a parallel?

• *Modify?* New twist? Change meaning, color, motion, sound, odor, form, shape? Other changes?

• *Magnify?* What to add? More time? Greater frequency? Stronger? Higher? Longer? Thicker? Extra Value? Plus ingredient? Duplicate? Multiply? Exaggerate?

• *Minify?* What to subtract? Smaller? Condensed? Miniature? Lower? Shorter? Lighter? Omit? Streamline? Split up? Understate?

• *Substitute?* What else instead? Who else instead? Other ingredient? Other material? Other process? Other place? Other approach? Other tone of voice?

• *Rearrange?* Interchange components? Other pattern? Other layout? Other sequence? Transpose cause and effect? Change pace? Change schedule?

• *Reverse?* Transpose positive and negative? How about opposites? Turn backward? Turn it upside down? Reverse roles? Change shoes? Turn tables? Turn other cheek?

• *Combine?* How about a blend, an assortment? Combine purposes? Combine appeals? Combine ideas?

Checklist for Evaluating Ideas

• Have you considered all the advantages or benefits of the idea?

• Have you pinpointed the exact problem or difficulty your ideas is expected to solve?

• Is your idea an original, new concept, or is it a new combination of known elements, a new adaptation?

• What immediate or short-range benefits or results can be anticipated?

• How will it contribute to profits, and how much?

• Have you checked the idea for any possible faults or limitations?

• Have you checked the operational soundness of the idea?

• Are there any problems the idea might create?

• Have you considered the economy factor or its implementation? What person-talent, time for development, investment, marketing costs, etc., does it entail?

• How simple or complex will its execution or implementation be?

• How well does it fit into the current operation of the company?

• Could you work out several variations of the idea, to afford those who will judge it a freedom of choice?

• Does it have a natural sales appeal? How ready is the market for it?

• Have you considered the possible user resistances or difficulties?

• Does your idea fill a real need or does the need have to be created through promotional and advertising efforts?

- Is it compatible with other procedures or products of the company and its overall [goals and] objectives?
- Is it a right new product area for your company?
- Are there any specific circumstances in your company that might make the acceptance of the idea difficult?
- Have you estimated the time it will take to prepare?

9

Newspapers

When and How to Use Them

To hear salespersons from competing media tell it, newspapers are dying. And they try to prove it by saying that circulation penetration—the ratio of copies sold to households—is falling. But you as an advertiser are interested in readership facts—a more accurate, informative measure of a newspaper's value. And the Newspaper Association of America (NAA) has the facts: daily newspaper readership is holding steady, and Sunday readership is up.

Daily newspapers may have had a struggle through the economic downturn of the 1980s, but weekly community papers, the newspapers that may serve your advertising needs best, are and have been hale and very hearty. According to a Veronis, Suhler industry report, ad spending growth in weeklies outpaced the rate for daily papers during most of the 1980s. And those weeklies, especially the fast-growing free suburban papers, are expected to stay strong, as low overhead continues to translate into affordable ad rates and city folk maintain their migration to the suburban weekly market.

Newspaper technologies are out in front: document-tracking systems accelerate the assembly of files for pagination; better color-editing programs allow quicker and more accurate electronic processing of images; page layout and photo editing software are common; and faster software for faster image processing speeds pages to the press. These changes have meaning for you because along with these there are such advances as programs to test the effectiveness of newspaper ads against direct mail and electronic commercial verification that you're getting exactly the ads you pay for. Additionally, newspapers are beginning to take advantage of and offer to both small and large businesses customer databases and a daily distribution system.

An example shows the strength you may already have at your local metropolitan daily or that is predicted to be available soon over most of the country. The *Spokane Spokesman-Review* culled its subscribers and identified 7,000 dog owners for a local pet and seed store. A letter to the dog owners told them to watch for an upcoming ad in the newspaper that would entitle them to a discount on any purchase and on the cost of a picture of the owner with pooch. When asked how well it worked, the store's owner said it had worked too well; nearly 600 people and their pets stood in line waiting to have their pictures taken. The owner stressed that he wasn't complaining; he figured the campaign introduced 200 to 300 new customers to his store.

An Attitudinal Change

One of the biggest changes in newspapers has nothing to do with technology and that favors advertisers: a new willingness to negotiate advertising rates. The change is quite remarkable in the eyes of long-time newspaper advertisers and good news, particularly to local business advertisers who are interested only in placing local advertising messages in their local newspapers.

Media buyers at advertising agencies were the first to notice a willingness on the part of newspaper management to negotiate in terms of breaking their rate cards. Now it is broadly accepted that newspapers have undergone a dramatic attitudinal change. This doesn't mean that they are willing to break rate for a single insertion ad, but often they will deal on multiple placements.

Even the often inflexible *The New York Times* is changing. The gospel of customer service is being spread to all business departments at *The Times*, the corporate relations manager for *The Times* tells *Advertising Age*. "Instead of 'that sounds impossible' or 'it can't be done,' the first response to advertisers now is 'we'll get back to you' and then see if it can be done."

Gannett Co., the largest newspaper chain, with eighty-one daily newspapers, also is telling its dailies to help their advertisers. Gannett has developed a program it calls ADvance, designed solely to make its newspapers more sensitive to and understanding of advertisers' wants and needs.

Knight-Ridder, the nation's number two chain, has an ongoing sales training program that focuses on better ways to serve advertisers' needs.

All of these changes may be appearing at a newspaper near you. Look for them, and ask about them.

Incentive Programs

Not only large newspaper chains and papers the size of *The New York Times* are working to help advertisers; local daily newspapers are offering special incentive programs too. *Value-added* is the new catchword in advertising at these newspapers. Rather than lowering rates, some papers are adding bonuses. "Advertisers want more for their media dollars today," acknowledges the *Milwaukee Journal-Sentinel*'s vice president of marketing. "We have to become partners in ways that pay off for them."

Many of these value-added enhancements involve some kind of a charity sponsorship. For instance, in Clearwater, Florida, a drugstore made a grant to the Broward Public Library Foundation to support its annual Children's Reading Festival. The local newspaper ran ads to promote the event and named the drugstore as a sponsor. When the drugstore began running its own ads shortly before the festival, it urged consumers to visit the drugstore for a coupon good for a free children's book at the event. An official of the drugstore spoke enthusiastically about the value-added promotion; it boosted store traffic, increased impulse sales, and presented the kind of image—caring and concerned—the store works hard to project. Other programs of this sort are keyed to giveaways and sweepstakes. Another newspaper ties its programs to sharing data with advertisers from a large consumer analysis survey it conducts each year.

One of the biggest pluses so far is that most of the value-added projects around the country are tied to local advertisers rather than the usual practice of putting benefits in the pockets of big-time, big-spending national advertisers.

Programs to link subscribers and advertisers are showing up not just in the largest papers but in such diverse geographic locations as Boise, Idaho; Hartford, Connecticut; Reno, Nevada; Richmond, Virginia; Rockland County, New York; Tucson, Arizona; and Wilmington, North Carolina. Subscribers who pay in advance receive cards qualifying them to receive discounts from area merchants who are advertisers with the newspapers. The cards are valid for the life of the subscription prepayment period.

Advertisers gain in two ways: added store traffic and increased exposure through the advertising placed by the newspapers in support of the program. Subscribers realize savings from the discounts offered. The gains for newspapers are obvious: readers continue to renew their subscriptions.

Newspapers as an Advertising Medium

One page of newspaper print contains more information than the entire television nightly news, and readers can digest it selectively in a fraction of the time, says William B. Ziff, Jr., chairman of Ziff Communications Co. Newspapers are the medium that readers turn to for detail whenever any kind of event or crisis occurs, after they receive the headlines from electronic media. And most important for advertisers, only print has the capacity for the detailed product information in advertising that's needed to sell today's comparison-shopping consumers.

Newspapers not only provide more information to readers but also go far beyond providing customary data for advertisers. Now it's possible to acquire from newspapers information such as age, address, and psychographic and demographic information. Most metropolitan daily newspapers have advanced databases, and many offer highly sophisticated delivery systems for advertising messages so that not only can specific consumer types be targeted but so can the neighborhoods in which they live. Any of those reasons may cause you to choose one or more newspapers as the medium to carry your advertising message.

On the other hand, you may have chosen the medium because it offers services that none other offers, services such as those of *The Poughkeepsie Journal*. This New York State paper has a new program, Adopt an Advertiser Service, which covers everything from monitoring—checking placement, appearance dates, reader reaction and such—of individual ads to a telephone contact system that addresses advertisers' concerns. Or perhaps you chose newspaper advertising because of a special service such as *The Tallahassee Democrat* offers, which makes its extensive market research services available to advertisers in the Tallahassee market.

If you haven't yet decided newspapers are the best place—or at least a better place—for your advertising message, here are some points on both sides of the ledger. First the plus factors:

- Flexibility. You can buy just about any size space—from full pages and entire sections down to a single column inch. And you can buy that space in any part of the newspaper that you feel is the most likely place for your special audience to see it. There is no problem of space allotments, as with radio's and television's time allocations, with the added broadcast problem that the best time slots are not available because they are under contract to long-time advertisers. Newspapers can increase or decrease the size of each day's paper to accommodate the needs of all advertisers.
- Short lead times can be a mighty advantage if you need to change your message quickly—say, because of unexpected weather changes or unforeseen events. A newspaper's advertising deadlines permit preparation of your ad one day for its run the following day. In many cases, a standby ad on file at the newspaper for just such quickly needed changes permits same-day changes.
- Fast response times by readers give an immediate test of the effectiveness of your message. Same-day response always is highest, but reaction can continue for several days after the advertisement has run. The number of responses gives an excellent, almost instant, analysis of how well your message is pulling or whether it should be redone.
- One of the great pluses for small budget advertisers is that newspapers are the preference medium for co-op advertising. (Co-op advertising is explained in chapter 2.)

There are some less desirable factors too:

- Smudgy reproduction on newsprint, although less prevalent with offset presses used by a majority of newspapers, may be the greatest disadvantage to using newspapers for advertising. Even with offset and better-grade newsprint, larger type and bolder typefaces must be chosen for easy readability. You cannot expect fine-line art, photography, and type to reproduce as well as on slick, coated paper. Strong contrast photos with clean, clear black and white areas and a minimum of shadings are essential for good reproduction on newsprint.

- Each newspaper has its heaviest advertising days, usually at mid-week with a profusion of grocery ads, and pre-weekend with department store advertising. Sundays usually are also heavy with advertising. A small-space advertisement can get buried in the clutter on those days.

- Newspapers are read quickly by businesspeople in a hurry to get to work. On the other hand, retirees and others without time commitments may spend hours with their newspaper. It is important to know how your audience reads the newspaper, so that you can construct your message to be brief, to the point, and a fast read for overly busy readers or with longer copy and greater detail for the person with more time.

Producing the Ad

You've chosen newspaper advertising. Now you want to produce an effective, productive advertisement that will grab the eyes of every newspaper reader who fits your consumer profile—one that will send this person rushing to the telephone to call, to the post office to mail an order, or into your place of business.

One of broadcasting's best-known commentators, Charles Osgood, in his book *The Osgood Files,* makes a point worth remembering in constructing print ads:

> There is a big difference between listening to something on a broadcast and reading it in print. If something doesn't make sense to you on the air, you just shrug and figure you must have missed something. But if something doesn't make sense in print, you can go back a few lines and try to pick up the thread. If it still doesn't make any sense the reader has every reason to conclude that it never made any sense in the first place. What I'm saying is that you can get away with more in hot air than you can in cold print.

The components for producing newspaper advertisements that will meet qualifications are explored in the following sections. Earlier, in chapter 8, you thought through what it is you want to include in your message and how it should be presented. You decided:

- Whether the message is to be hard sell or soft sell. The decision matters because not only the words but the look ôf the ad will vary accordingly. Soft sell is to inform or to sell an image; hard sell is meant to move products or services.
- The best way to create reader interest.
- The most important reason people want or need to buy your product or service and to feature that single reason: to solve a problem, to gain benefits, or because your product or service has a unique quality that sets it apart from the competition.

Another decision you made was the way in which your message will inform, because today's buyers want substantive information in advertising.

Pull out those decisions you made earlier about content and the facts that will bring good responses to your message. Keep handy the draft copy you wrote earlier, or your notes, for reference as you construct this ad. And give it a little longer KIS-S-S: Keep It Simple-Sincere-Straightforward.

There is a simple formula described by advertising executive Hal Betancourt that many professionals resort to when copywriter's block hits them or just to keep them on track. It is the AIDA formula, which stands for:

Attention (headline)
Interest (subheadline)
Desire (text, or body copy)
Action (closing)

Headlines

Headlines Take Top Billing

The headline is the most important individual element in newspaper advertisements. It has two main functions: to attract attention and to provoke interest. A minor additional purpose may be to improve the look of the overall ad, particularly if the copy block (text) is long enough to give an imposing, dull, gray appearance. The headline and subheads are a means to relieve such a look.

A graphic (an illustration) may share importance with the headline, but it alone cannot accomplish what a headline can and should do. It may, for example, be the first component that stops a reader for an instant. If the graphic does its job, it will entice the reader to read the headline, and the few words that make up the headline should grab a reader's interest to a sufficient degree to persuade her or him to read the rest of the copy.

A headline has no place in a radio or television commercial; radio and television are, in effect, all-copy format ads. But a newspaper ad without a headline will accomplish its goal about as easily and safely as a bungee jump with a frayed cord; you're taking a huge gamble if your headline isn't as strong as you can possibly make it.

Get Out the Notepad

If you are able to construct a really good headline on a first try—or even a fifth or tenth try—you're in the wrong business. Advertising agencies all over the country will pay big money to hire your talent.

Don't try to write a finished product until you've jotted down all the possibilities that enter your mind. In this note-making stage, don't worry about the words you use or about length, and don't judge ideas. (If this preliminary task leaves you staring at a blank piece of paper, put the headline writing project aside for now and come back to it after you've written the body copy—the main text in the body of the ad. It's often much easier after the copy is written to know how to word the headline. Many professionals follow this procedure.)

After you've drafted all the headline ideas you can think of, pick the best one and begin the polishing job. Throw out every unnecessary word—*the* and *and* are examples of throwaway words—and check the thesaurus for powerful synonyms that strengthen reader appeal. Then polish, polish, polish.

If you think this is taking too much time, listen to what one of the biggest names in advertising, David Ogilvy, has to say in his book, *Confessions of an Advertising Man:* "On the average, five times as many people read the headline as read the body copy. When you have written your headline, you have spent eighty cents of your dollar. If you haven't done some selling in your headline, you have wasted 80 percent of your [advertising] money." Ogilvy never wrote fewer than sixteen headlines for a single ad before he made his final choice.

More Advice

The quickest and most effective way to grab readers' eyes and minds is to appeal to their self-interest. Go back to your consumer profile and check which benefit, what purpose, or what unique quality ranks highest in interest value to your present and potential consumers. Tell them up front in that headline what's in it for them. If the message is directed to a particular group—gardeners, diners, travelers, mothers of infants, African-Americans, Hispanics, signage shoppers, people needing an accountant—let them know it in your headline.

The personal approach is another basic means to reach readers. Imagine that your future consumer—in the person of a friend—is sitting across from you. Write both the headline and the body copy to this person on a one-to-one basis.

If possible, include your company, product, or service name in the headline or subhead.

Stretch the KISS-S-S- acronym still more: Keep It Simple-Short-Straightforward-Satisfying. Write in the same easy-to-understand language you speak. As an example, John Pullen, quoted in *Printer's Ink,* says: " 'Cease motion, observe carefully and note sound of approaching train,' can't compare with 'Stop, Look and Listen'."

Finally, ask yourself if the headline is a "say-nothing" headline. If it is, you're getting ready to throw eighty cents of your dollar's worth of advertising in the trash can.

How Long Should the Headline Be?

There are proponents on both sides of this question. David Ogilvy believes the number of words in a headline isn't as important as the selling promise that it contains. He says the best headline he ever wrote was a long eighteen words.

Wordy, rambling headlines, however, are not condoned by any advertising professional. An excellent example of a long headline that says it all even while breaking some headline-writing rules follows:

The
$99
affordable
Easy-To-Use,
Practical,
effective,
Top Rated,
Monitored,
Wire-Free,
Security System
you control with
your phone.

This headline took up almost the entire two-column by 7-inch ad.

On the other side of this fence are those who say no headline should have more than five or six words. Abraham Lincoln, a tall man, probably had the best solution. When he was asked how long a man's legs should be, he answered, "Just long enough to touch the ground." Make your headline just long enough to do the job.

Content is the best determinant of length.

Make the Headline Easy to Read

Newspapers for years printed headlines over news stories in all capital letters. Now they know that all-caps are difficult to read. Cash in on this knowledge, and use upper- and lowercase **boldface** type.

Headlines that are overprinted, as over a color block or a screened tint block or over part of an illustration, are difficult to read. Separate your headline from any distracting influences.

A Headline Can Get You Fired!

If you're not the boss, an unintended double-meaning headline can get you fired. If you are the boss, it could be mighty embarrassing.

Chuck Silverman today is a top-rated advertising man, but the first headline he wrote got him fired. *Advertising Age* tells the story:

Fresh from California State University in Northridge [California] in 1966, the born and bred Los Angeleno splashed this huge headline on a newspaper ad for a slacks sale at a local Sears, Roebuck & Co. store: "The big thing in men's pants."

Intended or purely unintentional, double entendre can be risqué; worse, it can be risky. And it surely will be misunderstood. Be sure you listen to your words—whether they are in a headline, body copy, print, or a television or radio commercial.

Sometimes Two Heads Are Better Than One

Sometimes subheads under your main headline and throughout your copy let you say more, and they can give an ad with a large copy block a more attractive look. Subheads are lines of copy in headline format that are spaced throughout an ad. They can appear in smaller type as an overline above the headline, immediately below it, or throughout the body copy in smaller type than the main head but larger than type in the body text. They are meant to add a new idea, make a point that appears in the copy that immediately follows, or merely add eye appeal. They are almost always in boldface type and may even be in color for added emphasis. Finally, they break up and overcome that "gray" look, make reading easier, attract readers' eyes to information you wish to emphasize, and give the entire ad a more attractive appearance. They are, in sum, an attractive, interesting way to offer your pitch in what might be called an outline format.

Subheads provide stepping-stones into the text. Keep in mind that a reader who merely skims an ad—the majority of all newspaper readers—often will read the headline and jump to subheads to judge whether to read the body copy.

Give the same effort to writing subheads as you did to constructing the main head. They can be longer than a main headline, but they too must use action words that nudge the reader to read on. Because they offer an additional opportunity to get across a sales point briefly, use words that persuade and sell.

A Raxco Software ad in a trade paper carries a headline across the entire double spread that says, "How To Prevent Head Crashes." The accompanying drawing shows a man experiencing a terrible head bump against a wall. Instead of a subhead, the first paragraph, only two lines, explains, "Not hardware head crashes, the soft tissue kind." Although the headline doesn't seem to name a consumer, it's likely there's not a computer user who would miss the arrow aimed in his direction or miss the meaning.

Widely spread throughout the copy are the following subheads:

Cut way back on what it takes to run production jobs.
Remove the chance of accidentally running a tape.
Imagine you had two full-time assistants.
Here's an offer you'd be mad to refuse.

Each subhead states a benefit but in a subtle manner that undoubtedly kindles software-interested readers to read on. The copy gives details, emphasizing problems and solutions, rather than just droning on about how wonderful the software is. It plays to businesses that are up against understaffing and underequipping. At the end of the ad is a large, boxed, mail-in coupon with a large Raxco Software logo and slogan—*Do More With Less Faster*—that you can't miss.

Body Text

Don't Mumble

The effectiveness of the body copy (text) depends almost exclusively on how well it is read and understood and on the response it receives. Readership is your immediate goal. There is no disputing that people read what they're interested in. It has been proved that people are eager to read in order to learn what you have to tell them *if* you connect your words to their problems, their wants and desires, and their needs.

The trick to cashing in on that desire is to avoid any blurry or obscure wording in this portion of your ad. This means you must know and understand exactly what you want to offer to be able to express it clearly. If you are muddled or in doubt, no one else will understand what you are trying to get across.

Body Copy Is an Expansion of the Headline

The beginning paragraph directly ties the headline to the rest of the copy. In it, expand on the promise given in the headline. Convince readers that what you offer will fulfill their desire or need.

Remember, you are writing to one person, to your imaginary friend sitting across from you who exactly fits the profile of your potential buyer (or client).

In the rest of the copy, expand further. Give believable reasons and good examples of uses. Keep the wording lean, but don't be stingy with believable reasons that readers should buy the product or service; the more uses you provide, the more likely you will touch the wide variety of interests among your readers. That's one of the extra advantages in newspaper advertising: space to include several points of interest to readers. And unlike radio and television, you won't lose the attention of readers as quickly as listeners.

Using Humor

The most important place to use humor may be in newspaper ads. As Dave Barry of *The Miami Herald* explains, "News editors have become too 'market-oriented' [in the news sections]. They choose what is acceptable to newswire and syndicate editors as an indication of reader preference." Most of the news they choose isn't fun to read or funny. Yet readership surveys indicate the importance of humor to readers.

Nevertheless, there has been a slow recognition that humor is important in newspapers, if only as an antidote to so much in the paper that is serious or disquieting. At last there is recognition of the degree of popularity of humor among newspaper subscribers and some editors are reviewing ways to use more of it on their pages.

Until news columns become overloaded with humor, you may wish to cash in on editors' shortsight and attract the paper's readers with humor in your ad—and ultimately make its subscribers your readers. Be careful, though. Don't equate humor with being smart-alecky. That's a difficult quality to judge, so ask people who fit your desired audience profile how they view your "humor ad" before you run it.

Humor is immediately evident in the photo in an insurance trade paper. A bare-chested man, shown from the waist up, is covered with dozens and dozens of bandaids. The expression on his face and the position of one hand on his chest says, "Who? Me?" The copy, which recognizes that "overutilization is a sticky subject," targets companies trying to keep healthcare costs under control. And it treats a somewhat delicate subject with a touch of lightness that makes the pill a little easier to take.

The Call to Action

Remember the AIDA formula? So far, you've fulfilled the first three steps:

1. Grabbed attention.
2. Created interest.
3. Built desire.

Now you must generate action. This is where it is easy for the message to fall apart. No matter how stunning your copy is to this point, it will fail unless you urge readers to act now—and then tell them how to act.

The Raxco ad generated action on the part of readers in its last block of copy, under the subhead, "Here's an offer you'd be mad to refuse," and an oversized mail-in coupon. The coupon is the action lure to entice enthusiastic computer users to send for a free "limited-edition" t-shirt.

If your ad includes an order form, place it in a section of the space that makes it convenient to clip—near a page edge. Prominently list the mail-in address within the order form, and make the fill-in lines long enough to contain the required information. If a check is to be mailed, tell the reader to whom the check should be written.

Keep all of this closing information together in one place—as part of the order form, adjacent to it, or adjacent to the logo/signature. Don't make readers search throughout the ad for information—price, your company name, your address, or your telephone number. Make it easy for them to act.

The sole goal of your action close is to keep the reader from setting the ad aside. Chances are, if this happens, that desire will cool, and your ad will be completely forgotten.

End with the Signature

Make the name of your company prominent in the ad, so readers know at first glance which company is speaking to them. Readers expect to find the signature along with address and telephone number at the bottom of the ad because that's where most advertisers have placed it for years. Be sure it's there, no matter how prominently it's displayed elsewhere.

You can build recognition and remembrance by also using the company name in the headline, the body copy, or wherever else it is appropriate. But when you sign off the ad, prominently display the company name along with address (including zip code), telephone number, and business hours.

The company signature should be your company logo (short for *logotype*), a distinctive design bearing the name or trademark of your company or business. Consistent, persistent use of your logo builds recognition and remembrance, so that a reader need only glance at it rather than "read" it.

Layout

To lay our your advertisement, place all the elements (headline, illustration, body copy, and logo/signature) in the sequence you wish the reader to follow. Don't draw the ad in detail; merely sketch blocks to indicate where each element is to be placed, and roughly indicate heads and subheads.

Concentrate on making the ad as easy as possible for the reader's eye to move from headline to graphic or photo—or graphic to headline (depending upon which is the more eye grabbing)—to explanatory copy, to price (if applicable), to your logo and company location and telephone number.

Keep typefaces in the same type family, and use a variety of sizes within that type family to avoid monotony. Use bolder faces for emphasis, but avoid distracting devices such as overly decorative borders and reverses (white print on a black block).

You Can Get a Two-Color Look with Only One Color

You can get a two-color look by using only one color of ink if you take advantage of screening. Screening filters the ink so the same color can appear in different shades. The screens can be adjusted to make them much lighter, or much darker, or any degree between. The cost savings is immense when compared to the costs of running more colors. You also can use screening with black ink to achieve graduating shades of gray, up to solid black.

Step Back and Evaluate

Now look at your layout as objectively as possible. Is it clean and uncluttered looking? Have you left enough white space throughout the layout? (White space adds greatly to gaining attention, particularly in newspaper ads.) Is the graphic large enough, and does it help the reader visualize your sales point?

Once you've determined a layout style and a type family you like, use them in all your advertising. Then as readers continue to see your ads, there will be instant recognition. If they like what they read or what you've previously sold them or done for them, there will be that warm reaction a person gets on seeing an old friend.

A Test of the Look

To get a preview idea of how your ad will look to potential readers, pick a newspaper page that has a substantial number of ads, and place your layout in among them. Does it show up? Or does it melt into the clutter? Does it need a strong border to set it apart? Does it need more white space to attract readers' eyes?

The example shown of an ad that stood out loud and clear from a half-page of other two-column ads for hearing aids, a weight loss center, carpet cleaners, and a mortgage company's home interest rate message was a Network Security ad. Network Security broke the rules. Instead of using a graphic, it made the graphic a variety of typefaces in different sizes and styles. And instead of listing lines and lines of benefits in a copy block of small, somewhat difficult to read type or stuffing the space with a reverse-type block and a mishmash of copy, Network Security used a layout that jumped out from the clutter in a unique way, at the same time it told its story in an attractive, easy-to-read manner that broke the rules but grabbed readers' eyes.

Test Your Finished Layout and Copy

Even the pros pretest to get audience reaction. You too may wish to try out your ad on friends, business associates, and customers. Let

Soldier's mom renews bid for truth after POW news

Continued from Page 1A.

Get the live men out."

According to the Senate Select Committee on POW-MIA Affairs, Mrs Ransbottom's family is one of 244 in the United States that recently were notified — many for the first time — that their sons' names appeared on some military agency's prisoner-of-war list.

Spokeswoman Deborah DeYoung said Senate investigators determined that 111 of the men died in captivity, but they were unable to account for the other 133. She would not comment directly on Maj. Ransbottom's case.

She said that when the special panel reconvenes this week in Washington, it will focus on reports that American servicemen have been seen alive in Vietnam during the past 20 years.

"There are big question marks at the end of the war that should have precluded President Nixon and others from declaring everybody accounted for," Ms. DeYoung said. "When Nixon and top officials said they had no information to believe any (servicemen) were alive, that's just plain wrong."

Capt. Susan Strednansky, a spokeswoman on POW-MIA affairs for the Department of Defense, referred questions about the letters received by Mrs. Ransbottom and others to the Senate committee.

U.S. News & World Report reported in its July 20 editions that

"The thought your own children might be constantly abused and mistreated, no food, is more than you can tolerate. You have to find your own mechanism, your own way of dealing with it."
— LaVerne Ransbottom, mother of missing soldier

Defense Secretary Dick Cheney had not ruled out the possibility that American prisoners may be alive in Indochina.

He also was reported to have told House Republicans in a private meeting that 109 cases involving the sighting of American servicemen were still under investigation.

POW-MIA experts contend that more than 2,300 U.S. troops were never properly accounted for in Vietnam.

Mrs. Ransbottom, who lives in the affluent north Oklahoma City suburb of Edmond and works for a real estate company, alternately hopes her son, who would now be 45, is still alive and frets that if he survived, he may have been mistreated.

Maj. Ransbottom, whose radio call name was Snoopy 7, was 21 when his reconnaissance unit was overrun by Viet Cong troops at Kham Duc near the Laotian border 24 years ago. According to other troops in the area, Maj. Ransbottom's voice was the last they heard before the radio went dead.

"He said he was shooting them as they came through the door," said Mrs. Ransbottom, who said she has talked with several soldiers who heard the radio transmissions.

Maj. Ransbottom, a graduate of Putnam City High School in northwest Oklahoma City, had attended Oklahoma Baptist University for one year, studying for a career in hospital administration, when he and his best friend, Clint Wheeler, decided to enlist.

Neither returned from Vietnam.

"They (the government) made it such a hassle — you had to report your grades every month and so forth" to avoid the draft, Mrs. Ransbottom said. "They decided to get it over with. They said, 'We'll come back in two years and get back in school.'

"He really felt an obligation to defend his country. We really thought we were defending our country. I think we were misled."

She said she and her husband, Frederick, who died of lung cancer three years ago, learned soon after

Please see WOMAN on Page 11A.

Consumer confidence lags despite drop in loan rates

Continued from Page 1A.

North Palm Beach, Fla., company that tracks loan and deposit rates and produces a weekly newsletter.

The Laughlands landed a two-year, $5,000 debt consolidation loan at 13.6 percent and four-year financing for their Mitsubishi Diamante at slightly more than 9 percent.

Mr. Laughland, 31, who sells computer software, is delighted with his double-dip loan because he found a car deal that he couldn't pass up.

"I had maxed out three or four credit cards, and I needed to get out from under them. That 18 to 21 percent was kicking me pretty good," Mr. Laughland said.

The replacement at 13.6 percent is "not great, but it's a lot better than what I was paying," he said. "I feel great."

Bankers would feel better if there were more borrowers like Mr. Laughland who found appeal in lower interest rates for car, home improvement and other consumer loans.

FALLING CONSUMER CREDIT RATES
Figures for July 31, 1992, compared with Feb. 7, 1992.

	LOANS							
	CAR		HOME IMPROVEMENT		PERSONAL		CREDIT CARDS	
	7-31	2-7	7-31	2-7	7-31	2-7	7-31	2-7
Bank One Texas	8.50	9.45	8.99	9.50	13.50	17.50	18.00	18.00
Dallas Teachers CU	7.25	8.40	8.50	9.50	10.75	15.00	14.90	14.90
First Gibraltar	8.50	9.50	9.25	10.00	NA	NA	17.90	17.90
First Interstate	8.25	9.25	9.00	9.50	18.00	18.00	18.00	18.00
NationsBank	7.99	9.25	9.00	9.60	13.50	13.50	17.90	17.90
Team Bank	8.40	9.25	9.25	9.50	14.00	14.00	17.90	17.90
Texas Commerce	8.25	9.25	9.00	9.50	12.75	13.75	17.80	17.80

NOTE: Auto loans: $15,000, 48 months.; home improvement loans: $20,000, 10 years.; personal loans: unsecured, $1,000, 24 months.; credit cards: fixed rates for purchases.

SOURCE: Bank Rate Monitor

The Dallas Morning News

Slashing debts

Instead, Americans are cutting their debt. The amount of consumer installment credit outstanding has fallen steadily since the first of the year, from $728.6 billion in January to $721.4 billion in May, according to Federal Reserve figures.

Total consumer credit dropped $3.6 billion in April and $2.4 billion in May.

"Demand is still soft" in Texas despite some of the country's most competitive rates, said Chip Carlisle, First Interstate Bank's executive vice president of community banking in the state. "We want to make more loans."

The nation's average rate for personal loans in the last week was 16.25 percent, compared with 13.72 percent in Dallas, Bank Rate Monitor found.

Americans paid an average 9.75 percent to finance their new cars in the last week, down more than two percentage points from 11.69 a year ago. In Dallas, the average rate of 8.49 percent was second only to 8.46 in Houston.

"You guys have got a rate war going on," said Hugo Ottolenghi, Bank Rate Monitor's editorial director.

Finance companies owned by the Big Three carmakers, which do not announce their loan rates, have joined the competition. Ford Motor Credit and Chrysler Credit recently cut the rates they charge auto dealers by 0.5 percentage points.

Consumers should carefully consider "away from the dealership" whether a rebate or lower financing is their best deal, said Jim Boerger, who operates a car-buying business in Fairfax, Va., and publishes the American Automobile Association *Car Buyers' Handbook*.

Chrysler, for example, offers the following financing for a LeBaron, according to the Center for the Study of Services, a nonprofit consumer group in Washington, D.C.: $1,500 cash back and 6.9 percent for 24 months, 7.9 percent for 48 months or 9.9 percent for 60 months; or 4.9 percent financing for 24 months.

Refinancing, Mr. Boerger said, generally is not a good idea for cars. Consumers are "ultimately ending up paying interest on interest," he said.

The changing landscape of Texas banking has put new players in the field. "You've got more institutions trying to create a presence in the market, and that's leading to price competition," Mr. Ottolenghi said.

Most institutions in Dallas have current or recently-concluded promotions for consumer products. With rates on interest-bearing accounts plummeting, banks and thrifts have focused on how cheap it is to borrow — how little you have to pay for a loan, rather than how little they pay you for deposits.

Lending increases

Despite overall softness, the competition has boosted lending. First Interstate said the number of auto loans it made increased 96 percent during March, April and May, and home improvement loans grew 239 percent over the previous three months, which are traditionally slow for loans.

"Most people have never had an opportunity to borrow at rates this low. Certainly there are some deals out there," Mr. Carlisle said. "People are just uncertain. And when they're uncertain, they're reluctant to commit to debt."

If there's an exception, it appears to be home improvement loans. For the first six months of the year at Texas Commerce Bank, the bank made 3½ times more loans than it did in the same period last year, said Larry Hysinger, the bank's senior vice president of consumer banking.

"We're beginning to see consumers open up just a little bit," although they are still resistant, Mr. Hysinger said.

Consumer resistance

That resistance continues to be a "very serious" threat to the economy's recovery, said Reese Overcash Jr., chairman of Associates Corp. of North America, the finance company.

"Our (credit card and other) portfolios are only up because of acquisitions, or we would've had liquidations in our portfolios every month" in 1991 and '92 until June, he said.

Credit outstanding from finance companies dipped to $116.1 billion in May from $127.9 billion a year earlier, the Federal Reserve reported.

"I'm still very cautious about there being any real turnaround here" in the economy, Mr. Overcash said.

Banks are trying to maintain interest spreads between the rates they charge for loans and what they pay in interest. Margins were squeezed in the late '80s during the collapse of the Texas financial sector, so consumer lending rates haven't fallen as much as those for businesses, said Dr. Hempel of SMU.

The most dramatic example: credit card rates. During the year that ended in May, credit card rates at commercial banks slipped to 17.97 percent from 18.22 percent, the Federal Reserve reported.

"That's kind of ridiculous in today's environment. But evidently a lot of people don't think the way I do" and won't hunt for lower rates, Dr. Hempel said.

Student loan rates, floated by the federal government, also are coming down — to 7.51 percent for the year that began July 1, from 9.34 percent a year ago.

Lower interest rates for consumer loans might not boost borrowing, lenders said.

"If you lower rates another 100 basis points, I don't think it would make people go out and borrow money. They have to be confident they'll have a job to support their debt level," said Randy Meyer, First Gibraltar's executive vice president of consumer lending.

them see and read the ad; then ask what message they received from the ad. You'll know after only a few tests whether the ad is successful in accomplishing its goal(s). If it fails, ask each person to suggest how you can better convey your desired message. Regardless of your own perceptions of the ad's high value, rework it accordingly. The savings in advertising dollars that would be wasted with an unproductive ad are worth all the extra effort required.

Free or Low-Cost Help

Part of all newspapers' services is preparation of your ads. Some newspapers perform the service without charge; others do it for a moderate cost. This appears to be an attractive offer, but remember that no outsider—not even professionals—can design and write as outstanding an ad as you to carry the best message to target your special audience.

There are other drawbacks to accepting a newspaper's help. Because of the enormous volume of work, it is difficult for the newspaper to give adequate attention to your job, and never will anyone on the newspaper's staff have the depth of interest in your ad that you have.

What you can and should call on the newspaper to provide are technical services: finished layout (according to your draft), typesetting, and graphics. All newspapers subscribe to graphics services, called clip art. The art may be in print form, which can be clipped and pasted into a layout, or it may be computer graphics. Your advertising representative can explain the newspaper's art services.

Co-op Advertising

Newspapers are the medium manufacturers and vendors prefer to use to do their co-op advertising. If you qualify for co-op and haven't explored the possibility, do so now. (Return to chapter 2 for information.) If you've already lined up co-op funds, recheck the specifications the manufacturer placed on your use of those funds, and check your ad to be sure it qualifies. Co-op can be a win-win partnership that adds dollars to your ad budget.

For information about newspaper co-op advertising, here is a source:

Newspaper Advertising Co-op Network (NACON)
10400 Roberts Road
Palos Hills, IL 60465
312/598–7070

NACOM, which was founded in 1970, has as its credo, "to promote and heighten the public's awareness of co-op advertising and raise the level of its effectiveness."

The Future of Newspapers

Newspapers, like all other media and the economy, have experienced a depressed advertising market, but the bright light of a potential new revenue source is on the horizon: alternate delivery (or private mail delivery). It targets home deliveries of magazines, catalogs, samples, and other advertising messages. If a brochure or other insertion is delivered by a newspaper, the newspaper is paid on a per-piece basis. The service offers pinpoint targeting of specific household segments. For instance, a photo equipment store could advertise only to subscriber households that receive photography magazines. There may be as many new programs such as alternate delivery to entice advertisers as there are newspapers in the country.

Newspapers are getting stronger, and although delivery methods may change, the newspaper as an informational and advertising medium will be around for the foreseeable future.

There's no consensus about the ways newspapers of the future will differ from those published today. But there is agreement that there will be differences. An *Advertising Age* special report about newspapers, published at the end of 1992, predicted such possibilities as newspapers being read on flat, tabloid-size, hand-held screens; evolving into faxed pages through high-speed machines; and in audiotext or videotext format.

Subscribers to Denver's *Rocky Mountain News*—for no extra charge—can get an all-day electronic version of the paper with local, national, and business news and sports, plus stock market quotes and advanced access to the next day's classifieds.

"To survive in the long haul, the newspaper industry will embrace electronic journalism. We won't see massive change in the next three or four years, but probably around 2000," an executive at an international advertising agency predicts.

Knight-Ridder, the second largest newspaper chain in the country, has proposed the most radical transformation of the newspaper, according to *Ad Age*. It is working on making general interest newspapers, with individually requested supplemental news items, available via a portable, tabloid-size screen. A person interacts with this information appliance by touching the screen or using a special electronic pen. A reader will be able to turn pages, clip and save articles, and call up background information with the touch of the electronic pen.

"I do believe the newspaper of the future to be electronic, not ink-on-paper-based," Roger Fidler, Knight-Ridder's corporate director of new media development said. He predicts the electronic newspaper will be dominant within thirty years.

Advertising too is calculated to change, according to Walter Bender, director of an electronic publishing group at Massachusetts Institute of Technology. He says, "I see advertising as being much more directed. The consumer will be asking for advertising rather than just receiving it."

The advantage to the proposed delivery by fax method is that "it allows for general as well as customized news," Fidler says. "That will let advertisers better target their prospects and also cut a paper's expensive distribution costs."

The MIT group is doing research on user modeling that will allow for creation of *The Daily Me,* a paper tailored to an individual's interests. This newspaper could be available in forms such as on a personal computer screen, a PC printout, the television screen, or by audio.

As these predictions for going high tech explode throughout the industry, there also are warnings against becoming too engrossed in technology. Cathleen Black, president-CEO of the Newspaper Association of America, says that "for a great majority of people, a portable product, like the traditional newspaper, will still be the newspaper of choice for a long time."

10

Radio

Sound Advice on When and How to Use It

President Lyndon B. Johnson was pictured in 1965 telling the press, "Ya gotta grab 'em by the ears!" Newspapers across the country carried photos that shocked the nation of President Johnson hoisting his pet dogs by their ears. He was not speaking of radio. Without realizing it, though, he was offering sound radio advertising advice to small business advertisers in the 1990s: "Ya gotta grab 'em by the ears!"

Radios are in offices, kitchens, bedrooms, bathrooms, on the street, in supermarkets and discount stores, fastened on bikes and belts, and enclosed in cars. With such a blanketing effect, radio is a popular and effective advertising medium:

- It has reach and frequency. You can figure how many households will be exposed to your message and how often each will be exposed.
- It has specifically defined audiences. Whereas television attracts mass audiences, on radio if 10,000 or 20,000 people want a specific type of programming, there's probably a station that has it.
- It has efficiency, which means you can measure the efficiency of your ad dollars with regard to the amount of money spent in relation to the numbers of people the message reaches.

- It has flexibility. You can change messages and schedules quickly and with relative ease.
- It has low production costs, particularly when compared to television.
- It has the loyalty of its listeners, who pretty much keep their choices to one or two stations.
- It has intrusiveness, perhaps the most valuable of all its assets. Except for television, no other medium can invade a listener's living room or bedroom without an invitation, and it's the only medium that rides along in a person's car or walks right into her shower and dares to sell her something.

The Radio Advertising Bureau reports a major study that shows radio is the medium used closest to the time of actual purchase. (The same claim is made for bus and subway card advertising. There is no conflict in these claims, however. One is the claim about automobile drivers and passengers; the other is about public transportation riders.)

At certain times radio has no competition. Radio is the only form of broadcasting most people receive in their cars, and most people spend large blocks of time in their cars. What more could a small business advertiser with a hardscrabble media budget ask for as an avenue to reach present and future consumers? However, if color is necessary to portray your product, you will have a hard time rationalizing the purchase of radio time.

Radio: A Sound Medium

It was August 28, 1922, when the first radio commercial aired on station WEAF in New York City. The 10-minute advertisement was for the Queensboro Realty Co., which had paid a $100 fee.

As late as 1945, when radio served as our principal home entertainment, there were fewer than 1,000 stations. Then television came on the scene like a bulldozer, and most people thought it was the destruction of radio. But today there are almost 5,000 AM and more than 4,300 FM radio stations broadcasting an average of 2.6 million commercials a day.

Each day radio reaches 77 percent of all Americans. On a national basis, there is not an age bracket from 12 years and up that doesn't register 91 percent or higher as regular weekly listeners. And the lowest average daily time they spend listening is more than 2 hours daily. The figures are impressive, but they are national averages for all radio stations. Only the figures from your local stations, which reach the specific audience segment that is your target audience, are important to you for your desired results.

A Sound Advertising Investment

Aside from special interest magazines, radio is the most segmented medium available to advertisers. It virtually invented targeting. That means that exactly the segment of the population most interested in your product or service or company—home workers, teens, young adults, businesspersons, African-Americans, Hispanics, older listeners, and a host of other special interest groups—can be pinpointed with your radio commercials in a handsomely cost-effective way.

As Lane Kirkland once said, "Go where the customer is and don't expect him to come to you. The only way to convert a heathen is to travel into the jungle." If you've made the decision to carry your message to radio, this chapter tells you a little about the medium, how to construct a radio commercial, how to time and record the spot, how to buy time, and what you can expect for radio in the future.

Advertisers, especially small business advertisers, can no longer afford the wasted dollars that are the result of untargeted advertising. The ability of radio to identify demographic, geographic, and cultural segments for advertisers is invaluable. Pros know this, and it's important that you know it too: effective advertising is cost-efficient and targeted. It also is well known that radio's listeners are far more loyal than television's viewers and seldom switch channels.

There are other reasons for small businesses to use radio in preference to other media, and we will get into that information later in this chapter. For now, though, let's assume you have a budget for radio commercials, and you're anxious to get right down to the business of writing a commercial.

Writing the Commercial

Write a Picture

"Advertisers should think of radio as a VISUAL medium," says veteran advertising agency executive George Arnold. "Radio is a kind of little theater of the mind for that 30 or 60 seconds . . . and a much more imaginative medium than television." Arnold also says that "a good radio message will completely absorb and involve a listener so the words need to paint a vivid word picture. The best radio spots are the ones where you can see what's going on in your mind's eye." In other words, use words that conjure up mental images.

Sometimes the most striking pictures are the ones you can't see. The mind's eye often is the best eye, so the pictures may be better on radio. The right combination of voices, copy, sound effects, and/or music evokes strong images and grabs attention faster than visual media, advises the Radio Advertising Bureau.

As you draft your radio commercial keep in mind the principles of writing good advertising messages in any medium set forth in chapter 8. The precepts remain true for radio. The format, however, is singular.

Guidelines

Before you even consider the words to use or the length of time you must fit those words into, make a list of the elements that must be included in this particular spot:

- Exactly what you want your spot to do: build an image (what kind of image?) sell a product or a service? Are you introducing something new or declaring a new use for an old product or service?
- Benefit(s) the listener will receive from the purchase of the product or service. List all customer concerns, and the answers to their "What's in it for me?" questions. This is important; when you write the copy, you are going to choose the single highest-priority benefit and tell listeners what it will do for their comfort, happiness, family, convenience, or

whatever else is suitable to your product or service. (If you feel strongly that more than one high-priority benefit should be promoted, it may be necessary to write two spots and divide them among the time slots you've purchased.)
- Special price and methods of payment.
- Special date(s), if it's a limited-time offer.
- Name and location of the business.
- Hours of business.

When the list is complete, write a skeleton description of the picture you want to create in listeners' minds. In many instances, it may not be as effective to describe the physical aspects of the product or service as to create a pleasant use for the product or service. For example, Eastman Kodak sells film as its product, but its advertisements describe not the product but memories. It thus sells the mental pictures of memories.

If you choose the latter method, can you find a way to paint a picture of enjoyable, beneficial uses of your product? Instead of merely reciting one or two benefits, can you picture enjoyable ways the benefit(s) can be used?

Decide on an Attention Arrester

The greatest problem for advertisers who use radio is that their potential consumer must be listening, or more accurately stated, the listener may not be hearing. People often have their radios on, but they're not actively tuned in. Often radio acts as background while the listener does something else: housework, homework, or office work, for example. How to catch the listeners' attention is your first consideration—before you tell your message. You must grab their attention in the first 3 or 4 seconds of your time slot.

Music and sound effects are attention arresters. An announcer's voice also can capture ears. Sometimes professionals in advertising search for an announcer with a unique voice quality that catches and hangs on to listeners. Such a voice used in every commercial becomes a symbol for a specific advertiser. The voice used, however, should be appropriate to the image you wish to create and maintain. There are extra charges for special voice talent, so you may wish to use regular station announcers, for whom there is only a small charge or no charge at all.

Humor is another attention arrester, but humor can backfire if it's not funny, and usually takes longer to establish.

An opening sound effect or music behind an announcer's voice can set the mood or image you wish to establish. Decide on the image or mood you wish to convey and the kind of sound effect or music that will help establish it.

Music and Sound Effects May Be Free

If you decide to use music or sound effects, call on the sales representatives at the stations from which you purchase time. Most stations have free music and sound effects libraries. Copyrights on some of the music have expired, which means it is in public domain and there are no restrictions or payments to the composer for its use. The recording artists may have copyrighted their recording, though, and that means royalties must be paid to them. Your station representatives can help you with this aspect.

Listen to station representatives' advice, but do not leave the choice of music or sound effects to anyone else. Only you know the exact effect and image you want your spot to convey. And be sure the music or sound relates directly to the message that follows. A dog barking may grab the ears of a large number of listeners, but what relation does that sound have toward creating a desire in listeners to come to your restaurant or your tire store? But if you're selling security systems, there is a connection.

Remember that whatever lead-off grabber you use, it should not be so jarring to the listeners that it creates an overwhelming desire in them to change stations. It need only catch a wandering mind long enough to spike curiosity about what you have to say.

Trigger a Need or a Desire

As soon as you think you have listeners' attention, use words to start building desire and show need for your product or service. Do it with enthusiasm.

From your earlier research you know exactly what your target consumer wants and needs. Now help that listener visualize how he or she can benefit from your offer, how it will make life better, more enjoyable, more profitable. Prove that your product or service will fulfill that want or need.

To accomplish this, professional advertising copy writers who are particularly adept at using radio as a medium know that using dialogue and a storyteller or a narrator can create a picture in listeners' minds that enhances the desirability of a product or service. How do they accomplish this? Many actually sit down at their keyboards, close their eyes, or put on a blindfold, in order to truly visualize the word-picture before and as they write it. Try it. It may work for you too.

Build Trust into the Message

Honesty and integrity are the cornerstones for building a lasting consumer base. Lavish promises and the use of extravagant adjectives may initially produce listeners, perhaps even yield some customers, but in the end, such artifices are not conducive to building lasting consumer confidence. Particularly in today's climate of general political and business distrust, they are about the fastest means known to professional copywriters to destroy faith in your appeals and in your product or service. When a buyer finds the promises don't live up to lavish claims, you've lost not only the customer but undoubtedly potential consumers among the buyer's friends, associates, and acquaintances.

False or lavish claims aren't necessary. If your advertisement in any medium contains honest information the listener needs or has a strong interest in, you would have a difficult time stopping the person from listening. Listeners care most about ministering to their own self-interests.

Make It Easy to Act

Finally, tell listeners what to do to satisfy their need or desire and how to do it. Give them all the information they need to act on your offer, and tell them exactly how to respond. If you provide response choices, listeners will like the idea even better, because they feel a sense of control.

Don't Forget to Mention the Name of Your Business

Include as many mentions of your business as possible throughout the copy—at least three in a 30-second commercial, at the beginning, somewhere in the main part of the copy, and at the end. The last company identification should be the last words in your commercial so that listeners mentally take that information when the spot leaves the air.

Numbers are difficult to remember without the added benefit of visual stimulation, so try not to use street numbers. Rather, give listeners a landmark to help them remember your address: at the corner of Surrey and Fifth, or across from State Bank on Sixteenth. Don't even try to get them to remember a telephone number unless you can turn the number into a phrase, such as "Dial: Top Tires"; "Dial: Best Buy"; "Dial: Battery." Use words a listener can easily remember. Be wary, however, of using phrases that spell one way and may be heard another, such as: "Dial: 4-savings," or "Good Buy," which may be heard as "goodbye."

Jumping to Confusions

It's easy to create misunderstandings in a nonvisual medium. People may not hear your words as you wrote them. Bil Keane in a "Family Circus" cartoon, gives a good example. A little girl excitedly tells her mom: "Know what we learned in Bible class? The Lord is my chauffeur, I shall not walk." And another time, one of Bil Keane's kids says: "That sure made me hungry when we sang 'Lasagna in the Highest.'" True, adult listeners aren't likely to confuse words in the same way children do, but listen carefully to your copy for words and phrases that can be misconstrued. Some perfectly proper words can sound like off-color expressions.

Eliminate the Negative and Throwaway Words

Accentuate the positive; eliminate the negative. There's an important point here. Why plant a negative thought in a potential customer's mind when every test ever conducted has proved that positives produce better results? Selling is 99 percent a positive attitude. Make your commercial reflect your company's positive attitude. Instead of saying, "You'll never find a faster, cheaper cleaning service," reword it so that the listener hears, "The fastest, least expensive cleaning service in town."

Eliminate questions too. Even people who are prime targets for your product or service can think of enough reasons not to react in a positive way, so why ask them to think of more? Instead of asking, "Why go without this benefit any longer?" restate it in the imperative: "Get this benefit . . . now!" The imperative saves words, too, and precious time, which saves dollars in terms of the cost of the additional time required for the longer wording.

Eliminate throwaway words, such as *the* and *and,* wherever possible. Time is so constricted and so precious that every word must count.

Sound Conversational

No matter who you're talking to—young rappers, dignified businesspeople, retirees—make the copy sound conversational. Use *can't* instead of *cannot; it's* instead of *it is.* In some cases slang is acceptable, but in every case, it's best to use informal, casual, everyday language.

Say What You Mean

Some newspaper classified ads are humorous examples of trip-ups that are easy to make. Here are the kinds of "guarantees" you do not want to offer, along with some other examples of not saying what you mean:

"At this price, these TV sets won't last long!" (*Salt Lake City Telegram*)

"Don't kill your wife. Let our Bendix washing machine do your dirty work." (*Tucson Daily Star*)

"With any Monarch Range purchased, we will completely cover your kitchen with extra-quality linoleum or a 42-piece set of fine dinnerware." (*Salt Lake City Deseret News*)

"This new rifle is the popular rifle for campers, trappers, and other small game." (*Devils Lake (North Dakota) Journal*)

Preparing for Broadcast

Listen, Really Listen, to the Spot

Always, listen to your spot before you type it into final form. Read it into a tape recorder, mentally move to the other side of the table into the imaginary seat of the person you've been writing this commercial to, and listen from that perspective. Consider the following points:

- Does the opening "grab 'em by the ears"?
- Listen to the flow. Does it sound like everyday conversation?
- Does the spot provide a word picture that captures and holds interest?
- Does the copy establish that the product or service will satisfy the want or need of the target to whom you're aiming these words?
- Do listeners know how and where to find the product or service? Have you made it easy for them to act?
- Are there adequate mentions of your company name throughout the spot, and is the name the last word(s) in the commercial?
- Are your claims honest, realistic, believable, and deliverable?
- Is the copy crisp and graphic? Joel Siegel of "Good Morning America" explains good copy in a way that bears repeating: "You could eat the dialog for breakfast, the way it snaps, crackles, and pops!"

Be Kind to the Announcer Who Will Read Your Spot

Alliteration can be catchy in print, but it can be a huge hazard for an announcer, particularly if he or she is reading the copy live, on the air. Try listening to yourself say, "Serious savings at Sam's special super sale Saturday." If the announcer is able to handle the tongue twisting series of S sounds, you may end up with a sound effect you hadn't planned on—one long, extended hiss.

Here are other ways to help the announcer:

- Avoid hyphenating words, a stumbling block an announcer can very well live without, particularly if reading the copy live.

- Punctuate to help the announcer read your copy. There was a time when copy was typed in all-capital letters. Now capitals are used only for emphasis.
- Dots between phrases indicate that pauses are called for.
- If a name or word is unusual or its pronunciation unclear, build the phonetic pronunciation right into the copy, each syllable separated by a dash, and with the accented syllable in all-caps. Type the actual spelling in parentheses immediately following the phoneticized word. There's an example of this in the sample radio commercial on page 129.
- If something is best known by its acronym, as with AIDS, write the acronym in all-capital letters. But if you use just the initials for something, as in USA, separate the letters with hyphens (U-S-A). Hyphens (dashes) are used to alert an announcer that the letters are an abbreviation and are meant to be spoken separately.

Type the Spot in Script Form

Radio commercials are distinctly different in format from print advertising layouts. Radio commercials are written in script form to indicate at a glance exactly which are sound effects (SFX), music, and spoken words. For easier understanding, as you read the following information, refer to the radio commercial script shown on page 129.

Just as with final copy for all media, follow these rules:

- Use a clean typewriter ribbon or new printer ribbon
- Use 8½ inch by 11 inch business letterhead.
- Type on only one side of the paper.
- Double-space the copy the announcer will read.
- Write sentences in upper- and lowercase letters except when you wish the announcer to emphasize something. For instance, type your company's name when it's part of the message in uppercase letters.
- Space down three or four lines below your letterhead, and at the left margin, type your name as contact. If your telephone number is different from that on the letterhead or if there is a special extension number, include your telephone number immediately beneath your name

INVESTMENT SERVICES CENTER
100 Allentown Parkway
Allen, Texas 75002

Contact: Mary Gregoriew   Start Date: June 23

727–0655   End Date: June 27

Length: 30 Seconds

Words: 47

Music: "We're in the Money"

Up and under

Announcer: Some financial planners recommend THEIR

investment plans. INDEPENDENT financial

consultant, Mary Greg-er-oo (Gregoriew) finds

the best returns for YOUR dollar investments.

Call Mary at INVESTMENT SERVICES CENTER,

listed in the Yellow Pages under "Investments."

CONTACT: (your name)
(your individual telephone number or extension number)

- Space down another two lines and type the number of seconds in the spot:

  LENGTH: 30 seconds [or whatever length is correct]

- Space down two more lines and type the number of words the announcer will read:

  WORDS: 47 [or the correct number of words]

- Opposite your name as contact, type the dates on which the spot will begin and end:

  START DATE: July 5
  END DATE: July 18

- Begin information and body copy four or six spaces below the word count. If a sound effect is to be used, type:

  SFX: Telephone ringing, then sound of receiver being picked up.

- If music introduces your spot, type:

  MUSIC: [give the title, then on the next line down . . .]
  UP AND UNDER (meaning the music is played at a normal level as the spot begins, then is lowered and played softly behind the announcer's words).
  ANNOUNCER: [Type announcement copy, double spaced]

- After the announcer finishes speaking, indicate that the music is to be raised again to a normal level by typing:

  Music up

- Indicate the end of the copy by spacing down two spaces and typing:

  # # #

Time Your Copy

The least dependable and most often used method for timing your copy is with a stopwatch, before it is taped. People speak at different speeds, and if you time a relatively fast speaker but the person who actually records the spot speaks even a trifle slower, you have a problem.

With available technology, a commercial that runs even a fraction of a second over time is cut off the air. A more dependable means of timing is by the number of words:

Seconds	Number of Words
30	75
60	150

People speak at different speeds, so this method is not completely reliable either.

The most accurate timing measurement in advance of recording is with a formula devised by station KABC-TV in Los Angeles: five syllables equal 1 second. But the only absolutely true timing test is the one done after a spot has been recorded.

Get More Words into the Spot

There are methods to speed up commercials by compressing them electronically. It's called the *time compressor-expander* and is used for both radio and television. As you might guess, it's costly, but it is done with such skill and subtlety that listeners are not aware of what has happened. When a speaker's words are time compressed, he doesn't sound as hurried as when he tries to talk faster. Part of the reason is that the percentage of time given to pauses remains the same as in normal speech, and word emphasis remains the same.

Speedups usually amount to about 15 percent, a substantial amount but not enough to distort voices. A 15 percent speedup allows a 38-second spot to be squeezed into 30 seconds without any deletions. That permits about ten extra words.

There is another important side effect that few people know about: studies show that television and radio commercials that have been given the speedup treatment have greater powers of persuasion and recall. Unaided recall is improved by 36 percent, and aided recall is increased by 40 percent over normally spoken commercials.

There is another way to achieve this end: choose a faster-speaking announcer. There is strong evidence that listeners prefer faster speakers, even in casual conversations, because they regard them as more informed, trustworthy, intelligent, and truthful. Don't just ask the announcer to speak faster, because then the words tend to sound slurred. Instead, choose someone whose normal speech is faster.

The Recording Session

It's time to remove your copywriter's hat and put on your producer's hat to tape the spot at the radio station. No matter the size of the station, the announcer and the people who will handle the session all are professionals. If the first run-through is not completely satisfactory, however, or you notice something that should be changed, don't hesitate to insist on the changes. You're the producer responsible for the success of the spot. You're also the client footing the bill.

Almost all stations will dub (make copies of) your finished commercial if your spot is to run on other stations, typically at a charge.

Alternatives to Do-It-Yourself

If, after all your do-it-yourself efforts, you absolutely believe you cannot write a good spot, there are a couple of alternatives. One is that many radio stations will script and produce your commercial for you. There may be a charge for the service. If you choose this avenue, you must give the station your facts:

- The specific purpose of the spot.
- Whether you wish it to be soft or hard sell.
- A detailed description of your target listener.
- The specific benefit you wish stressed.
- The kind of music and/or sound effect you wish used.

If you use this service, insist on hearing the final version before it airs to check that everything in it is correct, to be sure you approve of its tone and style and that it is consistent with your other advertising in other media, and to be sure it conveys the image and impression you wish communicated.

Another alternative to writing the commercial yourself is to contact a local college or university with an advertising or broadcasting program. Arrange with an instructor for students to get real-world experience by preparing your commercials. Perhaps the instructor will give academic credit if the spots are used. Point out to the instructor how a student will receive other benefits: the beginning of a job network through personal contact with individuals in your company that will be invaluable when he or she enters the business world; provide actual advertising and on-the-job experience; furnish sample work to show future employers as examples of the student's ability and experience. If possible, offer some form of payment to a student, which can provide incentive for the student and offer proof to potential employers that his work is deserving of compensation in a highly competitive broadcast advertising world.

Nevertheless, think twice before having someone else do your spot. "Pity poor radio, the ugly stepchild of broadcast advertising," says *Advertising Age*. "While TV remains the darling of agency creatives, an overriding lack of concern about radio results in the unrelenting march of offensive and unmemorable spots hitting the airwaves," the trade paper states.

The big ad agencies focus on television and print, so you have a much greater chance to turn out a notable ratio spot because you aren't required to compete against their expertise and experience. The argument for the do-it-yourself method is strong because not only can your spot stand out in a field of less than great competitors but because you are the one person who really understands what the spot should convey and to whom it should communicate your special message.

Radio Copycat Files

Perhaps you're not excited about the overall tone of your radio commercial and wish you could come up with another idea, or you want ideas for your next commercial. Recycling is a hot issue these days, and copycatting might be called a form of recycling. Of course, the copycat file you've been building has only print ads; it has no radio commercials in it. But there is an alternative: you can buy a taped radio copycat file.

Advertising Age offers an easy way to check out what has been successful in radio advertising and get some ideas for your own commercials. It annually sells tapes of "The Best Radio Commercials—the previous year's hottest, funniest, clutter-cutting radio spots." You can order by credit card, phone, or fax from:

Advertising Age Marketing Department
220 East 42d Street
New York NY 10017
Phone: 1–800–283–2724 (New York: 212–210–0287)
Fax: 212–210–0111

The Radio Advertising Bureau also offers tapes that you can order:

Marketing Department
Radio Advertising Bureau, Inc.
304 Park Avenue South
New York, NY 10160
Phone: 212/254–4800
Fax: 212/254–8713

Information should be requested by category: Creative Resources Tape (sample spots by category—name the category) or Clio Award Winners Tape. The Radio Advertising Bureau invites those who would like to know more about how to move a product using radio advertising to request additional information and suggests the possibility of scheduling a free radio consultancy meeting.

Another valuable resource is the book, *Radio Success Stories: A Reference Book,* available from:

Interep Radio Store
100 Park Avenue
New York, NY 10017
Phone: 212/916–0700
Fax: 212/916–0772

It comes with a cassette that contains a selection of creative, effective radio commercials and campaigns that have moved product for advertisers.

The smartest strategy can be in knowing what your competition is doing, what has worked for them, and then doing a bit of copycatting. This is *not* a recommendation to plagiarize, which is against the law. It is a suggestion that you climb on the back of a successful idea (ideas cannot be copyrighted), adapt it to your own use, and ride the idea to commercial success. Every highly successful idea is imitated, and when your spot produces a good response, you can be certain it too will be recycled.

On the Air

How Many Is the Right Number of Radio Spots?

That radio is an excellent, relatively low-cost advertising medium doesn't guarantee that it will yield dividends on your advertising investment or returns in the form of goals accomplished. There are factors in the way you use radio that can spell either excellent returns or money out the window. Disaster comes more readily from the purchase of the wrong number of spots or from buying time at the wrong time than from a less-than-award-winning commercial.

An insufficient number of spots spread over weeks or months amounts to tossing money into the wastebasket. For radio to be effective, listeners must hear a spot more than once; repetition is essential to build recognition and remembrance, both required before the desire to buy is triggered.

Since a listener can't call back a radio commercial to hear it again, he or she may have to hear the same commercial two, four, or maybe six times before the message sinks in. A listener who missed your company's name or its location the first time consciously or subconsciously is hoping the commercial will be aired again soon to get the necessary information.

Radio advertising should be bought in chunks, not by the spot. High frequency over a short period of time is much more effective than low frequency over a longer period of time. It is important for your audience to hear your spot several times within a consolidated time period to get enough information from it to want or to be able to take any kind of action.

The Small Business Administration gives excellent advice. If you want to advertise and you can afford forty-two radio commercials, the following buy would serve you well: on Tuesdays, Wednesdays, and Thursdays, place three spots between 7:00 and 9:00 A.M. and four spots between 3:00 and 6:00 P.M. for two weeks. Notice that both day and hour periods are concentrated. "By advertising in concentrated areas in tight day groups," says the SBA, "you seem larger than you really are. And people hearing your concentrated campaign for two or three days will think you're on all the time."

Time of Day Matters

Success depends on buying time in the time periods during which your potential customers are most likely to be tuned in. A lot of radio sales reps will try to talk you out of advertising during specific times. They'll offer you a reduced rate called TAP (Total Audience Plan) that splits your advertising time into one-third drive, one-third midday, and one-third nighttime. This may sound like a good deal, but airing commercials during times when your audience isn't listening is bad advertising.

If your budget is tight, you probably can get by with only a few spots if they are scheduled at the same time on the same station on the same day each week to catch roughly the same listeners.

If your product or service is meant to help people sleep, the midnight to 6 A.M. period, when people may be having difficulty sleeping, could be ideal. It undoubtedly is the worst choice, however, if you wish to attract eight-to-five businesspeople who are asleep then. Morning and evening drive time is a better time to reach this group.

There are organizations that measure radio, but they are not measuring listeners who hear your commercials. That measurement must come from the number of responses you achieve, which entails more than the effectiveness of the commercial itself. It includes the proper choice of stations and time periods.

Each radio station has figures to show numbers of listeners by days and hours, age and sex, and other characteristics. As with other media, rates go up in relation to the numbers of listeners in each time period. You acquired this information when you were assessing the best medium(s) to choose for your specific business and purposes (chapter 7). Again, however, remember not to let estimates of audience and other data that lean heavily toward favoring the station cloud your judgment. It's the most important function of each radio salesperson to get you to spend as many ad dollars as possible.

Hispanic Listeners

If your audience includes Hispanics, a recent study shows that separate advertising buys are required to reach many of them.

Many marketers think that special Spanish-language advertising efforts are not needed because Hispanics are so well assimilated they can be reached through regular channels. Not so, says a study conducted by Strategy Research Corp. Only children and teens are very assimilated, but "there's very little assimilation going on" in other age brackets, according to Dick Tobin, the company's president. Almost eight of ten Hispanic adults listen to Spanish-language radio.

Extra Exposure

"Stations must strive to originate inventive ways of forming stronger relationships with their clients," says Lisa Gergely of WBT-AM/FM in Charlotte, North Carolina, writing in *The Pulse of Radio*. Gergely offers a tip for stretching your radio advertising dollars. Ask your radio station rep whether the station is willing to help form a stronger relationship with you as its client. The suggestion is to tag a public service announcement (PSA) with, "This public service announcement is brought to you by AdCraft Graphics." As Gergely says, "The client gets additional exposure while showing increased community involvement," and PSAs are free. The only charge is for production, and there should be no production charge for a tagline.

Incentives

There are big plans in progress by radio to grab more of your advertising dollars. Radio 2000/An Alliance for Growth is a goal plan that calls for all facets of the radio industry—groups, networks, syndicators, and local broadcasters—to form an alliance to market radio against other media rather than against radio, reports *Media Outlook*.

One technique that radio stations might use to convince you to spend more on radio is to offer you a money-back guarantee that your spots will produce results or additional spots until you get results. Another tactic offers a one-week "thank you" ad schedule every time a rep gets a "no" from a legitimate prospect that the station wants as a advertiser. In other words, you tell the rep "no," and she comes back at you with the offer of an additional week of free spots in an effort to get you to change your mind.

Cable Radio and Digital Audio Broadcasting

Radio virtually invented the concept of targeting and has become the most accurate marketing tool along with special interest magazines to reach and motivate consumers, not only by age group but by socioeconomic and life-style characteristics as well, the Radio Advertising Bureau claims. But television has been the glamor medium and where the big money has gone. Now cable radio is promising to make radio red hot, says *Advertising Age*.

Cable radio, launched in mid-1990, uses cable television receivers to deliver static-free music via wires plugged into cable subscribers' stereos. "The thinking behind cable radio is that cable TV needs new revenue and [that] consumers are fed up with commercials on radio," reports *Advertising Age*. Some in the industry believe that cable radio soon will begin accepting commercials, which adds up to an even greater audience fragmentation.

Still a year or more away in the United States is another high-tech advancement already in use abroad: digital audio broadcasting (DAB). There are anticipated problems here, too. "If DAB services are allowed to be delivered via satellite, experts speculate that the existing local radio broadcasting system could be endangered. If DAB doesn't operate on the AM or FM bands, both AM and FM would be severely impacted," according to *Advertising Age*. But overall, "Given that DAB is essentially perfect quality audio delivery, radio and advertising would be helped. Commercials would be more effective, the quality of the sound delivered more effective, there'd be no noise, with perfect coverage areas," is the belief of Michael Rau, senior Vice President–science and technology at National Association of Broadcasters.

11

TV: Is It the Impossible Dream?

When and How to Use Television

Years ago gagwriters began including jokes about television never replacing newspapers—because it's impossible to carry a TV set over your head in the rain! Or wrap fish in it!

True. But it is no gag that, for small businesses, television will never replace advertising in newspapers, radio, magazines, or just about any other medium because it is far too expensive. The average cost for a single, high-quality 30-second television commercial is around $200,000—and that does not include purchase of the time in which to run it. Nevertheless, it's important to include this chapter about television and television advertising for three reasons:

1. There are some ways that small businesses may be able to afford to advertise on television, such as with co-op, using similar spare production techniques similar to those used for public service announcements (PSAs), or by hiring semiprofessionals.
2. Businesspersons, no matter the size of their businesses, are bombarded by television sales representatives who cheer the fact that television reaches more people than any other medium. It's important for you to know the facts in order to accept or resist sales offers knowledgeably.

3. Many businesspeople have a strong desire to include television in advertising schedules based on personal experiences of how it controls leisure hours. Research supports these feelings: over the past two decades, television as a primary activity has grown from 10.5 hours a week, or 30 percent of leisure hours, to 15.1 hours, equal to 38 percent.

These reasons can seem to offer strong justification for digging deep to pay the high cost not only of television time but also for beyond-the-imagination production costs. Without all the facts, it's easy to succumb to personal desire and to strong salesmanship.

Television: Pros and Cons for Advertisers

Advertising on television has distinct advantages:

- Television combines sight, sound, motion, and color so that it most closely parallels personal selling.
- Television brings your message right into people's homes, making it an excellent vehicle to introduce new products or services and to create the desire to buy. There is a flip side, though: people resent the intrusiveness of your bringing your product directly into their living rooms. They cannot avoid sales messages unless they turn off the set or change the channel. With other media—newspapers, magazines, outdoor, direct mail—the targeted individual can completely avoid your message.
- If your product is different from or better than your competition's, television is an excellent way to sell it because you have all the senses except smell and taste working for you. And you can even create the illusion of taste with visuals and words.
- Television advertising gives a product or service immediate authenticity and importance.
- The creative possibilities are unmatched in any other medium. The camera allows you to take your audience anywhere and show them almost anything your creative mind can envision.
- Some specific audience segments can be reached: children

during children's programs, homemakers during soap operas, sports-minded people during sports broadcasts.

If your goal is to disregard the precisely targeted consumer that your research showed is the best potential buyer of your product or service and to reach out to a mass audience, television is an excellent choice. It can reach a larger audience more quickly than any other medium.

There are also strong reasons *not* to spend limited advertising dollars on television:

- The most compelling reason is cost.
- The majority of its programming doesn't precisely target individual groups of people. Instead, it reaches practically everyone. Even a morning agricultural program that obviously is aimed to the interests of farmers delivers a mass audience of farmers whose individual farming interests are highly varied. And soap operas may reach homemakers, but they cover the entire demographic, psychographic, and geographic range of homemakers.
- There are sophisticated measuring tools designed to help the television time buyer select programming in which to place commercials. Programs can be measured by zip codes, wealth, family size, etc. The statistical validity of these new measurements is, however, in dispute, as an example shows: A retailer's trade zone might encompass three zip codes. She can ask the TV station to make a computer run that will sort out the most watched programs by those particular zip codes. The idea is to buy the time slots that have the greatest number of people living in the targeted zip codes. Some stations may charge for the computer run, but probably not for a new advertiser. Cost is not the issue here. The charge for this kind of a zip code run isn't apt to be high. The drawback in this case is in believing too much in the validity of the numbers produced. It's a good directional tool, as long as you realize that results are plus or minus 10 percent to 15 percent. In other words, it's not all that precise, but if you factor in some degree of uncertainty, then it's a perfectly good and valid tool to use.
- Whereas radio is known to command audience loyalty for all

the programming on a single station, television can claim audience loyalty only for individual programs. To reach your targeted audience with any frequency, you may have to buy spots on several different stations rather than one, which dilutes your negotiating power with any one station.

- Viewers cannot hear competing commercials simultaneously nor go back to review a commercial for missed information. Nor can they clip an item and tuck it into a wallet or purse for reference, or clip an order form and use it immediately.
- Production of television commercials is costly and requires great knowledge and expertise. Viewers expect high-quality commercials, and their sophistication has increased to a point that poorly produced spots endanger the message's effectiveness and actually may create a poor image of the product, the service, or the company that you're attempting to sell. Viewers can "zap" whatever is on screen. There's an interesting sidelight about who has charge of the zapper in most households. According to a J. Walter Thompson survey 43 percent of men take charge of the remote control compared to only 29 percent of women. The statistic may have some meaning if you're targeting women at a time of day when men are in charge of the remote control.

Purchasing Television Time

Consult the Experts

If you've decided television is a good medium for your advertising message but you haven't yet purchased the time, go back to chapter 7 and review how to deal with TV salespeople, how to get the information you need, and how to get the best for your money.

Before you purchase time, be sure the advertising dollars you've portioned are sufficient to cover the purchase of both quality airtime and the production of a quality commercial. If you buy time that fits your budget but doesn't reach your audience—for example, late night for workers who must be in bed early—that's money thrown away. Similarly, if you present a poorly produced commercial to run in competition with technologically sophisticated spots from other advertisers, few people will pay attention to your spot. Be sure there are adequate funds so that the commercial can be creative enough to capture their attention. If you don't have adequate funds to allow comparable production values, then you absolutely must have a selling premise so powerful that it will overcome viewer indifference.

The biggest concern in purchasing time is that the dollars allotted permit you to buy an adequate number of spots to build recognition and remembrance. Repetition and frequency are essential. Be sure your audience will see your spot at least five to seven times.

Try to purchase time within programs rather than in break time between programs. TV viewers' loyalty is to programs, not to stations, and more channel switching is done between than during programs.

Another important point to remember when purchasing television time is that audiences show seasonal differences. A recent study is of interest. A. C. Nielsen Co. studied viewing patterns during July 1993 in two of the country's most weather-battered areas. In heat-soaked New York and Washington, where the mercury shot up to over 100 degrees regularly, people decided it was smart to stay indoors, but they didn't sit in front of a television set. HUT (Homes Using Television) levels remained constant. But in the rain-drenched Midwest, viewing levels shot up substantially when people apparently parked themselves in front of the set to dry out—and to monitor flood conditions.

Winter HUT levels peak in late January and early February and then drop in the summer when weather lures people outdoors. They are lowest around the Fourth of July, according to Nielsen, which compiles data daily. If your business is air-conditioners, or any other hot weather product or activity, the facts could save you money.

How About Using 15-Second Spots?

If your advertising dollar allocation is small, there may be an option, but check the fine print before you buy. There may be serious penalties.

Fifteen-second commercials were a high-priority item for a majority of television advertisers, according to the Television Bureau of Advertising, until 1991. There are several theories and a couple of strong reasons for the decline in their use. Some say it's because of creative considerations. Others believe it is because of a soft economy that resulted in sharp decreases in advertising expenditures, which in turn generated bargain prices for lengthier commercial time. Changes in strategies by advertisers is still another explanation, but the hard-fact reason—that definitely isn't a theory—for the decline comes by action of television executives who are concerned about commercial clutter and are pricing the shorter spots out of existence. A 10- or 15-second spot might cost as much as 80 percent of a 30-second spot. As if that isn't penalty enough, stations reserve the right to bump the advertiser from a particular time position if a 30-second buyer comes in. The risk for buyers of smaller time units is that the spots don't run as scheduled, and the advertiser's campaign is not effective.

For some advertisers the short spots still may be attractive because they "are 60 percent to 80 percent as effective as 30-second spots, in terms of recall or the ability to persuade consumers," according to an article in *The New York Times. The Times* cautions that 15-second spots are most effective when used to hammer home the names of well-known brands, a point to keep in mind if your product is not well known or if your purpose is to build recognition for a locally offered service, or to build company image. Such spots do not permit enough time to explain user benefits or advantages.

They also are excellent as a means to direct viewers to your advertising that is running simultaneously in another medium, such as newspapers or Yellow Pages. The print medium can give information that is impossible to include in a TV spot. If it is used as a teaser to induce the listener to consult the other medium, the costs and risks may be justified—for example:

"Look for money-saving coupons in Sunday's newspaper."

"All the details are coming soon to your mailbox. Watch for this envelope with my picture."

"For a list of locations, look for this ad in your Yellow Pages."

"To get our free brochure, call 1–800–000–0000."

"See our ad in this week's *Sports Illustrated*."

Don't Forget Co-op

Although newspapers are the preferred place for co-op advertising by those who supply the added funding, small businesses need co-op assistance the most with television. And the time to remember co-op is while talking to the television salesperson.

Co-op is available to retail businesses that sell products made by large manufacturers. The ground rules for getting and using co-op money are covered in chapter 2. Check to see if you qualify and how to obtain these funds that may let you present your advertising message alongside the biggest advertisers on television.

Jim Winters, executive creative director for EvansGroup Marketing Communications who has excellent advice about co-op, says that co-op is available not just from the primary vendor but also from the vendor's vendors. For example, "Diet Coke has co-op dollars; Coke Promotions has additional co-op dollars; the aluminum can manufacturer has more co-op dollars, and Nutrasweet has even more co-op dollars." Winters recommends digging deep to locate these vendor's vendors: "It's surprising how much money is earmarked for co-op, but is never claimed."

Your station representative should have the information about acquiring co-op funding and preparing and presenting co-op commercials on television. If not, write for information to:

TVB Co-op
Television Bureau of Advertising
477 Madison Avenue
New York, NY 10022–5892
212/486–1111

Except for following the rules set forth by the company supplying the funding, the commercials are prepared like any other television commercials. You may be required to provide a script, notarized by the station, of the spot after it runs, and you definitely must supply a log, also notarized by the station, showing what spot ran and the times in which it ran.

Sometimes prior approval is required, but that too will show up in the agreement.

Writing the Commercial

It's Best to Hire Pros, But There Are Other Ways

Of all advertising media, television commercials are not only the costliest but the most difficult and the trickiest to produce. They require knowledge and experience. A do-it-yourself approach is not recommended unless you are willing to give the time to study in advance and in depth. Television is a whole new world where not even "adverbabble" is spoken. The pros talk about upfront and scatter; program and daypart; audience size, composition, and guarantees; network and spot; cable and syndication; CPMS and unit costs; underdelivery and make-goods. As if that's not enough, it's also a world of grazing, zapping, or channel surfing, of "shopping" for a program. When "B.C." cartoonist Johnny Hart looked up the phrase *ad nauseam* in his "Wiley's Dictionary," he found the answer was: "a condition brought on by watching too many TV commercials."

If you are located in a metropolitan center with large networks and independent stations showing professionally produced, technologically intricate, nationally circulated spots, there is no alternative to hiring professionals to produce your commercials, except to forgo television advertising. If, however, you choose a small, independent, local channel or a cable station, perhaps you can construct your own spots. Never forget, though, that viewers in even the smallest towns still have access to network television that airs commercials from the biggest and best corporations and advertising agencies in the country.

Perhaps You Can Hire a Student to Do It

If you live in or near a university town, check out the availability of students majoring in advertising or broadcasting. Such an arrangement could be profitable for both you and the student(s). Talk to the head of the communications or marketing department, and perhaps an arrangement can be made whereby all the students in a class can compete—for academic credit or a prize offered by you—to produce a commercial that will meet your needs and give them experience.

Get Out Your Copycat File

The first step is to get your ideas flowing. It's not easy to collect a copycat file of television commercials to get the creative juices flowing; in fact, it is nearly impossible.

In chapter 10, you read about taped collections of the best radio commercials, available from *Advertising Age*. This trade magazine annually produces two tapes (one for television and one for radio) that you can rewind and review again and again. Another source for ideas is *Creativity International Video Magazine,* a quarterly videocassette subscription. It is gathered by *Advertising Age* and is produced for "everyone interested in commercial production, breakthrough advertising, new creative ideas, great acting, insightful writing, sharp shooting and editing, inspiring music, dazzling graphics."

Costs of both collections are high—from approximately $400 to almost $1,000. Further, none of the spots is a low-budget production, but they may be worthwhile to stimulate ideas. For information or to order, mail to:

Advertising Age Marketing Department
220 East 42d Street
New York, NY 10017
phone: 1–800/283–2724 or 212/210–0287
fax: 212/210–0111

How to Do a TV Commercial and Live to Tell About It

Start with focusing on the goal you wish the commercial to achieve, and keep the goal clear in your mind the entire time you work on this specific spot.

Then decide the length of the commercial: a 15-second, 30-second, or 60-second spot? Or will it be constructed to run in more than one time format? For local advertisers, 30-second commercials are the most cost-effective and the easiest to purchase time for. Moreover, there are data to show that a 30-second spot is up to 90 percent as effective as a 60-second spot.

Next, decide the form the commercial will take. Will it be:

- A demonstration of the benefit(s) of your product or service?
- A human interest mini-drama, with real people (not actors) acting out the uses of the product or service?
- A testimonial, in which real people enthusiastically testify as to the merits of the product or service?
- An announcer telling the benefits and making the sales pitch?

If you are running advertising simultaneously in any other medium—newspapers, direct mail, or radio, for example—use the same theme, the same visuals if possible, and basically the same copy. Keep your advertising consistent across the breadth of your choice of media to build recognition and remembrance.

The Message Can Take Several Directions

Television viewers enjoy and are conditioned to hearing stories on their favorite programs, and storytelling works well in getting an advertising message across to listeners. Time constrictions limit how a story is developed; 60 seconds, and even 30 seconds, allows time to tell a selling story, but 15 seconds is too narrow a period.

Just as newspaper readers and radio listeners enjoy and respond well to high human interest features, so too do television viewers. A couple of famous commercials are examples that illustrate the point.

A few years ago Coca Cola took a group of singers to Rome to film a commercial that became a classic. It was so simple—a couple of hundred kids holding hands, offering to buy the world a coke. They could have sung the song in 15 seconds but it wouldn't have had any meaning. The story—a story with no words, only the song—took 60 seconds to unfold. A great part of the effectiveness of that particular message was the *un*told story and the imagination that the viewer brought to it.

Another example, also from Coca Cola, is what is now called the "mean Joe Green commercial." Joe Green was a defensive football player for the Pittsburgh Steelers and as he came off the field he encountered a young boy and offered him his chin strap. The kid took it and was thrilled, so thrilled that he in turn offered Joe his coke. Joe took it and gave him his jersey. Again, it was a story with no words, no script, but a story that was told visually and with timing—again in 60 seconds.

As with advertising in any other medium, humor can be a means for gaining attention and action and establishing recognition and remembrance for your product, service, or company. But as with every other use of humor, if it's good, it's very, very good and if it's bad, it's horrible. If you use humor, try it out in advance on a significant number of people who fit the profile of your potential consumers.

Here's a Pro's Advice

From his years of experience working with clients, Jim Winters makes reliable observations and offers advice worth paying particular attention to. All advertisers, he says, tend to use their ad messages to say what they want to say instead of what their consumers need to hear. "It's important that they do the perspiration before the inspiration, and figure out what the key benefit is to the consumer. After that, the actual writing and production of the commercial are almost incidental," Winters says. That should make you less apprehensive about writing and producing a television commercial. You've already done the perspiration, so you know the key benefit(s) your potential consumers want to know about.

Winters goes on to say that while an inadequate production budget can sometimes make the TV spot a failure, inadequate thinking will always make it a failure. An advertiser "must present his product or service as a real solution to a real human problem. Then, if the content of the message is strong enough, and the selling premise is clear enough—the commercial will work no matter how it is produced."

Winters gives an example. A British commercial had a young man in a plain white studio with one stationary camera showing the man, full figure. He was listening to rock music coming from the portable radio held on his shoulder. The music coughed, sputtered, and conked out. The young man looked at his radio, opened the back, and removed the batteries. He then threw the radio away and walked off screen, carrying the batteries. A simple logo came up with the name of the battery company. "Cost to produce that commercial was peanuts because the idea was so powerful," says Winters. "Did they need to say one more word, or add one more piece of video? I don't think so. In most cases of persuasive communications, less is more."

First Write a Print Ad

The best first step, according to many advertising professionals, is to write a print ad, even if you have no plans to use print. A print ad allows you to write everything that's applicable and appropriate, not just the few words that fit in 28 seconds of television time. Just as you did with your radio spot, first talk it into a tape recorder; then pinpoint the benefit, condense it, and hone it to a fine point; write the print ad, and define and refine it until you have a message you can be proud of. Now you're ready to move on to the script, which must be written for each time slot purchased.

Ready, Set, Write

All production elements are developed based on the script. Although script changes may be made up to the moment of taping or filming, to keep costs at their lowest the script should be as complete and as final as possible before it is presented for other purposes such as locating props and talent and for taping or filming. Even the smallest production change raises costs.

In the script, plan to promote the honest attributes of your product, service, or company. Because so many top marketers have used unsubstantiated or irrelevant claims, it is essential to tilt your message all the way toward truth and honesty. Eliminate exaggeration.

If your audience is in either of two particular groups, be aware of presenting a credible message. *Adweek's Marketing Week* found from a survey it commissioned that the age groups that most often show the greatest skepticism about advertising are the 45–54 and 55–64 year olds, the people who command the greatest purchasing power.

Catch Their Attention

Use sound effects (SFX), music, and other attention getters to grab the attention of your audience immediately and keep them from heading for the refrigerator or mentally tuning out. Don't be shrill or strident. Remote control devices also have a mute button, and a particularly thunderous or raucous attention getter may cause a viewer to use it.

Because television is a visual medium, use a striking visual image. A striking, moving visual image is even better. The images can be anything you can think of but should be within the following parameters:

- A visualization of a consumer problem that your product or service will solve for viewers later in the commercial.
- A consumer aspiration that you will show viewers how to achieve.
- A scene of mystery, beauty, drama, excitement, or anything else must relate to your selling premise.
- Avoid statements that seem to have no relevance to what is being shown or said—for example, a roller coaster ride to set up need for consistent quality, an old car's exhaust spewing smoke to sell new cars, children playing to sell the importance of good tires, beautiful women to sell men's cologne, or beautiful men to sell women's fashions or cosmetics.

Another way to get viewers' attention is to speak to them individually. "Attention computer users" may hold listeners for the few seconds until they decide the message is relevant.

If you use music, make it meaningful to your target: rock or rap for young people, classic rock for middle-age viewers, tunes that date back forty or fifty years for those 60 and older.

If you use a stimulating or interest-piquing opening statement, be sure it fits your target's idea of what is stimulating or piques his interest and fits the word message that follows.

You may wish to create a mood with visuals and sounds to set a scene. For example, the sight and sound of a crackling fire instantly sets a particular mood. Make sure it is the mood you want your commercial to convey.

Remember to include the company's name early in the spot, and always use the name as the last words for the listeners to carry away with them.

Make It Sell

The goal, the objective, and the purpose of your television message is to sell an image, an idea, a product, or a service. You may take any road to get to your destination—a simple dramatization, a testimonial, a spot that entertains—but the bottom line is that the message must ring the cash register. The test of whether the spot accomplishes its purpose is the amount it rings the cash register.

Benefits are the best means to sell something to a viewer. If the viewer sees a benefit she wants or needs, she will buy. So benefits become your sales points. Pull out the list of benefits that your research indicated are the wants and needs of your target consumers. Pick the priority benefit to them, not to you or your business.

Motivate the Viewer to Act

The spot may be an excellent sales message, but TV viewers may have difficulty getting off the couch. And busy people often don't— or won't—take time to respond unless you give them a reason to act. Offer something that stimulates action, such as a discount. Ryder's Truck Rental gave viewers who are planning a move a substantial reason to move on weekdays: a 40 percent discount on those days.

Have It Typed into Script Format

When you decide the script is acceptable, it must be typed in a special format, (see the sample script on page 154). That's when you hand it over to production people, who know the accepted final script style and format, including the appropriate notations about video to accompany appropriate audio.

As you did for your radio commercial, you may wish to read your script into a tape recorder before you finalize it. Hearing it may help you smooth rough spots.

Production Methods

It is said that there is no free lunch, but everyone knows there are less expensive lunches. Here we will look at basic instructions for producing your own television spots based on less expensive production methods. Each method is used by big-budget companies for high-competition network-type commercials but is easily utilized by a small business for spots on local television. None ends up looking like the inept, amateur spots often seen on late-night local stations.

These techniques came into use when the economy turned frail and some advertisers were faced with dropping television schedules or finding less lavish production methods. Imitating Public Service Announcements offered one solution. The second is a technique that showed up in 1992 political campaigns, and the third is called the "talking heads" format. As a for-profit company, you are not eligible to run Public Service Announcements on television or radio; they are available only to nonprofit organizations. But you can use similar production techniques that can get the desired message across.

PSA-Like Techniques

THE COMPUTER. Locate a self-service copying service company that offers hourly computer rentals, and sit down at one of their computers for a couple of hours. Choose a typeface and style for each title card. (Title cards are what in newspapers would be called a caption; they describe an illustration.) When each is designed, it is then printed out in color and can be taken to a local television studio and transferred to tape with an appropriate soundtrack.

The ratio of a television screen is 4:5, and the format always is horizontal. Therefore, you must work within the 11 inches from side to side, "floating" within margins of 1½ to 2 inches.

If your company has an established logo in printed form and can be mounted on a card, undoubtedly a camera can pick it up. If you do not have one, you can create a logo on the computer, using a scanner to read it or any other specific art into the visual.

Another suggestion is to use the video and the audio to advance communication on both levels—eyes and ears. For example, if you show a picture of a car, don't use the word *car* in your script. Viewers can see it's a car. Instead, say something about the car, such as that if has a three-year warranty.

Keep words short, sweet, and memorable. The soundtrack must support and enhance the video, without literally repeating the words.

STOCK FOOTAGE. There are companies that own the rights to footage from old movies, documentaries, and training films. This means that if, for instance, you want to show a Parisian street café, you don't have to go to Paris to film it. It exists as stock footage. Just about every place on the globe has been filmed by somebody, and whatever you need is available at one or another stock house to use in your commercial. Silent movies and movies from the 1950s offer clips of posses chasing bad guys, cars flying over cliffs, biplanes crashing, romantic kisses, barroom fights, pie fights, dogs, kids, cats,

Audio	Video
MAN: Some of you may not know what an electric heat pump is.	Man on screen, next to large wooden crate labeled "The Heat Pump".
Well, let me show you. In summer, a heat pump is a high efficiency air conditioner.	Man opens lid of box.
So you stay cool and comfortable.	Lid of box is blue, cold wind sound, man reacts to"coolness" coming out of box.
In winter, it's the most efficient heating system you can own. Mmmmm.	Man opens box lid again, revealing warm colors, reacts to the warmth while snow is falling on him .
So, uh, who don't you just see it yourself at your heat pump dealer.	As he speaks, the man turns to walk away.
(SFX: THUD!)	Money bag drops into scene from top with a loud thud.startling the man.
Oh, by the way, it can save you money too. A hundred and thirty dollars a year, or more.	Man turns and comes back to box.
The heat pump cools, heats and saves.	Logo appears on screen over box and man.

*Television Script (above) **with Story Board** (opposite)*

"Heat Pump" – Length 30 seconds

Man: Some of you may not know what an electric heat pump is.

Well, let me show you. In summer, a heat pump is a high efficiency air conditioner.
So you stay cool and comfortable.
(WIND)

In winter, it's the most efficient heating system you can own.
Mmmmmmm.

So, uh, why don't you just see it yourself at your heat pump dealer.

(THUD!)
Oh, by the way, it can save you money, too. A hundred and thirty dollars a year, or more.

The heat pump cools, heats and saves.

A COMMITMENT TO SERVICE

pigs, cows, ad infinitum. You dream up the action, and there's probably a clip available to depict it. Just be sure the action is relevant to your selling idea.

These companies are located in New York or Los Angeles. Most TV stations have a list of them with telephone numbers; or go to the library or the telephone company and check the Yellow Pages. Tell the stock house what you're looking for. It will research and come back with available clips, which you can view for suitability before making a purchase commitment. Cost usually is on a per foot basis and is surprisingly inexpensive.

Make the video as relevant to the main selling premise as possible. Otherwise, it can detract from the message rather than aid it.

SUPER 8 VIDEO CAMERAS. Videotapes made with home video cameras aren't suitable for producing television commercials. Don't even try it. If you've ever seen "America's Favorite Videos" or news clips that use home video cameras, you can see how flat and characterless the images can be on broadcast television.

Super 8 is a film process that is inexpensive, and its grainy look helps create a super-real feeling that's used on some network programming (on MTV, too). You could use this when you want to show you are in tune with the MTV generation—when you want to add visual interest to a scene that lacks intrinsic interest. It also is a good tool to help create emotions of nostalgia or to add vitality to action scenes: children playing, sports, busy street scenes.

Super 8 cameras are sold or rented at many camera stores, along with standard format Super 8 mm film.

Again, you may find a surprising pool of talent at the local college to handle such a shoot. Ask the professors; they're eager to give their students practical experience.

STOCK PHOTOS AND 35 MM SLIDES. Stock houses also have libraries rich in gorgeous photography of almost any image you might imagine. The charge is $100 to $500 a photo, depending on a variety of factors, such as the uniqueness of the photo, its artistry, whether models who must be paid are included, whether it's for local or national television use, and the size of the market in which the spot will run (it costs less in Omaha than in Los Angeles). The images can be projected on high-quality screens, and the station's video cameras can be made to zoom, tilt, pan, or anything else to create a feeling of motion (*kinestasis* is the technical term for making stills appear to move).

Interesting high-style effects can be created by projecting images on white boxes or white globes or on flat surfaces at angles to the camera. This technique makes distorted images useful for a futuristic look or for a dream sequence or simply to give the appearance of expensive special effects without the cost.

DESKTOP PUBLISHING. Many desktop publishing services now have added video capabilities, which includes video editing, to their desktop computers. With them, it's possible to capture moving images from CD/ROM, videotape, or off the air, and then edit them together in a way you prefer. The editing instructions are stored on a disc and, with the image sources, can be taken to a station for final editing. This process is especially useful for commercials in which you plan to splice together a number of different scenes. If your script calls for fewer than four or five scenes, it's probably not worth the extra step.

Trial and error is the best method for assembling footage into the desired sequence within the limited time frames of the commercial and should be done before you walk into the expensive editing bays of a station or postproduction house. It will pay you to make those decisions at what is a much lower hourly rate. All this technology is new and time-consuming but is substantially less costly than going directly to a station or editing house, where the hourly rates are much higher. You may have to check several services to find one that offers the technique.

The Reverse Screen, Voice-Over Technique

Perhaps you saw the Honda commercial. It could have been a radio spot, except for the changing hues on your screen. There were no graphics, no visuals, nothing—just colors slowly changing on the screen and a voice-over saying, "Imagine you're driving down a road to the sea. Imagine you're . . . " and the voice goes on as you mentally picture what the announcer is asking you to imagine. At the end, Honda's logo comes on the screen, in white type on an all-black (reverse) screen.

Aetna Life Insurance, with its zippy slogan, "A policy to do more," has adopted a policy to do much less in its television commercials. It has pared down its production technique to about as meager as it can get. One Aetna spot features a child's voice-over along with what the listener knows to be a father's voice speaking as the words they say appear in white scrolled down a black screen. Finally, as the screen reverses to white, black copy shows Aetna's identifying logo, and an announcer's voice-over gives the final words.

Motel 6 also used the "black screen" style in a 30-second spot featuring the folksy commentary of Tom Bodett, Motel 6's announcer for many years. Bodett's well-known voice was the only "appearance" he made. His off-handed comment was, "This is what your room looks like when you're asleep."

Still other national advertisers use a rolling script over a simple video background on a reverse/black screen. But any color can be used, which is generated by the editing equipment.

None of these corporations have sent out financial reports on the success of these leanest of the lean television commercials, but they are worth imitating to keep production costs to an absolute minimum.

You can chalk up another deposit to your savings if you use the television soundtrack for a radio spot. It works better the other way, however: put pictures to your radio commercial.

Another somewhat similar technique provides an effective way to keep the name of your company on-screen throughout the entire commercial. The moving, visual message runs within a boxed area, while the top of the "box" carries the name of the company and the bottom of the box gives address and telephone number.

Talking Heads

Perhaps the least expensive commercial uses an announcer standing before the camera describing the benefits of the product or service. But in the melee of visually stimulating, high-interest spots, this method—if it is designed without action—also may be a fast means to send viewers for a snack. When there's something on the screen— person, words, or colors—be sure it moves. Figure a way to have the announcer doing something, such as demonstrating the benefit. Be sure the words he speaks are interesting and spoken with enthusiasm. And place him in an attractive setting. One way to avoid the deadly dull look of a "talking head" might be to shoot the announcer on site at your company, walking through the business.

Often there's a temptation to use a company executive as an announcer not only to save money but to gratify an ego element. Unless the person is as well known in your local area as Lee Iacocca, has past experience, and excellent on-camera talent, hire an announcer—the best one you can afford.

Steps to Creating a TV Commercial

A storyboard can be developed for each script. A storyboard is a series of illustrations that shows the action sequence as related to the script; it shows both audio and visual elements. (There is an example of a story board on page 155.) A storyboard has dual uses: it helps the commercial's creator visualize images and a smooth flow, and it can be used to estimate production costs of the commercial and as a guide in the actual shooting of the commercial.

Captions beneath each illustration may describe the principal action in the segment—the video—and include the actual words spoken—the audio. Music, sound effects, props, and camera angles also may be described for each panel. The best way to ensure high quality at the lowest cost is to be specific in all storyboard descriptions.

Call for close-up camera shots of the announcer whenever possible. They are more dramatic and they require fewer set props which keep costs lower.

There is a special language spoken in television studios. You will hear jargon such as CUs (Close-Ups) and ECUs (Extreme Close-Ups), and LSs (Long Shots) and MSs (Medium Shot), Supers, Cuts, and Dissolves. These are terms used in scripts and a significant reason for turning the typing of your script over to experienced production people. The Glossary in the back of the book includes definitions of these and other jargon terms for your understanding.

A 30-second spot permits up to twelve visual changes, and about fifty to eighty spoken words. Because television is a visual medium, lean toward using fewer words. Unlike radio, there is no need to describe something verbally that a viewer can see on the screen.

Any props must be located and backdrops or sets arranged for. A rear-screen projection of a scenic slide or any other background slide is the least expensive set. Several changes of scenes can be effected through slide dissolves, cuts, or fades.

Music, special effects, and titles must be arranged for, either with the station where the commercial will be filmed or in cooperation with the students or others with whom you've contracted to develop the spot. Most television stations have a music or sound effects library. If the music is in the public domain, it is free, unless the artists who perform it have a current copyright on it. In that case, the artists must be paid royalties.

Talent must be chosen. Finding the right spokesperson for your commercial is important. Although people expect announcers and other talent to be telegenic (photogenic on television), this isn't a beauty contest. Choose people who look like people you know—ordinary people to whom viewers can relate but who personify the image you wish to convey of your company, your product, or your service.

When all of this preliminary work has been done, it's time for the taping or filming. This part of the work must be handled by studio personnel, students with their instructor(s), semiprofessionals, or professionals. If the filming is not done at the television station, arrangements must be made either to rent a studio or to shoot on location.

Close the spot with 5 to 7 seconds of on-screen time for your logo. Your logo is important as a means for establishing recognition and remembrance and should be in the same type style as that used in your print advertising. There are relatively inexpensive animation techniques to put some action into those 5 to 7 seconds it's on screen: it can appear a letter at a time; it can flash on and off slowly so that eyes aren't affected and it can easily be read; or simple color changes can be used.

All elements of the spot—sound, video, special effects, music—must be integrated by someone with sufficient experience and training and combined on a single tape or film master.

This is the time for a careful final inspection and analysis of the spot. Changes will be costly even this late in the commercial's development, but better now than after duplicates are made and the spot begins its run.

Before any duplicates are made, give the spot a test run before an audience as similar in nature to your profiled group as possible. Ask for—and listen carefully to—reactions, criticisms, and suggestions. Make only those changes you consider imperative, but make mental or written notes about blunders or mistakes so that your next effort will be better for having acquired this knowledge and experience. Arrange for duplicates to be made, and if more than one station will run your spots, distribute them accordingly.

Expensive Techniques

You've heard about the kid who had his bag all packed and was ready to run away from home but just couldn't pull himself away from the TV set until the high-tech special effects commercials ended! He probably was watching national network spots by big-big corporate manufacturers, which use morphing and digitalizing, extremely costly techniques you undoubtedly won't use but should know about.

Think back to recent car and truck advertising campaigns and the uses of special effects in them, such as watching the roll-down of a beautiful scenic screen and then seeing a car drive off into it. It's a computer graphics metamorphosis technique called morphing borrowed from the feature film *Terminator 2: Judgment Day*. Morphing is a means of transforming one image into another. You can buy a morph program for your personal computer, but it won't be broadcast quality. It is, however, a good way to look at the special effect before you pay to have it done.

Still another highly effective, but extremely costly, technique that has become almost commonplace for big-budget national advertisers uses digital computer graphics and single-frame edits. It can create effects such as a car driving up and down a brick wall. These are the kinds of special effects Frank Lloyd Wright called "chewing gum for the eyes," and which your commercial must compete against if it runs on network television or on high-visibility channels in large metropolitan areas.

What's in Store Between Now and the Year 2000?

The prognosticators see the future as overwhelmingly influenced by visual impressions rather than by the printed word. New technologies and new economic and social changes call for everyday use of audio-video messages, and in particular the long-delayed television-telephone.

Direct broadcast television, which permits satellite signals to be relayed directly to homes equipped with small satellite dishes, is set for 1994. High definition television will be distributed into homes via fiber optic telephone lines. There will be a national interactive television system, which will allow viewers to use their TV sets to order all manner of services and to shop, bank, and pay bills. Such a two-way television system already is off the drawing boards, and Hewlett-Packard expects to market it for under $700, less than videocassette recorders cost when they were introduced.

There are strong indications that there will be a single multimedia vehicle that combines television, newspapers, computers, and the telephone.

What does all this mean to you as an advertiser? First, your audience will be spread over 300 viewing options instead of 30 or 40. You will be able to segment your audience better to target specific individuals, but each delivery of your message will cost more. Additionally, the current network/local station symbiotic relationship will be vastly different, which will make it more difficult for small advertisers to buy television commercials the way they can now.

Be aware of possible changes, and be prepared to change the way you advertise. New technology is predicted to drive up the costs of production and placement substantially.

12

Is It True What They Say About Cable TV?

The Facts to Help You Make Sound Buying Decisions

Most people think of cable television as new. Instead it actually began back in the 1940s and is almost as old as television itself.

Even early cable systems, called CATV (Community Antenna Television), were around as early as the late 1940s. But it wasn't until the 1950s when microwave relay provided the technology for cable to extend its range for hundreds of miles that the public and ultimately advertisers began to take notice. It also was then that the cable industry began to recognize its own strength.

By 1969 the industry had 3.6 million subscribers, and one out of every 16 homes in the country was equipped with cable. Then, as the number of cable subscribers continued to flourish, advertisers began to pay really serious attention. Initially they didn't see it so much as an advertising medium as a much as they thought of it as a means for testing commercials. But in the 1970s advertisers realized that it was an excellent medium to target very narrow and specific interest groups. That's when the term *narrowcasting* came into use. At that point, advertisers could target precise groups in the same way they used magazines and direct mail.

Today, more than half of American households subscribe to cable TV services, and it's expected that by 1994, cable companies will offer as many as 500 channels. Basic cable's collective share of the primetime audience in 1992 was a full point higher than ABC's. Viewers tend to be upscale, and 68 percent of all cable subscribers watch at least one ad-supported cable system each day.

The focus of this chapter is on understanding cable and the information needed to use it intelligently and profitably rather than on the production of advertising messages on cable. Many production techniques are the same for both television and cable, so if you decide to indulge your desires for inexpensively produced television-type commercials on cable, return to chapter 11 for the techniques described there. Included here, though, are a few tips and techniques that are exclusive to cable commercial production.

Prophets of Boom

Those early advertisers undoubtedly didn't foresee the ratings and revenue struggles ahead for the television industry, nor did they recognize how big the business of cable would become in both numbers of subscribers and income from advertising. Nor did advertisers anticipate so much public antagonism toward the intrusiveness of television commercials. With cable, subscribers can choose commercial-free viewing on a number of channels.

Like newspapers, some cable channels have two sources of revenue: subscribers and advertisers. Because these dual revenues distinguish cable from other broadcast forms, these channels are able to provide the widest range of special interest programming in broadcast. (Both television and radio have advertising revenues, but they receive no subscriber fees.)

Today there are more than 56 million cable subscribers, and revenues top $3 billion—twice the revenues of ABC, CBS, and NBC combined. Americans spend more on cable programming than on movie attendance and videocassettes combined. Cable is expected to reach 70 percent of U.S. households by the mid-1990s. By 1995 advertising revenues alone are expected to increase more than 70 percent, to $5.2 billion.

Menu Television

No matter what your taste, there's a cable channel that serves up the dish of your choice. You can choose all movies, all news, all documentaries, all music—even all country music—or all courtroom trials. And the specialization goes on and on; the All-Book Cable TV channel is scheduled to launch mid-1994 with 24-hour-a-day programming dealing exclusively with information about books. A sci-fi network broadcasts science fiction, science fact, and fantasy 24 hours a day. The channel is eagerly seeking advertisers and maintains that it targets "difficult-to-reach, highly sought-after core audiences . . . audiences [that] are not just viewers, they're avid fans, so your message will be delivered in an environment where viewer involvement has no equal."

In addition to a national all-sports network, there are more than twenty-five advertising-supported sports networks that offer regional and local sporting events of interest to viewers in defined geographic areas of the country.

One network claims to be the only programming service that targets 43 million Americans with disabilities. One directs its programming to Christians. Other channels target African-American audiences and Spanish-speaking Hispanic-Americans, upscale decision makers who want live business and financial information, and those who wish undergraduate- and graduate-level courses as well as life-long learners who seek wider knowledge and enhanced creativity. There's even narrowcasting devoted exclusively to travel and the weather.

Michael Eisner, chief executive officer of the Walt Disney Co., told broadcast industry executives that the nation's viewers may become highly fragmented in their viewing habits because each viewer can satisfy a narrow taste; broad entertainment themes that appeal to huge numbers of citizens will become an endangered species.

All the better for target-oriented advertisers!

As with all other potential media time or space purchases, it's important to look at the medium's good and not-so-good points in terms of reaching your audience and achieving your goal(s). There are cable channels that will accept commercials, giving advertisers more access to consumers than ever before—not as mass audiences as with television but as finely pinpointed groups. A lot of advertisers who haven't been able to afford network television now can afford cable at far lower prices than broadcast networks charge.

It's almost impossible to make precise comparisons between network television and cable costs. The problem with using cable for small businesses is in not being able to determine how many people of what kind you will reach. Over-the-air television is measured by Nielsen Station Index (NSI), a rating service of the A.C. Nielsen Company. It assesses "audience composition, size of audience, demographics, and psychographics" and provides believable, highly scientific measurements. Literally billions of dollars are spent based on these rating measurements.

Cable has not been willing to develop comparable rating systems, so when you buy cable you're never quite sure scientifically what kind of an audience you will reach. It is reasonable to assume that with programming such as ESPN, for example, you will reach a predominantly male audience. Then there is information to show the kind of viewers who watch each sport—so you know the profiles of those watching baseball, football, or soccer. But at no point do you know how many males you reach, so there is no way to determine a cost per thousand, a cost per rating point, because there are no rating points. Because of this, major advertisers most often use cable to build frequency at a very low cost against an over-the-air broadcast that establishes reach.

You didn't know you had it so good! Always before it's been the national buyers who get the rate breaks, but now those national buyers are turning to local cable because local systems reach a much smaller audience than cable networks and sell their few minutes per hour of cable network time at a much lower rate. These national advertisers can thus eliminate waste and save money by choosing a series of small, targeted system buys instead of a single big network buy.

Among the advantages for small businesses are these:

- Lower advertising rates on local cable systems permit much greater repetition of commercials.
- In many areas, cable is the only opportunity for local broadcast advertising.
- Spot cable offers small geographic regions—sometimes as little as a few neighborhoods—so they can deliver an audience

that can be broken down by address, zip code, and life-style. So-called local radio and regular television stations usually serve large geographic areas and therefore have much higher rates, and they also waste dollars for an advertiser who wishes to reach only one or two communities within the total audience.

- The content of advertising messages is less restricted than in broadcast. You can contract for longer commercials and much bolder messages; you can even show beer drinkers actually drinking beer, which is not permitted on television that travels the airwaves.
- There is a high inventory of available time slots.
- Like television, cable allows you to make your selling points visually, in motion, with spoken words, and with music and sound effects. It has a matchless capacity to create an unforgettable image.
- Although cable reaches only 60 percent of homes, it reaches 85 percent of the buying power. Cable audiences have greater purchasing power and tend to be younger and better educated. Cable penetration is well above the average in high-income households: 74 percent in homes with household incomes between $60,000 and $74,000, 77 percent in homes with household incomes between 75,000 and $100,000, and 75 percent in homes with household incomes of $100,000 or more.
- Cable reaches 70 percent of children aged 2 to 11 years—14.5 million—monthly. Cable also provides more children's programming: 263 hours per week as compared to 69 hours on television. Furthermore, children in cable households watch more television: 5.9 hours to 2.9 hours on noncable stations.
- Cable offers a much wider variety of commercial time periods. An advertiser is not restricted to 15- to 30-, or 60-second spots. They can be just about any length, in seconds or in minutes. There are 30-minute infomercials as well as 2-hour sales programs known as advertorials that sell by demonstration and cater to impulse buying. They include two-way communication so that orders can be placed at the moment the viewer reaches a buying decision.

- For larger-budget advertisers able to use high-cost television, cable is a less expensive means to pretest costly commercials.

There are disadvantages, too:

- The high audience numbers cited are in the aggregate, and with thirty- to fifty channels to choose from, the audience for any particular program can be extremely small.
- Uncertainty about cable regulations is a problem, but deregulation has caused a negative side effect for viewers. Since government ordered deregulation several years ago, there has been a three-times-inflation rate increase for cable subscribers, which conceivably could cut audience size.

  In the few communities where cable has direct competition, subscription rates are more than 30 percent lower than in communities with only one cable company. Congress's solution is to eliminate barriers to competition as quickly as possible, and hold cable rates and equipment charges to competitive levels until new competition can get itself established.

  Cable companies had justified their immense rate increases by claiming that the years of regulation prior to 1987 had kept rates artificially low. Now, with regulation again on Congress's agenda, cable operators are claiming that regulation will drive rates up. But (as this book goes to press) there is a raging debate over the whole issue of regulating cable and the fact that some people's bills have gone up while others have gone down. It's doubtful anyone knows at this point what will happen.
- The effectiveness of advertising messages depends on cable penetration at the specific local level. But it's often impossible for advertisers to get local market ratings and statistics. Even at the national level, there is only limited research available on cable viewership.
- Audiences are fragmented, so it is difficult for advertisers who do wish to reach a mass audience on either a national or a local level, and it's difficult to cover the market because cable doesn't have 100 percent national coverage.
- Some cable is strictly pay cable, which means viewers are

inclined to watch these channels because there is a better selection of entertainment and no commercials.

* There are complaints that cable TV needs to become more user friendly to advertisers, that it needs to provide scientific, statistical data similar to that provided by Nielsen for over-the-air television and do more to assist advertisers. It was recognized as a problem by executives attending Cabletelevision Advertising Bureau's tenth annual conference who anticipate that advertising deals soon will be constructed in more innovative and different ways that are expected to be more favorable to advertisers.

Purchasing Cable Time

Chances are high that the costs of cable commercial time are significantly less than regular broadcast time in your area—10 to 20 percent less. Because frequency (repetition) is exceedingly important to establish name recognition and memory, the lower cost may permit you to run your spot a greater number of times. Be sure that your audience sees your commercial at least five to seven times.

Before you allow a cable advertising rep to call on you, dig out your research about your target consumer so you can give the salesperson an accurate profile of your designated audience. Although the station may not have all the data you request, it should be able to produce the basic information you require. Make the purchase only if you can be sure the station has the viewers you want to reach.

With cable, you can make better targeting decisions than with newspapers, which know only how many people they deliver their product to, their circulation figures—not the psychographics of their audiences. Newspapers produce products for mass audiences; cable's specialized programming gives you a leg up on knowing the interest of the people who watch each station.

The *Cable Spot Advertising Directory,* published annually, lists more than 700 cable systems in all 211 Designated Market Areas, covering thousands of counties across the country. It can be purchased ($125), or your advertising rep may be able to give you access to it. The information is useful to small businesses that have customers spread throughout the country. It can be ordered from:

1992 CABLE SPOT ADVERTISING DIRECTORY
National Register Publishing
121 Chanion Road
New Providence, New Jersey 07974
800/323–6772

Going Through Channels

The first step in buying commercial time on a local cable station is to check to be sure it accepts commercials. The station or system in your area may be subsidized only by subscription sales.

There are two broad methods to buy cable commercial time, but it is unlikely that many small businesses will have much call for the second way:

1. Cable companies have individual sales representatives or representative firms. Both work on a commission basis, and usually they can arrange buys elsewhere within their affiliated systems.
2. Advertisers who want commercial time over a broader geographic area than a local station provides should explore interconnects. Interconnects link up two or more systems so that they can share programming signals, which permits an ad schedule to appear across the breadth of the linked systems. Interconnects may connect many systems or as few as two small communities.

Just as local television stations offer both local spots and network spots, so does cable. Local spots appear within local programming. Many local small businesses recognize that this can create an image among members of the community that the business is a part of, active in, and cares about community affairs, so this kind of positioning can build image at the same time viewers are receiving your message. Network spots appear only during time breaks that networks permit local stations to sell. They are transmitted only to the local station's viewers, not nationally.

Ethnic Groups

If your desired audience includes any specific ethnic cluster, be sure to plan accordingly. There are individual cable stations and a cable network that provide programming in a number of foreign languages. Check the availabilities in your area. About 60 percent of the network's programming is in Asian languages, including Chinese, Japanese, Korean, Vietnamese, and Filipino.

Co-op

Check whether co-op monies or co-op-produced commercials are available to you for your product or service.

Ask your cable ad representative for details about funds that may be available for your purpose(s). (Information about co-op endowments, eligibility, and requirements as it pertains to television, and therefore, cable, is covered in detail in chapter 11.) Specific information about co-op for cable is available from two organizations:

National Cable Television Cooperative Inc.
14809 West 95th Street
Lenexa, Kansas 66214
913/599–5900

National Cable Television Association Inc. (NCTA)
1724 Massachusetts Avenue, N.W.
Washington, D.C. 20036
202/775–3550

NCTA also publishes a booklet, *A Cable Primer,* that provides basic information about cable television, including operations, economics, history, programming, and regulation.

Production Tips Exclusively for Cable

Although production basics are the same for both television and cable, there are some differences. The most important one is that with cable there can be commercials of 45, 60, 90, 120 seconds, and longer—up to hours—in length. Two-minute commercials are popular with advertisers who wish to extend a message to set a mood, as for travel spots that show magnificent scenery and permit high visual impact. They also are favored for direct-response purposes when, for example, an advertiser wishes the viewer to respond directly by telephone to place an order. Two minutes gives to adequate time to demonstrate a product, present the call-in number or order address, and allow time for viewers to make note of the information.

Longer commercials permit an advertiser to sell more than one product for the product costs of only one spot. The jury is out, however, about whether this works as well as single-product spots or tends to confuse viewers.

Purchase only the amount of time you require to present your message concisely and effectively, and use the time wisely. Don't extend a commercial merely because you think the overall costs might be less, or unless there is something important to include that a shorter time period doesn't permit.

Check before you produce an unusual-length commercial such as 15-, 20-, or 45-second lengths. Some stations don't offer uncommon length spots because they are more difficult to accommodate.

Some local cable stations are able to handle production of local businesses' commercials. Typically they can produce high-caliber spots that fit within a company's advertising budget, and some may have equipment that can produce technologically advanced special effects treatments. Keep in mind that the simpler the production requirements are, the less expensive the production costs will be.

Some cable systems have on hand what are called generic commercials. They are primarily visual in nature so that you can add your own verbal message. Because they usually are of a much higher visual and technical caliber than a small-budget business can afford, they tend to have a higher impact on viewers. The problem is that they may be too generic to fit a highly specific message.

Such a commercial might show an American bald eagle floating, swooping, and diving in the beautiful mountain and lake country of the Pacific Northwest. As your eyes watch the bird's actions, you hear ear-catching patriotic music. The production is the best, and if you can make the generics fit your message, buy it.

Although cable stations rarely have entire libraries of special effects as television stations do, some have small collections of special effects, including animated titles.

If you have established your company name or product or service recognition with commercials on radio and in other media, try to incorporate the same recognition factors into your cable commercial to build consistency and extend recognition.

Infomercials

Infomercials are information commercials that demonstrate and supply information about a product or service rather than solely present a sales message. They generally run about 10 minutes and often run up to 90 minutes or longer. Any time a viewer can gain a better understanding of your product or service through watching how it is used as opposed to merely citing its benefits and features in a sales message is the time to use an infomercial.

Infomercials can be particularly productive for companies that don't have sales staffs who can follow up to meet a prospect face to face, which permits a demonstration, a sales pitch, and the customary personal sales close. Infomercials allow adequate time to present an audience of prospects with all the information they need to make decisions.

There is a commonsense approach to producing infomercials: handle them as salespeople handle sales calls. Don't make them entertainment spectacles. Make the message straightforward, clear, and believable. Use the extra time in an infomercial to enforce—or reinforce—viewers' beliefs in your business's honesty, integrity, and friendliness. Don't make wild claims.

Keep in mind the short attention span most television viewers have, and buy only enough time to keep the message loaded with interesting information. Present it with enthusiasm. And use a spokesperson to whom viewers can relate—someone they feel is much like a dependable, friendly neighbor.

The Future Is Here . . . Almost!

The future may be increasingly cable heavy if the trend toward rising cable ratings continues. A ratings report in 1992 gave cable a 20 percent share of prime-time audiences, beating out a major network's rating of 11.9 by a 12.2 rating.

The country's largest cable television conglomerate, Tele-Communications Inc., will use digital compression technology to carry as many as 540 channels to the first of 1 million cable subscribers starting in 1994. Programming on the new service will include nonstop movies, scores of sporting events, replays of top prime-time shows, shopping by TV, trading stocks, and interactive cable-viewer game playing. In interactive cable, viewers can respond to polling, and both station and viewers gain a greater understanding of the rest of the program's audience. Or they can vote for a particular end result. The best interactive use from the perspective of an advertiser is the ability by users to place orders. Perhaps a better description might be "direct response cable."

Others in the cable industry are planning a future menu that will add four or five more niche services, such as animation and all-talk programming, and to refine the targeting even further, they plan subniche services, such as all-golf, -photography, or -automobiles programming. Some of these new channels will remain subscriber-funded only, so the only way advertisers can have their names used is by sponsoring programs. This is done on public television to promote an image.

By the mid-1990s, new cable technologies should be firmly entrenched, offering hundreds of viewing options and revolutionizing how cable TV time is perceived, priced, and purchased.

Already infomercials are putting advertisers in direct contact with potential buyers, but consider the potential when cable TV systems are intertwined with the telephone and the computer. *DM News* describes the functions:

> Through a menu, a catalog of specific products much like a traditional printed catalog and an interactive, remote keypad, the customer accomplishes the order-entry function. All relevant shipping and billing information is already maintained on the cable system database. The purchase is invoiced by the cable service with one consolidated monthly invoice—rather than several to numerous vendors.
>
> Consider these, and you're considering the possible decrease—perhaps elimination—of not only paper advertising but also of the direct mail industry's uncontrolled and insatiable silent partner: the U.S. Postal Service.

There will be a continuing fragmentation of audiences, which will offer even greater opportunities to target a specific segment of buyers narrowly.

There will be multiplexing, which involves using satellite feeds to show a program in different time periods or in different languages. Multiplexing is possible because of video compression, which reduces the size of television signals. This means a nearly unlimited number of channels will be available. "It would be like having a video store or a multiplex theater right in your own home," explains the president of a cable company. Already the fragmentation makes cable similar to specialized magazines in its ability to target specific interests.

Cable executives are concerned that consumers will not be willing to pay more for traditional cable channels. They believe, however, that the problem can be solved with a pay-per-view approach, which allows viewers to pay only for programs they wish to watch. That is the direction the trend is expected to take.

All this boils down to a few facts that already exist but undoubtedly will multiply in the future. Unit costs to advertise on these new channels probably will not be lower, and cost on a CPM basis may even be higher, but there can be no denying that advertising dollar waste will decrease still further because audiences can be targeted even more precisely.

13

Direct Mail Advertising

Generate Sales with Direct Mail Advertising

You may have seen it. The Charles Schulz cartoon with Snoopy atop his doghouse sitting at his typewriter pounding out his somewhat less than memorable prose:

First panel: *Tears formed in his eyes as he read her letter of farewell.*

Second panel: *"We will always have our memories," she wrote.*

Third Panel: *Suddenly, he realized it was a form letter.*

Form letter! A lot of people call it junk mail—any mail that is unsolicited, unwanted, and inconsequential. Professionals in advertising sometimes call it direct response or direct marketing, but business people call it direct mail. Direct mail usually is unsolicited, but if it's properly planned and well prepared, it is not unwanted or inconsequential.

If *mail* is merely communication with a postage stamp on it, what then is *direct mail*? It is *advertising* with postage on it: form letters, enclosure letters with statements or billings, highly productive and personalized sales letters, printed letters, postcards, folders, booklets, miniature newspapers and newsletters, brochures, reprints, circulars, fliers, bulletins, handbills, samples, catalogs, novelties, package enclosures, invitations, calendars, pamphlets, and self-mailers. It can be as small as a postcard or as large as a thousand-page, four-color mail order catalog.

Direct mail can be in a new format—a video mailer—which sky-rocketed in popularity during the 1992 election year when politicians used it to develop a kind of video campaign mailing. The concept combines the visual impact of television with direct mailing's ability to target a specific audience, according to Lisa LeMaster, one of Dallas's (Texas) best-known political consultants. LeMaster says that instead of mailing voters campaign leaflets, a candidate mails them videotapes. It costs $2 or $3 a tape, not expensive when compared with television advertising, and unlike a commercial, it can be as long as you like—or at least, as long as the viewer will tolerate. The idea caught on fast with businesses, as when Dallas–Fort Worth Ford Motor Co. dealers mailed 33,000 direct mail videos to area owners of 1985–1989 model vehicles.

What all this direct mail variety and popularity adds up to is that 40 million direct mail pieces are sent to millions of Americans each day.

There's a belief, undocumented, that the smaller the business, the more productive direct mail is. But many of the largest corporations also use it, obviously because it works for them.

The Appeal of Direct Mail

Small business owners have found that direct mail is the least expensive (per sale) communication method for reaching their customers. It's perhaps the easiest way to tell targeted individuals exactly what you want to tell them, at exactly the time you've learned is the best time to reach them.

Your direct mail piece can be sent to the specific geographic location where your targeted individuals live or work and at a time of your choosing, and you can reach special groups—by age, income level, or ethnicity—with exactness. This is an opportunity to convince recipients to buy now, and you literally hand them the order blank with which to make the purchase. Additionally, you can measure results in terms of cost and effectiveness with dependable accuracy.

Beyond its appeal as bargain advertising in terms of the number of returns, it offers pinpoint coverage and complete control. You can mail to a city block or to an entire state. You can even mail to only those left-handed Irishmen with handlebar moustaches who live west of the Mississippi in manufactured housing. You're in control, and you can narrow your targeted recipients to precisely and exactly who your research has selected as the best, most receptive potential buyers of your product or service.

There are even more advantages:

- You can single out your prospects and extend your personality beyond the limits of impersonal contact to create confidence in you and the product or service you are selling.
- There is no waste circulation. You pay only for directing your messages to those you want to reach; thus, direct advertising is economical.
- You can tell as complete a story as is needed, with as accurate and fine illustrations as may be called for.
- Your messages need not shout for attention. They are alone with the reader.

Let us say that you are a retailer selling car batteries, and you have three retail locations in a large metropolitan area, but your budget won't permit the use of radio or television. This is an example of when demographic and geographic targeting is the best way to go.

You know from chapter 4 that you can call a direct mail list house and get a roll call of every person within a specified radius, say 3 miles, of each of your three retail locations. You can narrow it to a list of everyone who has a car that is between twelve and fifteen months old—the time period when first batteries typically fail. Then you can use direct mail to send an individual message to people with a predisposition to buy a battery.

If the battery hasn't yet failed and the recipients haven't yet realized that they are predisposed to buy your product, you can point out the odds of its failing within the next 90 days, and enclose a certificate or coupon that gives $10 off on the purchase of a battery. Chances for making them sure-purchase customers will skyrocket if you also give them some reason to come into your store before the battery fails. Give them something as simple as a free offer to clean the cable connections on their present batteries.

Basic Strategies for Direct Mail Pieces

It's time to put on your copywriter's hat and get busy preparing to write your direct mail message. It also is time to recall the decisions you made in chapter 8 when you assembled the primary ingredients you wish all of your advertising messages to contain, regardless of the medium in which they are used.

Letters are the most widely used, largest-selling kind of direct mail, and however you use a good sales letter, it will produce for you. Sent by itself, it will sell. Sent as the lead-off piece in a direct mail package, it will increase the pulling and selling power of any folder, brochure, or booklet it accompanies.

Because letters are direct mail's best sellers, let's use them as the primary form to describe and demonstrate the basics of most direct mail messages and how they should be constructed. The copy principles pertaining to direct mail letters apply to most other types of direct mail copy.

Short or Long?

Advertising professionals are on both sides of the fence with regard to keeping direct mail copy short. There is a time-worn advertising maxim that says the more you tell, the more you sell. But others say, just as decisively, "Make it short." Support for the latter advice is stronger if you agree that the more a person says, the less people remember. Be wary of long copy for people, such as working mothers, whose time already is stretched to its limit; they don't have time to read it. And avoid long messages when your readers are teenagers whose impatience quotient doesn't make reading a top priority. On the other hand, retirees with plenty of time to read may react well to longer messages.

If you believe more information must be given than the reader is likely to read in a letter format, keep the letter short and attach or enclose a brochure or a flier with the added information.

There is evidence, however, that people will read information in which they are genuinely interested, no matter how long the copy, if it provides answers to their problems or promises to satisfy their wants and needs—and if it is easy to read.

Don't be afraid to write a long letter *if* every sentence is as concise as you can make it. If, however, one paragraph is enough, don't write anything longer.

There is nothing more important in writing of any kind, and nothing more time-consuming, than honing—writing tightly. Benjamin Franklin recognized the amount of time good writing requires in a letter to a friend: "If I'd had more time I'd have written a shorter letter."

The following, said in 1978 by David C. Jones, chairman of Joint Chiefs of Staff, could be the basic rules for all your direct mail messages. You may want to frame the words and hang them alongside your computer or typewriter. "My guidelines are simple. Be selective. Be concise. Don't tell someone what you know; tell them what it means [to them], and why it matters[to them]."

We add an edict: Include information about only one product or one service in each mailing. (Catalogs sent by direct mail are the exception to this mandate.)

Set the Right Tone

Don't be too formal in your writing. Think of your letter as merely talking to someone on paper. This "you-in-an-envelope" can be warm and friendly or give an impression that your company—and you or whoever signs the letter—is stuffy, dull, pompous, or uncaring. If you have the computer or word processing ability to mass produce individualized letters or there are funds to have others do it for you, address the reader by name. If it must be a form letter, give it the next friendliest salutation, such as "Dear Neighbor," "Dear Fellow Photographer," "Dear Pet Lover," or whatever else is appropriate. Or just say, "Hello, Friend."

Make Everything Clear

Murphy's mother probably told him that anything that can be misunderstood will be misunderstood. Be very careful that your words transfer your meaning. If you're not sure what you mean to say, that too will be very clear. Blurred or hazy thinking is reflected in a blurred and hazy message.

Keep the Facts Accurate

Be sure that the addressee's name is spelled correctly and that everything in your message—whether in direct mail letter form or in any other advertising form—is accurate and honest. If a refresher course will make constructing your direct mail message easier, return to chapter 8 for a quick review.

Open with a Grabber

Make your opening sentence and opening paragraph short, but include something that will immediately grab the reader's interest. Your opener is essentially your headline, and your recipients won't read past it if it doesn't grab their attention and capture their interest. A primary benefit that your research showed is something your potential consumer really wants—or better yet, needs—is probably the best opening grabber.

Journalists' techniques for grabbing readers' interest include opening a news story or feature article with a provocative question, a little-known fact, or a quote. These may work for you, too, when you don't have a benefit or the word *free* with which to grab interest. (*Free* is at the top of the list of words that capture readers' eyes and interest.)

Stress Benefits

It never hurts to repeat yourself if by doing so you build readers' desires to a point that they think they'll miss something essential if they don't obtain the product or service and decide that doing business with the company is imperative.

Offer an Incentive

You want readers to act quickly, so tell them that if they buy before a specific date, they will receive a free premium or a bonus. Or offer a discount off the purchase price if an enclosed coupon is redeemed before a specific date.

Offer a Guarantee

It is said that only two things in life are guaranteed: death and taxes. Whoever said it forgot about product and service guarantees. Even though no one wants to test Uncle Sam's or the Grim Reaper's guarantees, everyone appreciates and looks for other kinds of guarantees. If your company is not well known, a guarantee of satisfaction, with return privileges in the case of products, can be a deciding factor in convincing a reader to respond. Offering services such as a maintenance contract also can build customer confidence in the integrity of your company and its advertising.

Close with a Clincher.

Repeat the incentive offer, and urge readers to act now. Make it easy for them to respond immediately by including an order blank, a reply card, or a return envelope, and tell them to mail it today.

It is believed that giving potential customers options makes them feel more in control and leads to higher response rates. If possible, give the reader an option to order by mail, by telephone, or by fax. Both telephone and fax orders mean speedier responses for you.

Add a P.S.

Some advertising professionals believe that postscripts in direct mail letters have the highest readership of all the other parts of a direct mail package. Some believe that a P.S. may catch the eye of readers who never intended to read your letter and send them back to the beginning to read it all. At the least, a P.S. is an opportunity to restate the primary benefit for the reader or remind the reader of your offer or incentive.

It's OK to Be a Bad Copywriter Your First Time Out

If you've just taken the plunge and written your first direct mail piece but are fearful of turning out less than a masterpiece, don't worry. Actually, you can hope your first effort is not much of a success, because it's the fastest way to learn what works and what doesn't and to become good at the job.

There is a terrible result from giving in to concern that you might write bad copy: you will write bland, innocuous copy that ends up making you a bad copywriter anyway.

The best advice is to take the plunge with enthusiasm—and write the copy with enthusiasm—the surest road to success in whatever kind of do-it-yourself advertising you produce. Suggestion: do a little wading first. To be sure you are on the right track, don't plan an immense mailing that costs the entire ad dollar allotment. Try it with a small sample.

Appearance Guidelines

Do multisentence paragraphs in textbooks or business or scientific journals turn you off? The mass of words become great gray blobs that are less than the friendliest invitation to read. Even letters from favorite friends sometimes are a chore to read when sentences run on and on in long paragraphs.

Now look at your favorite newspaper, the one you enjoy reading every morning. Its news columns are loaded with words, but the sentences and paragraphs are short, which adds white space around the blocks of type. Another thing newspapers do is break the writing rules our teachers taught us: only one idea or thought to a paragraph, and the paragraph must contain all of that idea. In newspapers, a thought or an idea may be spread over several paragraphs, broken into snippets of information to make reading easier and more inviting. Newspaper writers also introduce a new idea or thought in the last sentence of one paragraph to capture readers' interest and nudge them to read on to the next paragraph.

Give the Letter an Appealing Appearance

Give your letters a reader-friendly look: short sentences, short paragraphs, and wide margins. Indented paragraphs add a little extra white space at the beginning of a word block. And avoid copy blocks with words and lines that are jammed together, whichmakes readingsomuchmoredifficult.

These practices are wise rules to follow when typing your direct mail letter so that the reader's eye is able to keep its place as it skips across the page.

Give your letter as personal a look as possible. A typed letter says "personal," whereas a typeset letter almost shouts that it is mass produced. Today's high-tech computer letters and photocopying reproduction processes make copies of computer- and word processor–produced letters look as if each was typed individually. If you don't have a laser printer, be sure to use a letter-quality printer, and if it's a dot matrix, be sure it has a fresh ribbon.

Make the Signature Look As If the Letter Is Personally Signed

Another way to make any letter look more personal is to use blue or green ink for the penned signature. And if each letter is not signed by hand, be sure the reproduced signature—in blue or green ink—is first quality. Fine-point pens may give adequate reproductions if the writing is dark enough and the paper is smooth. Otherwise, use a medium-point pen.

Type Styles Are Important

Make the typeface easy to read—no script or "Olde English." The easiest to read of all type styles and the best for faxing and copying is Helvetica, a sans serif ("without the serif," the decorative heads and tails attached to some typefaces). Times is the easiest to read of the serif styles.

Paper Indicates Class

The caliber of your company can be subtly indicated by the quality of the paper you use. If it matters that readers think high class and high quality when they think of your company, then spend the extra dollars and use a bond paper. If the appeal is to sell a product, strong colors of paper will do, but if you're selling a company image or a business service, keep to the more dignified image implied with white, beige, or light gray papers.

A letterhead helps to establish the name and build recognition and recall for your logo. Regular letter-size (8½ by 11 inch) paper saves money over costs for odd-size sheets and the odd-size envelopes they require.

If your message is in a long-letter format, keep it on only one side of each page if the extra pages don't add extra postage to the mailing cost. Readers tend to miss reading the backsides of pages unless the pages are in a brochure format (on a folded larger size paper: for example, a four-page letter on a folded 11 by 17 size paper.)

Never staple pages together. Staples can tear paper, fingers, and fingernails, and many readers resist handling anything clipped together with staples.

Use Enclosures to Repeat the Story

Very few sales are made with one recitation of the sales message, so one of the dictates of salesmanship is to repeat your sales message. Never expect one "telling" in a direct mail piece to make the sale.

Enclosures allow you to go into detail by repeating with reworded copy the important information in the letter. They also permit much more dynamic visual images with the addition of colors and graphics.

Inserts are less restricted in format than letters, although they must conform to the constraints of the envelope size and shape. Experiment with insert sizes, shapes, and folds, but remember the limits of your mailing costs allocation. Weight considerations must be kept in mind. The cost of a one-stamp mailing can mean twice as many mailings as a two-stamp mailing.

To check the weight of your mailing, include everything—letter, enclosures, envelope, even paper clips—and weigh it all to the precise fraction of an ounce. The smallest fraction overweight can mean an immense increase in postage costs—even to doubling this expense.

When designing the fold(s) of your enclosure, remember that the part that is first seen by the recipient must have the greatest impact. The rest of the folded piece should present information in diminishing importance as it is unfolded and seen by the reader.

If you enclose a prepaid reply card, check postal regulations as to size and weight of paper, but keep the card at the lightest allowed weight so postage costs remain as low as possible.

Make Sure the Envelop Says "Open Me"

Be as personal with the envelope as you are with the letter in it. Bar codes and zip code sorts on envelopes literally shout, "This is a mass mailing! This isn't a special letter to a friend!" In terms of reader reaction these postage savers probably lose as much for the sender by being tossed before opening, as they gain in postal savings.

An individually addressed envelope (rather than one addressed to "Occupant") gets the highest ratings for readership, but window envelopes that show an individually addressed letter inside also get good grades. They may cost a little more, but they save on addressing expenses.

A teaser on the envelope about the benefit inside for the reader can be a means to get a recipient to open it. If your company's product, service, or image doesn't require portraying a high degree of dignity, you may wish to print teasers on both sides of the envelope.

Odd-sized and odd-shaped envelopes may attract attention, but they are more costly and seldom are worth the extra money, as measured by response rates.

Some direct mail advertisers use a technique to keep the recipient from guessing about what's inside and who it's from. They use no outside message—not even the sender's name and sometimes not even the return address. And when a high-quality paper is used for the envelope, recipients seem more likely to open it out of curiosity, in the belief that it must be from someone they know or because they are concerned that it contains valuable or confidential information. (Credit card mailings, for instance, show only a small-type-size return address and no company name).

Example of an Effective "Open Me" Envelope and Message

Even though your company is a small business, profits can be reaped from hitchhiking on some Madison Avenue expertise. Pay attention to, and add to your copycat file, examples that you feel may adapt well to your circumstances.

An example of a sure-fire "open me" envelope could easily be adapted for a service company that wants to maintain a class image. This one was a direct mailing from the Smithsonian Institution. The plain white 9 inch by 12 inch window envelope has no return address on the front. (The return address is in small type on the flap on the reverse side.) In relatively small letters just above the window is the question: "Will you please do us a favor?" On a slant in the upper left quarter is an all-caps boldface warning: DO NOT FOLD. Although the size of the envelope in effects says "advertising inside," an impression of dignity is maintained. And a recipient's curiosity is definitely nudged to wonder what the requested favor is and to speculate that something inside must have some value if it is not to be folded.

But it's a whole different approach once the envelope is opened. It contains a four-page letter, plus an order card and prepaid envelope. Almost every ploy known to advertisers is used to catch and hold the recipient's attention:

- An indented box at the top of the first page uses the word *free* three times in four one-sentence paragraphs.
- Although the type throughout the letter is a dignified standard typewriter style, there are color handwritten notations is both margins and within the body of the copy.
- The word *free* is handwritten in color three more times alongside the four-paragraph boxed opening paragraphs.
- Although the letter is single-spaced, not one paragraph in the entire four pages is longer than one sentence, which leaves blank, white-space double spaces every few lines.
- Each of the handwritten color notes in the margins shouts a benefit, using words such as *discounts, super, rainy day delight, expect the unexpected, join the fun, send no money* and so on.
- The letter is signed with the writer's full name and with his title below it, but the remaining space on the fourth page includes a typed "P.S." plus a penned "P.P.S." personal note in color that signs off with a friendly, "Thanks," and the first-name initial of the letter writer.
- The fact that this is a limited time offer is stressed in several places, and the ending note asks you to reply even if you cannot accept the offer, "so we can [make the offer] to someone else."
- Each of the four pages contains some underlined text—not enough to make readers eye weary but enough to catch their attention and to accentuate specific information.

Except for the added cost of using a color ink in addition to black, the devices used in the example do not add greatly to the cost of a regular letter mailing. The order blank, however, uses more costly devices that a small business advertiser can do without: detachable stickers in different colors: "I accept," "I decline," and "Free TV," which the recipient is supposed to detach and affix in special spaces.

The order blank is not, but could be, a self-mailer. Instead, the sender encloses a self-addressed, stamped envelope, which also somewhat increases the dignified image feeling.

Nowhere inside the envelope is there anything that even mentions the favor requested on the envelope. Nor is there anything inside that cannot or should not be folded. But by the time a recipient has read through and responded to—or merely glanced through—the messages inside, undoubtedly all thought of or curiosity about the grabbers on the envelope are forgotten.

Pretesting Is Worth the Effort

Before you invest the total dollars planned for a single mailing, try small samplings to test for copy effectiveness. One excellent way is to send different versions of the same direct mail piece to two different groups that are as nearly identical in makeup as possible. Code response cards, return envelopes, or order forms to indicate which version of your mailing brings in the larger number of returns. A simple "A" on one and "B" on the other is adequate.

Timing

Some times are better than others for mailings. The leading months for direct mail results are December, January, February, July, August, and September, in that order. A consensus of advertisers shows that household product mail generally brings the greatest response in December and January; self-improvement products and services are best presented in December, January, and February.

The most productive receiving days within any month follow commonsense guidelines. Avoid getting lost in the clutter of end-of-the-month bills and first-of-the-month notices that cram mailboxes. It's better to mail mid-month, between the tenth and the twenty-fifth. Also, time your mailing to arrive on Tuesday, Wednesday, or

Thursday. Mondays don't allow much mail reading time for most businesspeople because usually there is an increased amount of mail from two-day weekends, and there are catch-up job activities. And Fridays, when most people's minds are on weekend demands and plans, are equally unproductive times to talk business to people. Testing can be conducted to determine the best mailing times for your letter in much the same way you conduct tests of the effectiveness of your copy.

Mailing Lists

It only makes sense not to send your direct mail pieces to addresses where people no longer live or to people who have died. Keeping database information up to date is one of the greatest problems for direct mail advertisers. Twenty percent of the population moves every year; in some areas it is 25 percent or more.

The post office will provide corrections, for a fee, for mail that weighs more than 6 ounces when the envelope carries the request: ADDRESS CORRECTION REQUESTED, RETURN POSTAGE GUARANTEED. The return postage guarantee notation must be included, and the return postage cost will be added to the fee. For third-class mail, the envelope must carry the notation: ADDRESS CORRECTION REQUESTED. The post office will correct your mailing list, for a fee, if the list is provided on cards. The savings in postage more than covers the charges made for these services.

Address change requests on your envelope, however, like bar codes and zip code sorts, say without words that this is not a personal letter, that it even may fall within recipients' concept of junk mail and be tossed away without opening.

TRW Information Services in Orange, California, recently won a U.S. Postal Service license to offer a Delivery Sequence File address verification service. According to TRW, mailers can match their files to more than 100 million addresses or sort addresses into walk sequences that are useful when the advertiser uses nonpostal door-to-door delivery. TRW also offers such computer services as address cleaning; data overlay, which matches records in one file to records in another that lacks some of the information in the original file; and merge/purge, a process of combining two or several lists at the same time that it eliminates duplications and unwanted data. If you use such a service, you may have to increase your advertising expense allocations.

Response

What kind of response should you expect? With direct mail, you always know how good your letter copy is, because you can count how many people respond. A typical response for, say, a $10 offer, is 5 percent. A principle that many mail order specialists follow in determining potential returns for mailings is a three-to-one ratio: $3 in trackable returns for every $1 in mailing costs.

Telemarketing

Telemarketing (direct marketing by telephone) has been a very hot medium—it is believed that 18 to 20 million people are called by telemarketers each day—but serious negative consumer reaction that threatens the procedure has developed.

Consumer reaction to telemarketing calls has been intense.

The Telephone Consumer Protection Act of 1991—often called the junk phone legislation—gave the Federal Communications Commission regulatory authority over the entire process of telemarketing. Its principle provisions called for a ban on unsolicited faxed advertising mail; mandated that calls must be placed only between 9 A.M. and 8 P.M.; and required each company using telemarketing to maintain an in-house suppression list, which means that recipients of a telemarketer's call may direct callers to never telephone them again. The TCPA also banned automated dialing, commonly referred to as the recorded message file, but that was challenged in the Oregon Supreme Court, which reversed the FCC's ruling.

The TCPA legislation must be working—complaints dropped 10 percent this past year, according to the Direct Marketing Association.

Although most telemarketing is legitimate, "telefraud" has become a serious problem for all Americans. Every year consumers lose $3 billion to $15 billion as a result of telemarketing fraud, says the director of the U.S. Office of Consumer Affairs.

Beyond fraud, there are issues of invasion of privacy that could bring the medium under governmental regulation. The bottom line here is that more and more of the public is resenting and resisting telephone solicitation. In chapter 18, a pro gives basics for conducting a successful telemarketing campaign.

The Future

The Report of Its Death is Greatly Exaggerated

No one is ready to put up a headstone saying R.I.P. or buy burying space for direct mail, but at this point a caveat is in order. Although the prospects for growth of direct mail, are auspicious, dangers lie ahead. The immediate threat comes from public backlash against companies that perpetrate fraud and deception or engage in direct response advertising that is misleading. In an attempt to overcome consumers' outrage, the Direct Marketing Association provides a means for anyone who doesn't want to receive direct marketing solicitations to be removed from lists.

Substantial postal rate increases already in place, with predictions of more to come (now postponed until 1995), undoubtedly won't mean the death of direct mail advertising, as has been predicted, but they doubtless will mean ongoing searches for better, less costly substitutions for an advertising medium that has had no peer to this time.

14

Yellow Pages

Yellow Fever or Gold Rush?

Some of the best salespeople in the media business are those who sell advertising in the Yellow Pages. A businessperson can catch a bad case of "yellow fever" just by listening to them. Where else, they ask, do you find an advertising medium where 160 million buyers seek sellers, rather than vice versa? These salespeople are effective too. Businesspeople are buying space for their listings or display ads. The questions then is, Is purchase of space for your advertising message in a Yellow Pages directory a good decision or a poor one? The answer is that a Yellow Pages display ad is a necessity for some businesses and unnecessary for others. A listing, however, is something else. Almost every business needs a listing, just as individuals need a listing in the white pages.

Yellow Pages display ads probably have the highest importance for repair service businesses, such as plumbers, electricians, fencers, and roofers. Next come businesses that offer commodities, such as appliances, carpets, gifts, computers, signs, restaurants, and videos. Lower on the display ad priority list are professional services, such as doctors and attorneys for whom buyers want more personal recommendations than a doctor's or attorney's own advertised declarations of ability. But consumers do use Yellow Pages to search for other professionals, such as accountants, computer programmers, real estate and insurance agencies, tax auditors, and CPAs, among others.

If your consumer profile includes Latinos, you'll be interested to know that an *Ad Age*/Gallup survey shows that 57 percent of Hispanics say they typically use the Yellow Pages primarily for price information and comparison shopping. That compares with 40 percent of the total sample and 35 percent of blacks.

A Popular Advertising Format

Yellow Pages advertising is not glamorous or dazzling. No one sits and watches it by the hour like television. It's not known for its exciting graphics like magazines and newspapers. But it's one of the most popular advertising formats available. And it is the fourth largest advertising medium, behind newspapers, television, and direct mail.

Statistical Research Inc. found in a major national study on Yellow Pages usage that, aside from the Bible, Yellow Pages may be the most frequently referred to publication ever. Yellow Pages salespeople claim that more than 160 million people shop in their books. (That's *shop*, not *sell!*) They maintain that their pages are consulted more than 46 million times a day; in an average month, 77 percent of all adults use the Yellow Pages; and in 8 billion cases a year, use of the Yellow Pages leads directly to purchases.

Yellow Pages is the medium most often referred to by people making purchase decisions. Whirlpool found from a study that next to the recommendations of family and friends, consumers turn to the Yellow Pages most often to find products or services they need. Whirlpool also found that consumers consult and then buy.

Statistical Research also found that 83 percent of advertisers agree that the Yellow Pages is an important source of new customers. Over 82 percent of Yellow Pages advertisers say that Yellow Pages reaches customers that are not reached by other media.

A smooth-talking Yellow Pages salesperson is happy to expound on the numerous benefits. There are, however, some negative points you should know before you decide to invest precious advertising dollars in this medium.

One problem is a war among directories that is creating havoc and confusion among advertisers. The full-scale war broke out when there was realization that anyone could use the "Let your fingers do the walking" logo because it wasn't copyrighted. There are currently more than 5,800 local Yellow Pages directories published annually in the United States, and no slowdown in numbers is in sight. Some are only a few pages in size. Others can be as large as several thousand pages.

NYNEX, publisher of more than 300 directories in the Northeast, calls its directories "phone books" and competitors' books "clone books." The plethora of directories poses an enormous problem for a small business as to which one(s) is best for it.

Competition among directories isn't new; for many years, there have been books to target specific ethnic or professional groups, even neighborhoods. But the unprecedented explosion in numbers of directories came following the 1984 breakup of AT&T. Before the breakup, the Telephone Publishers had a monopoly because other Telephone Publishers couldn't come into their markets; after the divestiture, AT&T and the Bell companies were joined by independent publishers, and all proceeded to invade one another's territories, resulting in a glut of directories.

Now, in addition to regular telephone company Yellow Pages directories there are independent directory publishers with publications aimed to students, marine businesses, the industrial security industry, the travel and leisure market. Just think of a group, and there probably is a directory aimed to their interests—and to grabbing extra advertising dollars for the publisher.

That's great! you say. You believe in target marketing. But in this case, it can be great or not so great. There can be an advantage in finding a directory that pinpoints an audience, but you may miss out on substantial numbers of your target audience because vast numbers of the newer directories provide incomplete target market coverage. They don't distribute to all telephone subscribers in the specialty area, whereas the major directories are distributed to every telephone subscriber.

Also, business telephone subscribers of the major directories usually get one free basic listing (not a display advertisement). With these larger directories, however, there is an offsetting problem of clutter. Without spending extra money for a large-size display ad, your listing can get lost among the competition.

Listing or Display Ad?

A few pointers may help solve the dilemma about your need for Yellow Pages display advertising or merely a Yellow Pages listing. If your regular customers know your company, service, or product well enough to have need only to use the Yellow Pages to locate your address or telephone number, all you need is a listing. On the other hand, do people who want or need your product or service browse for it in the Yellow Pages and make their decisions based on the kinds and amount of information in your ad that satisfies their search for answers to their questions? Finger-walkers require more than a listing, because they will choose among display ads that offer benefits they seek and the best pre-use evidence of your dependability, honesty and integrity. The soundest advice is not to bust the budget with a large space ad unless the Yellow Pages are your best and main source for reaching new customers.

If a listing rather than a display ad is all you need, remember two points:

1. Pay a little extra for boldface type to make your listing stand out, particularly if the alphabetical placement of the company's name puts it far down the list.
2. If you use both a listing and a display ad, be sure that the listing refers the reader to the display ad and states the page number where it—with all the information the reader wishes to know—can be found.

Placement

If you choose only a listing, your name will appear alphabetically in its section. If you choose a display ad, it may be a whole different ballgame. Half of the Yellow Pages publishers in the United States publish display advertising alphabetically by size, and the other half publish by seniority by size. If the publisher you purchase space from is in the latter category with seniority given preference and this is your first time to buy display space, your ad will be at the end of the section. Ads for those who have purchased space for years are given choice beginning-of-the-section placement. It may be years before your ad works its way forward in the section.

If you are already running Yellow Pages advertising, do a little examination of the response you are receiving. Is the amount of business you can directly trace to this advertising up to your goal? And ask yourself perhaps the more important question: How effective is my ad in comparison to those of my competitors?

Competitors' ads are not separated as they are in other media. Your ad must stand up to—and against—your biggest and stiffest competitors' attractions and attractiveness in terms of graphics and copy. Obviously, this calls for a higher degree of expertise in writing and producing the advertisement.

If even a simple analysis indicates that competitors' Yellow Pages ads pull better than yours, take a hard, objective look at your ad. Is your listing bold enough to stand out from others? Does your display advertising message give solid information your customers want or need? Is the layout so dull it gets lost among the clutter of all the competitors' display ads on the page? Don't be concerned with the information your competition presents, just with the reasons their ads are pulling well. Their strengths may not be yours, but your strengths are exactly what a portion of that potential market is looking for.

Rates

Yellow Pages salespeople often say their ads are an inexpensive way to advertise. A small community's small directory may offer relatively inexpensive rates. But be aware. Most rates for Yellow Pages advertising space are quoted by the month. That means that when the salesperson quotes what sounds like a tempting figure, it may actually be a per month rate, which commits you to an annual contract for twelve times the figure mentioned, usually adding up to thousands of dollars.

Rates vary around the country and even within cities where there are competing directories. A few annual rates are listed below for fundamental listings and for half-page display ad space, as cited in YPPA's July 1993 *National Yellow Pages Advertising Rates and Data* publication. The name of the publisher also is indicated.

Shreveport, Louisiana - BellSouth Advertising & Publishing Co.

Listing:	Regular	$154.20
	Boldface	$222.60
Display:	$9,765.00	

Des Moines, Iowa: Telecom USA Publishing Co.

Listing:	Regular	$ 63.00
	Bold	$138.00
Display:	$5,880.00	

-U S West Direct

Listing:	Regular	$ 78.00
	Bold	$174.00
Display:	$15,338.40	

San Francisco, California: Pacific Bell Directory

Listing:	Regular	$ 90.00
	Bold	$210.00
Display:	$17,484.00	

Syracuse, New York: NYNEX Information Resources Co.

Listing:	Regular	$ 22.56
	Bold	$262.10
Display:	$18,769.90	

Ad Size

The size of your ad tends to denote your stature in your field and how well established you are. Patey Signs in Portland, Oregon, ran a half-page for years. Owner Karma Patey says she feels her ad, because of its size, denotes stability, an image she wants to project for her corporate customers. Patey also uses the size of her ad to put as much information as possible in front of potential customers, listing all the types of sign jobs available. She says that this weeds out callers who are looking for different types of signs.

Some companies believe that Yellow Pages ads bring in only small jobs. Griffon Signs, in Fort Lauderdale, Florida, agrees that a lot of the jobs that come through the telephone directory are the less expensive ones, "but enough 'good' jobs come through that way to make it worth while."

Display Ad Tips

Your listing and display ad must compete head to head with every competitor in town and maybe with a few from other towns or states. The bigger the town or area is that the directory serves, the greater the number of competitors. Lucky for you, however, most of those competitive ads are flat, punchless, and without any real selling ability.

As you write the copy and design the layout for your Yellow Pages display advertisement, take time to figure out your unique selling proposition—how you outsell even the most aggressive competitors. Remember how America West Airlines dug out information that it shrewdly used to grab customers from larger rivals? Pull out your heaviest artillery, and go after the prospect.

Companies have personalities just as people do, and people react to companies' personalities just as they do to people's personalities. Do all you can to convey your company's personality. Don't decide to present a neutral company personality on the premise you don't want to drive anyone away. That is the quickest way to drive off everybody. Again, remember the America West strategy. After bankruptcy forced the airline to take a close look at itself, it set about developing a 180-degree turnaround in company personality—one that concentrates on respecting customers and caring about them. Then it spelled out this guiding principle in advertising messages for the public. What this means is, don't count on people knowing your company's personality or hope they'll perceive a warm, friendly, caring one. Tell them what you want them to know in your advertising.

Keep these guidelines in mind for the copy:

- Reach out and grab readers' attention and convince them that yours is the company to do business with instead of the competition. This is no time to tiptoe, on the premise that hard sell isn't dignified.
- Keep the copy professional and businesslike.
- Use a KIS-S-S-S formula: Keep It Simple-Short-Straightforward-Satisfying.
- Establish honesty, integrity, dependability, and experience. Something such as "in business since 1985" helps to establish these qualities, but be more specific whenever possible.

- Offer a specific guarantee to indicate integrity and dependability and build confidence for new customers.
- Offer a benefit, but don't exaggerate it.
- Offer specific reasons for shoppers to call you.
- List the brands you carry or the services you offer.
- Mention any financial plan you may have and whether you accept trade-ins.
- List all the credit cards you accept and whether orders may be placed by telephone.
- List service benefits: free estimates, a give-away (be sure your stock of the item will last the lifetime of the directory ad, which may be six months to a year), delivery service (a strong motivator for some customers), or a specialty (a person looking for someone who knows and understands copyright laws, or Honda repair, or brickwork, will stop at the ad that states the service or company is a copyright specialist, or a Honda specialist, or a mortar and brick matching specialist.) If you have many specialities, think about spreading them over several smaller-sized ads instead of listing them all in one ad. If you are proud of the service you give, spell out exactly what that service includes. For instance, "good or excellent service" is meaningless, but "fast service" is something everyone hopes for.
- Give your store hours. Perhaps one of the greatest customer activators is that you have "after-hours" hours. If you're available on Sundays or you take calls 24 hours a day, say so. That can be a major influence for people whose time is limited or who have a problem that needs immediate attention.
- Give your telephone number a prominent place in the ad, and if you serve a wide area, not only list the communities you serve but give prominence to toll-free numbers.
- No matter how well known you believe your company's name and location is, always give your address. There always are people who don't know who you are or where you're located. Show the address with the logo so readers don't have to search throughout the ad for it. If people have even the smallest difficulty in finding your location, give a landmark such as "Next to Good Foods Supermarket" along with the street address, or include a simple map.

Artwork and Layout

Yellow Pages directories are printed on newsprint, a porous paper that does nor reproduce sharp images, so strong-line artwork and typefaces are called for.

A graphic can attract readers' eyes and set your ad apart from the majority of other advertisers who never use any kind of graphic. Use high-contrast photos, drawings, and decorative designs that show greater differences (contrasts) between light and dark areas. High contrast is required because of the poor reproductive qualities of the paper.

The paper on which Yellow Pages ads are printed calls for bold, crisp lettering. Two standard typefaces you can count on to reproduce well are Times (serif) and Helvetica (sans serif). Use boldface lettering for emphasis of the telephone number, and the service or product you offer, but don't overdo it.

In your layout, follow the same general look of your other print advertising. Use the same logo that is in all of your ads and on your letterhead to help create and build recognition. If a border is called for, make it simple but bold enough to set your ad apart from others on the page.

More than sixty directories (of the more than 5,800 Yellow Pages directories in the country) now offer color. *Advertising Age* tells how it profited one company:

> When much of [Bloomington, Illinois] was flooded by spring rains and swollen rivers last year, Peoria's WEEK-TV went to the Yellow Pages to find a plumbing contractor to interview on the air. They told [company owner Morris Sunkel] he was selected because his 5-inch-by-6-inch, four color ad in GTE's local *The Everything Pages* directory gave Sunkel & Sons the image of a reputable outfit.
>
> Mr. Sunkel reports a 25% increase in overall profits since the ad first appeared in March 1990, and he attributes "quite a bit" of that increase to the $600 he spent on the multicolor ad.

GTE's marketing director says, "Our research has shown that a four-color ad is 64% more successful than a two-color ad of the same size." No data were given as to comparisons between the standard "yellow and black" and two-or-more-colors ads.

If you use newspaper ads, you undoubtedly know and understand how to increase visual impact with screening, which can be used with both black and color ink to achieve graduating shades of gray or a light shade through to solid black or the full tone range of a color. The ink is filtered, and screens can be adjusted to give lighter or darker shades.

Directory Specifications

Request information about your directory's specifications before you sign a space purchase contract, so you have it before you begin construction of your ad. The specifications may cover such matters as:

- point size of borders
- maximum typesizes
- use of comparative statements about competitors
- use of superlatives
- whether guarantee may be mentioned

If the regulations called for by the directory's publisher do not permit use of the last three items above or of crisp, punchy, selling copy, a display ad may be a waste of money. An anemic advertising message actually may turn consumers away. In these cases, choose a listing, and use the directory dollars for a newspaper ad or a direct mail piece instead. However, the ad undoubtedly will be accepted in credible Yellow Pages directories if you use the same measurements you use for good advertising in newspaper and magazine ads.

YPPA at the end of 1992 announced a plan to standardize ad offerings. It is meant to reduce time and confusion for advertisers and save money in production costs, since advertisers using different books won't have to recreate the same ad in slightly different sizes for different directories. Standardization is expected by 1994 in six areas: graphic specifications, ad sizes, standard codes, copy content, pagination, and space/sequence precedence. This plan offers the greatest benefits to national advertisers, but others also may benefit where it's necessary to advertise in several competing directories in the same city or area inasmuch as 80 percent of the directories throughout the country are expected to implement the standards.

Testing Your Ad

There are three ways to measure response to your Yellow Pages ad:

1. If you have an 800 number, it can be metered as to the number of calls coming directly from your ad.
2. Key the ad with an offer that measures response.
3. Arrange with the telephone company for all telephone numbers to be unlisted except those in your ad.

There is, however, another way that—much like focus group research—gives far more than mere statistics, and it doesn't cost a cent. Ask every new customer how he or she heard about your company. If the Yellow Pages ad was the cause and the customer is receptive to your questions, ask what about your ad caught his or her attention, what information he or she wishes had been included, and any other questions that will help you construct a better Yellow Pages advertisement next time.

Keep a tally of answers. Although it may be six months or a year before you can put the answers to use, a composite of the answers will be invaluable in making decisions about increasing or decreasing the size of your ad or retaining or changing next edition's copy, configuration, or look of your ad.

Just as you're continually updating your database about customers, keep your Yellow Pages advertising message up to date. Get an agreement in writing from your salesperson that copy changes will not affect its seniority policy.

Co-op Dollars

There are co-op dollars available for this medium, too. YPPA is available to help its members take advantage of the maximum co-op dollars available to them. If the directory company with which you plan to do business is a YPPA member, it has the information you need.

YPPA has created a co-op database and handbook that lists approximately 900 co-op programs for Yellow Pages advertisers to participate in, as well as support materials that include clip art and ad layouts for co-op ads, a co-op reference manual, and co-op training materials.

Request this information through your Yellow Pages advertising representative.

Choosing Among Directories

As directories continue to proliferate, small business owners face the choice of either appearing in several books and busting their normally tight advertising dollar allotments, or sticking with one and risking the chance that the fingers of potential customers walk through the other directories.

To most businesspeople, the new offerings and competing claims pose difficult choices. Three examples come from *U.S. News & World Report:*

- A lawn service was advertising in four of Bell Atlantic's Baltimore-area editions but decided to "plunk down an additional amount to be included in Southwestern's Baltimore book. I don't have any choice," the president of the company explained. "The competition will be in there."
- A moving agent is sticking with NYNEX, although some other rates are just a sixth of NYNEX's. "A small business cannot make a profit and pay for ads in all the books. As it is, the monthly bill is choking my company," the moving company's president said.
- In Los Angeles, where there are more than eighty competing books, a cab company spokesperson said, "All these directories are causing confusion. All you had to do before was open the phone book and find what you wanted. Now, nobody knows where to look."

Although five of the nine largest directory publishers subscribe to measurement services for some of their books, intramedia research—comparing competing books and rating individual Yellow Pages directories on consumer usage—is lacking. Complicating matters even more, much of the research has been done by the publishers themselves, which makes it suspect as mere self-promotion because it seems always to put the publishing group presenting the data in first place.

The bottom line of all this is—if you decide to use Yellow Pages display advertising—you still are on your own in choosing a directory or directories to target your audience. But keep demanding third-party research from your local Yellow Pages advertising representative. It will help you assess which space to purchase or whether you should purchase any display space at all.

If you have questions you can't get answered from your local directory representative, perhaps two groups can give you answers:

Yellow Pages Publishers Association
340 East Big Beaver Road
Troy, MI 48083
800/325–8455
Fax: 313/880–8880

Association of Directory Publishers
105 Summer Street
Wrentham, MA 02093
508/883–3688
Fax: 508/883–3717

A Warning

The Federal Trade Commission is issuing warnings. Across the country businesses are receiving what appear to be invoices for space in their locally circulated Yellow Pages directory. Some carry the familiar "walking fingers" logo and the name "Yellow Pages," neither of which is protected by any federal trademark registration or copyright. Some of these so-called invoices are in fact solicitations for listings in alternative directories. The FTC explains that alternative directories differ from traditional Yellow Pages in that they often aren't widely distributed and some aren't published at all.

Some of these solicitations make such confusing statements as "directory listing renewal invoice," "renewal payment stub," "present listing information," and "prompt payment is necessary to guarantee ad placement in the directory."

There are several ways you can protect yourself, according to the FTC:

- Examine the so-called invoice closely.

- Investigate the company and its product before responding.
- Ask the publisher for a previous edition and for written figures about distribution numbers, the method of distribution, and the directory's life span.
- Call your local Yellow Pages publisher to learn if it is associated with the company soliciting your business.

Industry Advances

"Talking Yellow Pages," or audiotex, may be coming to your neighborhood soon—or perhaps your area is one of 160 cities in the United States and Canada that already offers consumers news, sports, weather, financial information, as well as information on advertisers in that particular directory, at the touch of a button. The services, available to consumers for the price of a local call, range from soap opera updates to local movie listings to season games and activities listed in Yellow Pages directories—all available for advertiser sponsorship. Sponsors typically receive taglines—short announcements at the end of the message, called trailers.

Videotex is another technology with the potential to reshape the industry. Videotex uses personal computers to provide access to information in much the same way as audiotex does. The Integrated Services Digital Network may soon be able to hook every home with fiber optic cable and be one of the most important new advertising vehicles since television.

With Yellow Pages' new, sophisticated distribution systems and consumer databases, advertisers are beginning to use the medium to reach consumers in new ways. Some are paying to have coupons, free-standing inserts, product samples, or even videotapes delivered with directories.

The wide-ranging future services include electronic directories with which Yellow or White Pages listings would be available by computer and telephone. The concept could include on-line classified ads and catalogs. Products could be ordered electronically.

Another future technology, predicts *The Dallas Morning News,* is an "electronic post office," whereby telephone companies can be clearinghouse/post offices for small businesses and consumers who can't afford expensive technology.

Database information also is expected to improve and be more attainable for small businesses. Baby Bells would work more closely with information providers to make databases useful and easy to use.

The belief is that it will be the late 1990s before all these advances will be in place.

15

Billboards and Transit
Hot Media. But How Do They Work?

For over two hundred years, outdoor advertising has been an important part of American life, but it was the advent of a motorized America that sent advertisers rushing to outdoor advertising to extol on poster panels and painted bulletins the excellence of a wide variety of products and services.

Wooden structures of the past have been replaced with modern monopole displays. Computers are able to paint an advertisement in minutes that once took days and weeks to complete, and the number of new advertisers taking advantage of outdoor ad space is increasing daily.

Outdoor advertising is one of the most tightly controlled industries in America today. Most Americans are familiar with random size "on premise" signs, promoting everything from hot dog stands to entertainment emporiums. Such signs are controlled by local ordinances only. Traditional off-premise billboards, however, are subject to highly restrictive local, state, and federal laws governing size, height, lighting, and placement.

Outdoor advertising is high in the popularity polls with certain businesses that have specific advertising needs and want to reach customers at specific locations. And it is plainly what it says: advertising that is presented outdoors.

Most outdoor advertising is done on billboards along streets and highways. It also includes posters and circulars that are displayed outside. But it has a close relative, transit advertising, the "billboards" on the sides of buses and other transit vehicles. Transit also includes car cards that are displayed inside buses and subway trains.

According to the experts, every day millions of Americans are confronted with over 500,000 billboards and painted bulletins, and 1.5 million car cards and posters appear in buses, subways, and commuter trains.

Billboards, the 7-Second Medium

You have 7 seconds to get your message to a passerby from a billboard. Actually, it's more like 3 to 5 seconds in crowded, congested areas to catch the eye of drivers who are battling traffic.

Think about it the next time you're on an open road, without the jam of rush-hour traffic. As you approach a billboard, count off 7 seconds. (1000 and 1, 1000 and 2, 1000 and 3 . . .). Check whether you are able to take your eyes off the road safely for the full 7 seconds and really read the message.

The job of a billboard is to create a quick impression and to remind the viewer that a product, a service, or a nearby business exists. A McDonald's board, created by Arnold & Company advertising agency, fulfilled those specifications well. It sent its message in six letters. The entire board, from side to side, in McDonald's traditional colors of yellow-gold on red, showed six golden arches, separated by hyphens, that spelled out:

M-m-m-m-m-m

The only words used gave the location.

Basic Outdoor Structures

The two basic standardized outdoor advertising structures are the poster panel and the painted bulletin. Posters are the smaller boards and painted bulletins are the larger boards.

The poster panel, measuring 12 feet by 25 feet (300 square feet overall, with molding), is typically leased for thirty-day periods, which permits advertisers to change copy on a monthly basis. Special time change requirements can be written into contracts.

The painted bulletin measures 14 feet by 48 feet and customarily is sold for a period of time that ranges from four to thirty-six months. There are two types. The rotary bulletin can be dismantled and moved to a different location every thirty to sixty days so that an advertiser's message can be seen throughout a market. The permanent board remains in one location and usually is placed at extremely high-traffic locations such as freeways or busy intersections.

Rotary bulletins have some attractive selling points. A business, such as a paint and body shop or a restaurant, that wants to attract people from all over town, buys a rotary board that is moved every two months instead of a board that sits in one location for six months. The big plus for rotary boards—instead of paying the usual costs of, say $3000 for a freeway location, gets that location for $1400 a month, it stays two months, and it's moved to another excellent freeway location for two months, then to still another high cost freeway location for another two months.

Painted bulletins (or "paints," as they're called in the industry) are usually purchased on a unit rather than a package basis, and production is included in the monthly rental cost. They are usually hand-painted in an outdoor company's studio and put up in sections on location or painted directly at the location.

Painted bulletins are placed where traffic is moving at a faster speed than on secondary streets, arteries, and thoroughfares, where posters are usually placed. The larger size is related to readers' ability to view and understand a message while traveling at a higher speed. And because they're larger and are on high-density arteries, far fewer painted bulletins are required than outdoor posters.

As an example, an advertiser can do a good job of blanketing the entire Dallas/Fort Worth market with about a dozen painted bulletins strategically located on high-traffic freeways. It may take as many as a couple of hundred posters to do the same job—to get the same reach in terms of the number of people who see the message and the frequency with which they see it. So painted bulletins—per board at least—may build reach and frequency more slowly as a result of fewer locations throughout the market area, but reach exceeds frequency usually within four months because of their placement.

In a nutshell, both are signs. One is bigger and reaches more people more quickly. With the other, you must have many more of them in order to reach as many people with the same frequency.

What are the advantages and disadvantages of each? From a production standpoint, obviously it's less expensive to produce five, six, or ten painted bulletins than the seventy or eighty outdoor posters for an equivalent reach and frequency. Production costs are typically somewhat less for painted bulletins than for posters, which are made up of overlapping sheets that must be pasted in place. Because they're paper, they tend to have a fairly short life; they won't stand the heat, the rain, or the sun much longer than thirty to forty-five days, whereas the life of a painted bulletin, without need for refreshing or refurbishing or redoing, generally is four, five, or six months. Moreover, the lithography of imprinting a poster is specialized and expensive. It costs far too much to produce 100 or so posters.

The time frame in getting the message up is considerably shortened for painted bulletins because they're put together in a different way. They are composed of a dozen to fifteen metal-backed panels that are assembled in the outdoor company's warehouse. The message then is either painted on or stripped on with a vinyl overwrap and slid into place on the framework of the painted bulletin. It's a bit quicker and considerably easier to get painted bulletins up than it is to go into the field where you must take the pieces of paper of a thirty-sheet poster and glue each piece in place—in wind, sun, or rain.

There is a relatively new kind of outdoor board, a moving message board that you rent by the day. They're similar to the time and temperature message run by the bank down on the corner and offer no possibility of graphics. There's another important drawback: they usually are not in quality locations because the big outdoor companies have the best spots under contract. They may be set so far away from a street or highway that they are virtually unnoticed unless there is a major traffic snarl and car occupants have an opportunity to let their eyes wander.

For most businesses, they are a waste of money unless you have an event to promote, or you want to draw attention to a specific location for an event, or you want to tell the world someone turned 40. But you may be confronted by their sales people, so you should be informed in order not to fall prey to their hard sell tactics.

These boards are not offered or regulated by the big outdoor board companies, which would not consider them a legitimate use of an outdoor medium. They're presented by individual promoters.

They can rightly be called BILL-boards because they require big bills to rent them.

Is Outdoor for You?

Outdoor is good for impulse items and for disposable items like bread and beer—to remind people to stop on their way home to pick up a loaf or a six-pack.

The best way to think of outdoor is as a quick reminder or a directional sign. It also works well when there's an on-site signage problem that makes it difficult for people to spot your business and you wish to direct them to it. It's effective when you want advertising to reach people in one specific geographic area. If you're opening a restaurant, for instance, it can be highly profitable for the first six months of business to have boards six blocks in both directions from the restaurant that say, "Now open. Wendy's six blocks ahead."

Outdoor boards work well for hotels, motels, and restaurants. There's no better way to catch hungry, weary travelers than along a highway a few miles on either side of the establishment. They are also good for recreational facilities and any kind of business that is buried in an area bypassed by a major highway, as a recent survey by the U.S. Travel Data Center confirmed. The research came as the outdoor industry was under fire from the Visual Pollution Control Act, which charged that the outdoor boards "provide very little information to the motoring public." The survey found that 83 percent of those questioned said the information on outdoor boards was helpful in locating restaurants, motels, tourist attractions, service stations, and other travel-related services.

Banks have found billboards are an excellent place to tell potential customers about ways to boost their earnings when the audience is on its way to and from earning those funds—to and from work. Other businesses that use outdoor boards to their advantage are car and tire dealers and real estate and insurance agencies.

There is another big plus on the side of outdoor: it can't be turned off like television, tuned out like radio, or discarded like newspapers and magazines. It's there all day, every day, and the person traveling to and from work or shopping will see it every day.

George Arnold, whose advertising agency creates Wendy's advertising, provides a rule-of-thumb law that also dictates when outdoor advertsing is for you. Can you keep the content of your message to six or seven words maximum? That is all that can be managed in a 7-second reading time by passing motorists, under the best of traffic and weather conditions.

Considerations Before Buying

Location

When a media representative tells you about a board location that is available in an area you want to be in, personally check it out.

The first consideration, particularly if the board is to include a message in words rather than just a graphic, is that the board is visible for a minimum of 100 feet up to 300 feet. Check that there are no distracting features nearby or around it, such as other boards or close-by trees, that will obscure or divert attention from your message. There are enough distractions beyond your control, such as car radios or passengers in animated discussions. And be sure that it's not located just around a curve.

Costs

A single outdoor board may be an excellent, economic way to get your message across if production costs are kept low.

Rental costs differ by area, controlled not only by the size of the community but also by the type of board and its street or highway location. A cost comparison gives an idea of the affordability of billboards. A single-color page in a women's fashion magazine could cost $70,000, but a standard 14 by 48 foot board in Times Square goes for just $4,500 a month, according to *Advertising Age*. The average cost for this size painted bulletin runs from $1,200 to $2,500 a month or higher, depending on location, circulation, size of market, bulletin dimensions and other factors. Poster panels run from $200 to $400 per month depending on size of market and illumination. The average cost of poster panels is only an index, however, since panels are usually sold in "showings"—groups.

Even in large metropolitan areas, small boards are available at reasonable, affordable rates. And although boards are not as selective as direct mail, they are the most local medium.

The principal drawback, according to many advertising professionals, is that you can't establish a brand through outdoor. A brand is established when customers call for the product by the brand name—when, for instance, they ask for Kleenex instead of tissues. The brand must have already been established through some other medium before outdoor boards are effective and cost-efficient.

All bulletins are sold on a monthly unit rate schedule, based on yearly contract periods. Contracts include the dismantling and moving of rotary units, as well as several repaintings per year to keep color bright or to allow for changes in copy.

Billboard rates are determined by gross rating points. GRPs are used in all media, but in outdoor advertising, they determine the number of people in terms of percentage of the total population who pass a billboard each day. They are figured by multiplying the total reach (unduplicated audience) by the frequency (average number of exposures)—in other words, the number of showings each board has.

Boards are given GRP ratings—of 25, 50, 75, or 100—depending on their size and their location. A board with a 75 GRP rating is exposed to an audience equal to 75 percent of the total likely viewers.

Let's say your business is a bank or savings and loan that wants to reach men and women ages 25 to 50 years on their way to work. Your city has a population of 100,000, and your audience adds up to about 60 percent of the total population, which means your potential audience is 6,000 people. If the GRP for the board you plan to rent is 75, your market exposure would be about 4,500 (75 percent of 6,000.)

The Institute of Outdoor Advertising states that "during a thirty day period, an average #50 GRP showing will reach more than three of every four adults in a market, with a frequency of 15 times each."

The Outdoor Advertising Association of America is the nation's oldest media trade association, and the Institute of Outdoor Advertising is the marketing information and creative center for OAAA. It offers the Buyer's Guide to Outdoor Advertising, which contains information about rates, allotments, and names and addresses of outdoor companies. OAAA is a library of data that range from audience measurement to creative testing. To contact this organization, write to:

The Institute of Outdoor Advertising
342 Madison Avenue
New York, NY 10173
212/986–5920

Designing a Billboard

This is not a medium where you can sit down with a pencil or at your computer and drum out a block of copy. There is virtually no copy-writing process. Unlike other forms of advertising such as newspaper, magazine, and television, which are a combination of editorial and graphics, outdoor is almost totally graphics. It is the primary medium in countries where illiteracy is high.

Production and construction services are part of the contract. But the decision about what the message should convey—in words and graphics—is your responsibility.

There are no good and bad billboard examples in your copycat file, so begin at once to notice every board you pass. Determine whether each passes a single test: does the message come through in a momentary glance? On those boards that have high attraction, take particular note of the impact of the visual used. Note the amount of plain space and how it is used. Effective billboard messages are never cluttered, and they are always simple.

Here are some tips to help you catch the attention of fast-moving readers:

- Use a large, dramatic graphic that is uncluttered with background artwork.
- Use no more than five or six words, set in a bold, easy-to-read typeface.
- Use brilliant, contrasting, eye-catching colors. Remember the effectiveness of that McDonalds' board featuring strong "golden-arch-color" yellow on red.
- Leave no doubt about the identity of your product, service, or company name. Spell it out in big, bold, beautiful brevity.

An example comes from a bank that wants to get its message out about its renewed commitment to small and minority-owned businesses. The graphic, occupying about half of the right side of the board (the portion farthest from the street viewer), is of one white and one black hand in a handshake. The message on the other half of the board, in strong white type on a reverse dark background, says, "While other banks tremble, we shake." The only other items are the bank's symbol and its name, Northpark National Bank, in the same reverse type.

The Future of Billboards

"Outdoor Forecast: Sunny, Some Clouds" headlined a story in *Adweek's Marketing Week* in July 1991 about the future for outdoor advertising, which, like every other medium, is becoming more high tech. The story says that this is a high time for billboards; new technology has the outdoor board business up and jogging away from the recession that threatened all media spending and made lower-cost outdoor boards more appealing. True. But there are problems, and they've come mainly from two groups: environmentalists, who call billboards "pollution on a stick," and those attempting to establish location and content controls. Those who run the industry challenge anyone to name another medium so controlled by regulators, both elected and self-appointed.

Despite all the obstacles and the political pressures to limit them. 15,000 new billboards are constructed each year. And the very features that bring the environmentalists to their feet remain the ones that captivate advertisers. No one has invented a zapper that will blank a billboard, and you can't skip the message by flipping a page, but with a billboard, drivers on their way to work will see your message five days a week. Rent several boards in a neighborhood, and they will probably see it five times a day, every day.

The sunshine in the forecast comes from technological innovations such as those contracted by MCI Communications. MCI has unveiled sixteen electronic signs in nine U.S. cities where a digital display lists an ever-increasing dollar figure—the amount the company says MCI customers save on telephone calls. These are not the moving boards described earlier, which merely run the same moving message repeatedly. The electronic signs are similar to any other outdoor board, except they include a "window" or a portion of the board that presents constantly changing numbers, as in the MCI signs.

Another technological novelty shows up on a Los Angeles billboard touting Universal Studio's earthquake adventure ride. Fiber optics create the illusion of motion and flames.

Outdoor and Transit

The overall field of outdoor advertising also includes "billboards" on the sides of buses and other public transit vehicles and car cards and bus posters on the inside of the vehicles.

Interior transit offers a captive audience and a unique item that makes it popular among advertisers: "Take Ones." Take Ones, one of transit's biggest advantages, are stock pads of coupons or post-cards attached to interior car cards that can serve special purposes: offer a coupon, a sample, a brochure, or some other means for an interested targeted individual to contact you and become a buyer of your product or service, or provide himself or you with information—for example:

- Coupons can be carried to a sales location for purchase of a product, to seek a service, or to locate information the consumer is interested in. Usually an incentive, such as a price reduction or a giveaway, is a part of the redemption offer.
- Postcards from an attached stock pad can be placed in the hands of consumers by an advertiser who wishes direct response to an advertisement or to make an appeal for information.
- Pocket attachments to hold brochures can be attached to car cards, providing information to potential consumers. Most sellers of interior car card space permit the attachment of Take One pockets or pads, which provide excellent response tests.

Advantages and Disadvantages

Transit isn't targeted enough for any business requiring a special, highly selective audience, but it does cover specific locations, and it reaches all ages and lower and middle-income individuals. Moreover, it reaches more than one-third of the monthly riders on any given day.

An interior transit advertising message is presented at a time and place where there is little else to hold the attention of passengers; it reaches a literally captive audience. A transit ad may be the closest point to a store to present shoppers with your sales or reminder message along with Take Ones that can influence riders to visit the store.

A business or event promoter whose target audience is centered in an urban area can use transit advertising to advantage. So can food and beverage product distributors, local insurance agencies, banks, and cleaners. However, inside and outside transit signs attract different audiences. Outside signs are seen by people riding in cars; public transportation riders see interior transit.

If your concern is a need to remind, remind, remind, you may wish to use transit. An advertising agency head described why it has caught on big as a preferred medium for movies: "Outdoor advertising is so cost-efficient and so great as an awareness generator. With a motion picture, you sort of have to keep pounding [consumers] over the head."

One of transit's best selling points is its low cost in relation to other media. Costs vary city to city and region to region, and by size of the display and its location on the vehicle. This is information you must gather in your area in order to compare its cost to that of other local media and to decide if your allocated advertising dollars will permit its use.

Sizes

Interior and exterior displays are available in a variety of sizes.

Exterior "billboards" on buses come in various sizes, with smaller sizes for front and back and larger sizes for the sides of the bus. Front-end displays usually are 21 by 44 inches or 11 by 42 inches. Rear-end displays usually measure 21 by 72 inches. And side panel displays most often are 24 by 12 inches, 30 by 88 inches, or 30 by 144 inches.

Exterior bus cards have even greater limitations than the reading time limit for billboards. Both the reader and the vehicle holding the transit board are moving, so "read time" may be only 1 or 2 seconds.

Although exterior bus cards are seen at closer range than billboards, the same kinds of bold-but-simple graphics and type styles must be used. Limitations on message content are even more restricting than for billboards, which means that copy must be extremely simple, and type should be as large as possible. Keep in mind that letters 4 to 6 inches high are *minimum* size; 1-inch letters are wasted because viewers can't get close enough to read them.

Interior bus or subway ads also come in various sizes. Most common sizes for inside displays are 11 by 28 inches, up to 11 by 56 inches. Inside car cards need not be as restrictive as outdoor boards since riders have plenty of time to read them, but the card must be attractive, with an arresting graphic, and the headline and copy must be easy to read and sufficiently interesting to carry the reader through the message.

Rates

Transit advertising is quoted on a monthly basis, and discounts may be given for three-month, six-month, or year-long contracts. Although sales quotes vary from market to market, typically outside displays are sold on a per unit basis, whereas inside displays are quoted on the basis of using all the vehicles in a fleet or only half or a quarter of the vehicles.

16

Magazines

How to Make Them Work for Small Businesses

There are about 22,000 magazines in circulation in the United States, and no matter how focused are the interests of your company's present and potential consumers, doubtless one or more magazine is aimed specifically to that highly vertical audience.

Where mass media were the vogue in the 1960s, now the spotlight is on special interest. There are magazines for interests literally from A to Z. A media buyer describes the scope: "There's an environmental magazine for preteens who think green, and another that is promoted as a [kind of] *Reader's Digest* that both baby boomers and highbrows can love." An excellent illustration of a magazine with a highly defined special interest is *Vibe*, focusing on the hip-hop culture, the underground music that was born on South Bronx playgrounds and now dominates the music charts. It marks the entry of the corporate mainstream, which sets it apart from the crowd of small-scale competition.

There used to be many more general interest magazines—*Life, Look, Saturday Evening Post,* and *Liberty*—but in the late 1970s, not many in the media business were taking bets that magazines would be around much longer because of their severe decline. Advertising revenue fell from 60 percent to its present level of 50 percent. In a search to find readers to gain circulation and attract advertisers, specialization took over and recuperation began. Magazine publishers now believe it's only a matter of time before advertisers fully recognize the advantages these so-called niche publications offer and bump their ad budgets back up in their favor.

Advantages and Disadvantages of Magazines

There are substantial values for advertising in magazines. Like newspapers, copy can be long and detailed, and readers can have "hard copy" to tear out and carry with them. Magazines have long lives, and people save them for reference. A monthly magazine may last up to a year, and even weekly magazines remain in a home or office for at least a week.

Magazines and newspapers have some similarities. Because they are in print form, they are more believed than spoken messages from radio and television. And magazine ads allow tear-out coupons or reply forms that are automatic response tests of the ad's readership and effectiveness.

Unlike newspapers, the majority of magazines uses a good-grade paper with a high screening ability that permits higher fidelity in the reproduction of photographs and illustrations. Also, color reproduces much better on the higher-quality magazine stock.

But if you're in a hurry, magazines are not the way to go. One of the chief criticisms of magazine advertising is the necessity for long lead times—as much as three to four months. That kills their use for messages that have any immediacy at all. And there can be sizable difficulties in making copy or placement changes.

Another disadvantage is that positioning your ad may be a problem. As with newspapers, right-hand pages attract greater readership, but right-hand page space may be hard to come by, and there is no reduced rate for left-hand page placement.

Do advertisers have control over placement of their advertising? The answer is yes and no. There are certain positions that an advertiser can pay a premium to have—for example, opposite an inside cover, an outside cover, or across from the table of contents. You can buy the space for a premium. But if you're buying "run of publication" then you have no leverage in the placement of the ad.

As an example, Mercedes Benz had a policy for years that they did not want to be adjacent to any story that had any negative connotation about Germany or Germans or the European Common Market. They made that part of their space contracts. Recently, the publishing industry rebelled and Mercedes Benz has recanted and apologized. The line between advertising and editorial in magazines, just as in newspapers, is one that you cannot cross. All advertising space is for sale, however, including right-hand pages—even page 59, if that's what you want. You just have to pay a premium for it and, if you're not willing to pay the premium, then you take your chances. Also, most publications will work with frequency advertisers to give them better positions. The bigger the ad, the more frequently it runs, the better position it will be given, on an automatic basis. That's the way it works.

Still another disadvantage is that most magazines are not local, although some have regional editions or regional sections. Most magazines usually are best for national or multistate businesses.

Selecting a Magazine

For advertisers, magazines can be like network television and local radio. There are general magazines that speak to everybody, as does television. And there are those that speak to special interest audiences or to listeners in specific geographic areas, as with radio. Some national magazines offer regional editions, and some offer demographic editions that may, for instance, reach only doctors' offices or business offices.

There are newspaper-delivered Sunday inserts such as *Parade* that call themselves magazines and may reach a national audience, or they may be published by the newspaper and reach only the geographic area covered by the newspaper. These insert magazines differ from other types in that they have shorter lead times—sometimes as short as forty-eight hours. They are not printed on equally high-quality paper.

Others fall in the local category and include city magazines in many of the larger cities in the country. They may be published by chambers of commerce or independent publishers. In each instance, local magazines can narrow geographic range, but they have broad demographic and psychographic ranges.

The yardstick for selecting a magazine is much the same as for selecting a newspaper. Generally special interest magazines are far more productive for small businesses than the across-the-board mass audience appeal of general interest magazines.

Marketing consultant Michael Anthony offers questions that can be your gauge for selecting a magazine for your advertising message:

- Does it reach the people I want as customers?
- How many people does it reach in that category?
- How often does the publication reach these people?
- Is it local enough to produce business?

Buying the Space

Buy Enough Time So the Message Will Be Noticed

Advertising professionals repeatedly stress that hit-and-run advertising doesn't work in media the public doesn't see on a daily basis. (In daily media, a two-week campaign can give the impression of consistent, constant advertising.) Steady exposure is the key to recognition and remembrance in magazines because each advertising message builds on previous ones.

No matter what publication(s) you choose, give your advertising time to build—a minimum of three months, and longer is even better. The readers of a particular magazine need time to get to know your company, what it is, and what it stands for. If your first or even the second ad fails to bring reaction and response, you may be ready to walk away. Don't do it. And don't advertise in any magazine until you can afford to stay long enough for a proper test period.

Magazine Rates Can Be Negotiated

Magazine rate cards are comparable to radio rate cards: not to be accepted as unchangeable. It may help you from being intimidated by magazine salespersons to know what an executive at a major New York advertising agency had to say: "Rate increases are going to be announced [on the rate card] at a significantly higher level than what is actually going to be delivered on a negotiated basis." Another agency executive put it this way: "When it gets to negotiation, we'll be paying last year's rates. Our clients are not raising their budgets next year so if magazines raise rates, they'll drop off the list. There are a lot of people in broadcast who would love the money." You can and should apply the same thinking and tactics to your negotiations.

As a buyer of advertising space for a small business, you will not have the negotiation clout of large corporations, which buy great amounts of space, or of agencies, which may meld a purchase for several clients into one buy. Nevertheless, rates can be negotiated, so dicker for your best rate.

Consider frequency discounts, based on the total number of insertions on a regular basis. A frequency discount has nothing to do with the total space purchased; it has to do with the number of regular insertions regardless of the size of each insertion.

Negotiate for Write-Ups

There is another possibility that may be available from the magazine(s) in which you wish to buy space, something that is not available from newspapers: free editorial write-ups. It's not generally acknowledged that such agreements are available, but some magazines, when asked, will permit one editorial space story for each paid ad—called a "one-for-one" deal—or one write-up for every two purchased ads—a "one-for-two" deal. The magazine's representative may absolutely deny that such deals are available from the publication. A hint about whether these deals actually are or aren't available will show up when you check advertisers in the mail order or new products sections and then look at the editorial sections to see whether there are write-ups about these advertisers.

Still another boost to your magazine advertising investment is spelled out by the publisher of Times Mirror Magazines, which publishes a number of niche-interest magazines. "[We] have to go back and offer more than a page of space. If I present a package that is one-fifth advertising, the advertiser may say to me, 'I can get a better deal at Hearst.'" Their outdoor magazines stage events for advertisers such as ski races, or they give tickets for a ballgame, or a page of free space in a trade magazine.

None of these deals may be available if you're a one-time-only buyer, but at least make a serious effort to negotiate lower rates and then try for a write-up or another "perk."

Preparing the Magazine Ad

Rate cards may be useless in reporting rates, but they are valuable for other information: sizes of space available, mechanical specifications, restrictions, deadlines, publication dates, and circulation figures.

If you've been using newspaper advertising, you may be a bit spoiled by the production assistance they offer: graphics, copywriting, mechanical preparation, typesetting, or reproduction. Magazines seldom provide such help.

When you write a message to people with highly focused interests, be particularly careful to speak to them in their language. If the magazine is published for a finely targeted group and you aren't quite sure what their language style is, read the articles and some of the ads.

Because magazines have such extended lead times—up to three or even four months—pay particular attention to the season during which the ad will be read. You may have to write the copy during a February snowstorm but readers will be thinking summer vacations and how to stay cool when they receive it in June.

Because the paper is of a much higher quality than the newsprint used by newspapers, the screen used for magazines is much higher. A screen is a dot process used in halftone and four-color printing that is easier to reproduce than a "continuous tone" image. The number of dots per line—the screen—for a magazine can range from 110 to 133, and sometimes as high as 200 lines per inch. A newspaper screen may be as low as 65. The higher number of lines per inch produces a higher level of detail in the images.

Preparation of your magazine ad undoubtedly demands some professional help. Perhaps there are college or university classes in your area where competent students can be enlisted through their instructors. Otherwise, locate a commercial studio or an art studio to do the work, for which you will be charged.

One bit of help you may get from a magazine is free reprints—depending on the number requested—of your ad. There may be a small charge if you require numerous copies. Reprints can be used effectively for direct mail advertising. Reprints, mounted on cardboard, carrying a line that says, "As advertised in . . ." also can be used with in-house displays.

The Future

Although the magazine industry has suffered a serious slump, it appears now to be on a long road to recovery. Publishers are, however, looking at every means of cutting costs. One of the more significant changes is showing up in a trend toward decreasing frequency. One publisher of a monthly magazine explains, "There are no rules that say we have to publish 12 issues." There are a number of reasons for the change, according to the publishers, but the most compelling is that few advertisers buy space in all twelve issues of a monthly. Monthly magazines that are cutting from a 12-times schedule often publish combined editions, such as January/February and July/August, times when newsstand sales and advertising are soft. The physical size of magazines also is being trimmed to reduce the costs of paper, printing, and mailing.

To keep abreast of the times and advertisers' demands, magazines are being forced to develop more extensive intelligence about their publication's subscriber characteristics. Require this information before you purchase, to ensure that their readers fit your audience's profile.

There is another acknowledged trend that can benefit you and your advertising program. According to *Circulation Management* magazine, "Smart business publishers today see themselves as being in the information and communications services business. The 'smart' business publishers' portfolio[s] for the '90s will include expositions, conferences, newsletters, contract publishing operations and varied direct marketing services."

As yet another means to counter advertising dips, publishers are seeking to develop new revenue by means of audiocassette versions of their magazines. *People* magazine expected to test an hour-long audiocassette version of one issue, which they planned to sell at supermarket checkout counters, newsstands, and bookstores for $5.98. *Newsweek,* with the Associated Press, planned to market cassettes of a weekly hour-long radio news program. It also planned to test the program selling ten-week subscriptions, going to fifty-two week subscriptions, that cost the listener $149 if the test indicates consumer approval.

Buzz, an upscale life-style magazine, plans to involve advertisers, thereby permitting the magazine to circulate free cassettes twice yearly to its 30,000 subscribers.

The nation's largest weekly news magazine, *Time,* became a trendsetter in April 1992 when it announced, "This issue of *Time* contains the most significant changes since the magazine's creation in 1923." Its redesign reflects editorial changes—"a shift from re-hashing last week's news to breaking original news"—according to the magazine's managing editor.Need for the changes is attributed to both decreasing advertising sales and to the intensified and shifting marketplace created by the widespread expansion of electronic news media such as CNN.

What possible effect could these changes have on your advertising program? Obviously, production changes require changes in the presentation of your advertising. Beyond that, editorial changes such as those by *Time* magazine will be picked up by other magazines, including those that small businesses use, and that can affect your audience and change the types of readers/listeners, as well as their numbers. All of these changes, and no doubt there will be more ahead, demand your attention and regular reevaluation.

17

Publicity

A Great Companion to Advertising

Publicity is news. It may be news of your company, and it may be the same news you plan to use in your advertising. But if a publicity release is used by media, it will be because it contains news of interest to a number of readers or listeners, not because it is meant to persuade readers or listeners to buy something. It will be treated as news and used in the news sections of print media and on news programs on broadcast stations. In credible media there will be no charge for the space or time in which the news is carried.

Together, advertising and publicity can be a legitimate and effective solution to a large problem among small businesses: making buyers aware of the seller.

Speaking of 'Free Advertising'. . . Don't

Right here, quickly, before there's any misunderstanding, there are those who profess to be advertising authorities, who make a very misleading statement. In fact, entire chapters in some books are devoted to what the writers title something like, "Publicity—It's Free Advertising."

Publicity is not *free advertising.* It is important to know the difference and to respect it. True, publicity may be advertising that money cannot buy, but if you ever have a news release that you want used, never call it "free advertising." News people in any medium—print or broadcast—resent that kind of thinking.

If an editor or a reporter believes that your publicity story is an attempt to get free advertising, you can be sure that it will end up in the wastebasket quicker than you can say the two words "free advertising." Perhaps more important, you will have made no friends in the newsroom—people you may need as friends down the line, if you plan to send other publicity releases.

There's good reason to believe you may really need those newsroom friends in the near future. The best brains in the marketing and advertising business are now saying that in the future what a company stands for will be as important as what it sells. Publicity is a means to get a message across about what your company stands for in an even better fashion than through advertising.

Publicity together with advertising can be a legitimate and effective solution to a large problem among small businesses—making the buyer aware of the seller and to demonstrate that the seller is credible.

What *Is* Publicity?

Publicity is the fundamental instrument for courting and gaining public opinion. It boils down to getting a positive message about your business out to the public. (Publicity is also known as public relations.)

But the same definition could also be given for advertising. Right? Yes, but there are substantial differences between publicity and advertising. The biggest is that publicity is telling the story of your business without paying for space or time to do so.

In fact, though, there are publications, usually special advertising sections within publications, that do accept payment for publicity articles, but the articles are recognized as advertorials. Readers know that such articles are merely advertising in an editorial format and may discount their content accordingly.

Publicists

As your company's publicity representative, you are in effect a special reporter on the staff of every publication in which the company wishes its publicity to appear.

Even with all the news services available, editors cannot cover every event and all the activities of all companies, groups, and organizations. Your news release can be of great value to an editor but only if it contains information of value to the public—specifically, to the public that is that newspaper's readers. An editor will gratefully accept a qualified publicity representative as an unpaid extension of the staff, to route news to her.

Medium-sized and small papers have small staffs to cover events, so they need copy; if your releases are well written, they will be used. (Larger metropolitan papers often are more difficult to crack.)

A publicist may be anyone with the following five qualities:

1. A nose for news. In a company, finding news takes little thought. But milking a story requires hunting for unusual angles, adding an original twist, and sometimes digging deep for information beyond obvious facts.
2. The ability to present news. This means knowledge of the mechanical production of copy by certain specifications.
3. Energy to do the work: digging out facts, data, and information that make up a news story, putting it into an acceptable release format, and typing it. (Every news release must be typed, never handwritten.)
4. Persistence and determination, which, next to integrity, are a publicist's top attributes. Not all releases are used, for reasons that have nothing whatsoever to do with whether the story is well written, newsworthy, and interesting. There may not be sufficient space to include it or, more likely, breaking news knocks it off the page. The only way to accomplish a publicity goal—to keep the good name of your company and its people before the public—is with persistence and determination to maintain a regular, ongoing publicity program.
5. Integrity, the most important quality a publicity representative must have. If an editor does not have faith that information is true, correct even to minor details, and will not backfire on him when printed, he will never use your releases. Editors guard their reputations for accuracy with zeal. Accuracy is an editor's job, because readers count on what they read in credible media to be accurate and exact.

As publicist, your job is to win public confidence for your company. If the information released cannot be relied on, the publicity representative will be perceived by newspeople as unreliable, untrustworthy, and undependable. Worse, the company will gain the same reputation by association.

From the company's standpoint, you, as the owner or top executive, are the best person for the job of publicity representative. A fundamental reason is that there is no guarantee that everything about your company, your product, or your service—or even about people within your company—will always attract good press. Therefore, if at some time in the future a difficult situation arises, it will benefit the company when the press reports the negative news if they already know and respect you. Newspeople who know your name and your reputation through personal contact or by the dependability of your publicity releases will listen to, or seek out, your explanation of a problem and include an accurate account of your company's position in their news reports.

There can be times when a good quote from a top executive or additional information about a situation, a new product or service, or a new development will add substance and interest to a news release story or actually be required if the story is to be used. Editors and reporters are far more likely not to toss the story but take the extra time to call a company head whom they know has answers, or fast access to answers, than a staffer who must track down the information and whose name with a quote won't be as impressive.

There also is a sizable personal benefit for you as a publicity practitioner. All skills improve with practice, and over time as you do the job, you will continually improve your writing skills—no small benefit in business.

To ease any concerns you may have about your writing ability, know that good writing is not a natural gift. You have to learn to write well. And because good writing is not a talent, it can be learned. The copycat method makes the learning easy.

The bottom line is it's good PR for you to know the newspeople. If time doesn't allow you to take on the job, select someone who is willing to put in the time and extra effort needed and who will represent the company well in manner, demeanor, and attitude.

The Copycat Method

To make writing news releases a much easier task than you ever expected, start a copycat file of published news stories on topics that you anticipate are similar to the news stories you will offer newspapers. The file should contain only newspaper stories, for a very particular reason. Unless your news release has a "stop the presses" rating—which usually means it has high negative or scandal content—only newspapers will have interest in it because only they have adequate space to include news of small businesses. The time constrictions of television and radio news programs don't permit reporting positive small business news, and lead time for magazines is so extended that your news will be history before a magazine can use it. There is an exception: trade magazines or journals in your field or industry. They want news of your industry, and the companies and people in it, and often will use the news even when it is weeks old.

Each newspaper is distinct. As you begin to gather news stories for your copycat notebook, it will pay you to notice the personality of each newspaper, particularly those to which you will send releases. Most news about small businesses appears on the business pages, so pay greatest attention to the writing and style used there.

Use a notebook of adequate size because your notebook eventually will have four sections.

Section 1 will contain published model news stories. Be on the lookout for news stories about:

- new products
- new services
- product or services improvements
- new company executives or board members
- results of research
- company relocations and expansions
- company tie-ins with charity, education, or other nonprofit events
- awards given to or received by companies or their employee(s)

Your collection of stories need not be about small businesses only. The same journalistic principles apply to stories about large corporations and the smallest businesses. The published stories need not come from only small newspapers. Often the writing in metropolitan dailies is better, so they will be better role models for your copycat efforts.

As you gather the news stories that will become your "copycat instructors," cut them out and paste them into the notebook—one to a page—with the publication's name and date of publication. Separate the stories by types.

Sections 2 and 3 will contain dated copies of your news releases and dated copies of the news stories published as a result of the releases.

Section 4 is your media list; it will be as big or as small as your needs require. If your releases will have interest only to the local newspaper, the list will be short. But even that list requires names of editors—correctly spelled—with whom you will have contact, their titles, and the sections they edit, along with the newspaper's address and telephone number, and perhaps the editors' direct-dial telephone numbers.

If your releases will be sent to a broader list, you may have to consult the current edition of *Editor & Publisher International Year Book* or *Bacon's Publicity Checker*, at your local library, for the names and titles of editors at each publication. Remember that although the information any directory contains is correct at the time of publication, there can be numerous changes in the personnel listed after only a few weeks. It will pay you to check each newspaper by telephone every few months as to who is the current editor, because that person will have a far better reaction to a release addressed to her rather than to the person who occupied the chair earlier.

In addition, jot down pertinent information about the types of material that particular newspaper, that special section and editor, uses, and the style of writing.

Make a note of publication day(s) if the newspaper is a weekly or a suburban paper and the deadline day if the story is for a Sunday edition. Sunday editions have much earlier deadlines, and the deadlines may vary from paper to paper.

Not only will this notebook give you direction in how to write your news releases by following the writing and style of the examples you collect, but later, comparisons of your releases and their printed results will show changes the editors made in your news releases. The editor's changes indicate ways you can improve your future releases to comply better with style and content requirements.

This handbook will become a written record, with dates, of the happenings that made news for your company, and it will become the guide for a successor or anyone else you may assign to do the job.

The Rules of Newswriting

Before you see how to copycat a news story and then go about writing your news release, it helps to understand how a straight-news newspaper story is constructed because it is unlike any other type of writing.

There are basically three parts to straight-news stories (which are different from feature stories in newspapers): a headline, a lead, and the body of the story.

Although your news release will carry a headline (typed in upper- and lowercase) it is only for the editor's benefit. It summarizes the information that follows and is designed to catch the attention and pique the interest of the editor. (The head that actually appears over the published story will be written by a newspaper staffer.)

The headline should include the most significant point in the story that follows while remaining short and concise. Something that describes the benefits to the newspaper's readers makes an excellent eye stopper. Some of the most effective words used in heads that attract readers' eyes are also words that attract editors' eyes, such as *new, innovative, breakthrough, announces, better, more, revolutionizes, changes, improved,* and *discloses.*

The lead is a roundup of facts of the story—a one- or two-paragraph summary of the who, what, where, when, why (the five Ws), and possibly the how of the information that follows in the body of the story.

As you construct these segments remember that the editor is YOUR most important reader! If the editor doesn't read the lead, the entire release will be given an instant burial in an oversized wastebasket alongside the desk. Remember that an editor's priority is information that interests the newspaper's readers.

Keep the lead short—no more than fifty words. The reason is that large blocks of type are like watching a blank television screen. They're boring, tire the eye, and force readers to turn to more appealing eye matter. The following lead is an example:

> Data For Less Inc. said today that it plans to franchise five service operations in adjoining counties over the next year, beginning with the recent opening of an operation in LaPorte.

If fifty words won't do the job, extend the lead to a second short paragraph:

> Allen Realty Services, Inc. and Lakeside Food Store plan to begin construction within two weeks on a 3-acre shopping center in West Allen at 16th and Park streets.

Along with Lakeside Grocery, Jones Drugs already has signed as a tenant in the strip shopping center on the northeast corner.

The head and the lead are the most important parts of a release; they are the only parts of a story you can count on editors—and later, if published, readers—even to glance at. The head catches the eye; the lead determines whether to read further. Put your best efforts into these elements.

The body of the story fleshes out the story, with the most important information presented immediately following the lead. Information decreases in importance in each paragraph that follows the lead. This style is called an inverted pyramid because it presents the information in an upside-down style. The inverted pyramid allows editors to cut a story at any point to fit space without cutting the gist of the entire story or the most important information.

A News Story Is Timely Facts

Make your news release immediate, not just current; otherwise it's history, and newspapers aren't in the business of reporting history. For instance, in the Data For Less Inc. lead, if the publicist had taken his time in releasing the story, thereby having to indicate that the announcement was made a few days earlier, the story would be about a current happening, but an editor would consider it history. And, further diminishing its importance, the newspaper's readers in LaPorte may already have read it in that community's newspaper.

Release your information before the event happens if possible, or immediately after it happens. Mailing a release too early, however, is almost as bad as mailing it too late. If it arrives too much in advance, it may get lost in the newsroom melee. Good timing calls for the information to arrive three to five days before an event to give an editor time to assign a reporter if the story warrants it. If the story is about a decision, such as an election of a chairman at a board of directors meeting, it should be delivered in person or by fax the day the decision is made.

News stories are factual. Facts alone, however, make pretty dull reading. Your job is to flesh out the facts and make them interesting. An editor usually will find space for a newsworthy release that is written with a little resourcefulness and originality or is loaded with human interest.

Newspapers have much the same writing requirements for news stories turned in by their own reporters as for those turned in by publicity representatives, with one exception: as a publicist, you are not required to report negative aspects in your publicity releases.

There is abundant news in every organization. Names make news because people want to read about other people. They also want to read about programs, projects, and items that make their lives or jobs better, easier, more enjoyable, or more attractive and about ways to save or about alternatives that save them money.

Your publicity job is to make everyday people or more-or-less commonplace programs or events in your company sound interesting and like news to the newspaper's readers. It's also the editor's job to find information for readers.

A lead for a release about ordinary people doing ordinary things might be something like this:

> Gary Ferris Sr. and Gary Ferris Jr. have dedicated their lives to building one of the city's premier restaurants—Seven Gables—so it was natural for Mason College to name them recipients of the Jonas Entrepreneurs of the Year Award.
>
> The awards will be presented Tuesday by college president John Smith at a 7:30 p.m. ceremony in the auditorium at Mason College.

Write It Right

Murphy's Law is operative in publicity too: if it can be misunderstood, it will be.

Even the Associated Press, journals of higher education, as well as newspapers can write it wrong! All of the following examples were reported by *Reader's Digest:*

> Notice in the *Ashland (Ohio) Times Gazette* about a local barbecue: "Prices for the dinner are $4.50 for a half chicken, $3.50 for a quarter chicken and $4 for senior citizens."

> From an AP item: "Nine women who bared their breasts on a city beach last summer were not covered by the Constitution, a judge ruled."

In North Carolina State University's *Official Bulletin:* "The Water Aerobics Club will meet Wednesday in Room 2037. It is vital that members attend this meeting. The club is in jeopardy of dissolving."

There probably is no need to explain the writing mistakes made, even by excellent organizations. However, just in case you have a question, that first item would more correctly be written: "Prices for the dinner are $4.50 for a half chicken, and $3.50 for a quarter chicken. Senior citizens will pay $4.00."

There's an old saying: "You get what you inspect. Not what you expect." In other words, proof and reproof your copy, and remember that clarity begins at your desk and within your company.

Never Doubleplant

Editors may refuse to work with you if they see the same information from your release in another section of their newspaper as well as in their own section. It's called doubleplanting and is almost as big a taboo as sending incorrect information. Almost always the error is inadvertent: the sender neglects to choose between two editors on the same paper before sending the release. If your media list includes more than one person at each newspaper, always decide which person would be most likely to use this particular information. Then send it to just that one person.

How to Copycat

Shown are part of an actual news story copied from the business pages of *The Dallas Morning News.* Directly after it is a fictional news release written to emulate the published report in news release format, to demonstrate the manner in which an actual news story can be used as a model. All people and companies named and the publicity release itself are fictitous.

The Press Kit

Often an attached release package means the difference between a release's being used or discarded. Although your news release must be able to stand alone, often additional material provides details

Annual casino night fund-raiser set Nov. 21 by Wylie chamber

WYLIE—An annual casino night fund-raiser will be from 6:30 p.m. to midnight next Saturday at the National Guard Armory at 700 N. Spring Creek Parkway in Wylie.

Casino night is sponsored by the Wylie Chamber of Commerce and features Las Vegas games, including blackjack, roulette and craps. Dealers for the games are provided by Vegas Touch of Dallas.

Proceeds go to the Wylie Chamber of Commerce for community programs and services.

Tickets can be purchased for $30 per person in advance or $35 per person at the door.

Admission includes a buffet catered by Maria's Restaurant of Wylie and $5,000 in playing chips. Entertainment and a cash bar are available.

At the end of the evening, players will cash their chips for prizes, including two airline tickets for a trip anywhere in the United States and tickets for a trip to Las Vegas. A silent auction also will be held.

Tickets can be purchased in advance at American National Bank, Wylie, Provident Bank, Wylie, First National Bank, Sachse; Maria's Restaurant in Wylie and the Chamber of Commerce office at 108 W. Marble St.

For more information, call the chamber at 442-. . . .

MINIATURE ITEMS FOR COLLECTORS
2832 Smith-Jones Avenue
Centerville, Georgia 11536
Tel. (123)456–7890   Fax (123)0987–654

Contact: Howard Hanson   *For Immediate Release*

Saturday fund-raiser sponsored by Centerville business will benefit learning disabled children

CENTERVILLE—Children with learning disabilities will be recipients of proceeds from a day-long Saturday event sponsored by Miniature Items For Collectors at the city's convention hall in Centerville.

Activities, which include an old-fashioned quilting party, will be followed by a barbecue dinner and dance.

Proceeds go to The Children Fund, a Centerville nonprofit organization founded in 1991 by Cheryl Wilkerson, owner of Miniature Items For Collectors.

Tickets may be purchased for the daytime sessions ($15) which begin at 10 a.m.; for only the evening barbecue and dance ($25), which starts at 6 p.m.; or for both day and evening events ($30).

Admission for the day's schedule features sessions to teach quilting and other crafts and booths where handmade craft items will be sold. Evening admission features a barbecue dinner prepared by volunteers enlisted by Ms. Wilkerson.

Dance music will be by The Honey Tunes who are contributing their services.

Among those who will assist with the buffet-style dinner are Mary and Herbert Kraft, Sue and Thomas Feldman, Joanna White, Betty Topham and Joseph Applesby.

—more—

Children's Fund fund-raiser 2-2-2

Tickets can be purchased at the door or at Miniature Items For Collec-

tors, 2832 Smith-Jones Ave. For more information, call Howard Hanson at

456–7890.

The Children's Fund was established when Cheryl Wilkerson was un-

able to locate special classes for a family member with a learning disabil-

ity. Her company, Miniature Items For Collectors, is underwriting costs of

the Saturday event.

###

that give a reporter a handle on who and what is behind the news, some quotes to spice up the report, and possibly technical data that make for better understanding.

Businesses that conduct sophisticated, often expensive publicity programs assemble Press Kits that contain such backup information. Smaller businesses on limited budgets may elect merely to enclose the extra information with the release.

The Press Kit may include the following information:

- A backgrounder. There are different kinds of backgrounders. If the release is about the company or its executives, the backgrounder may be a history of important high points in the company's background. In the case of a merger or an acquisition, there should also be a historical backgrounder of "the other" business. Backgrounders should be written to strengthen the firm's reputation and standing in the community.

  To accompany the previous fictitious release, a backgrounder could contain straight facts about the nonprofit group, including names of its board members, founding date, goals, and accomplishments to date. The backgrounder also might include information about the retail store that sponsors the fund-raising event.

- A quotes sheet. Reporters like to use quotes. They add zest to a story and provide a means for the writer to make a point, commend or praise an individual, or add meat to a news report. Give the name of each person who is quoted, with title or position in the company, or his or her identification with reference to the product or event that is the subject of the release. Quotes to accompany the previous news release might include several from Cheryl Wilkerson, owner of Miniature Items For Collectors and Founder of The Children's Fund such as: "We have so many advantages that my young learning-disabled relative doesn't have, that I just felt we should be doing more to help. That's why I started The Children's Fund. Now there are all kinds of classes that volunteers conduct. If we can just raise enough money we can expand that help."

- Bios. Biographies of individuals named in the release add substance to a reporter's rewrite of your release. Bios should be concise and include only information that is pertinent to the news story.
- A brochure. If the release is about a new product or new equipment, a brochure or an operating manual that describes or explains complicated features can help the reporter give a more understandable description of the product, its operation, or its use.
- An annual report. A company's annual report is an excellent fund of information for reporters to draw from.
- Photos. Often photos tell a story as no words can. Readers who haven't the time or desire to read a story almost always will scan a news photo and its caption. It may even tempt them to read the story. Head-and-shoulders or mug (head only) shots of person(s) depicted in bios also may accompany a release about an individual.

Submitting Publicity Releases

There is a format for producing news releases and a major reason for following it: the easier you make the editor's job, the more likely it will be that your release will be used.

A metropolitan daily newspaper processes about 8 million words each day from staff reporters, wire services, and feature syndicates—and that doesn't even include all the publicity releases received daily. Then consider that it's all done within a matter of hours, and you're suddenly aware that it's only common sense that an editor won't struggle to read anything that isn't earth-shattering news. There isn't time. So at the very least, be sure your release looks professional and is easy on the eyes.

You will need the following tools:

- company letterhead and matching second sheets
- fresh typewriter or computer printer ribbon
- dictionary and thesaurus (optional)
- *The Elements of Style,* by William Strunk, Jr., and E. B. White, (Optional) an eighty-five-page style book of rules of acceptable English usage, principles of composition, commonly misused words and expressions, and tips for clear writing.

To prepare copy, use these guidelines:

1. Typed, double or triple spaced, one side of paper. Keep a dated duplicate file copy. The original is undated except for inclusion of a possible release date.
2. Upper left-hand (beneath letterhead), single space: "Contact:" [your name and title, or name of the company's publicity contact]; "Phone:" [if there is a direct-dial number or it's different from that on letterhead].
3. Upper right-hand: "For Immediate Release," "Release at your convenience," or "Release Date:"
4. If you are giving one newspaper an exclusive, let the recipient know. Type "EXCLUSIVE" above item 3. Then don't give the story to any other news source.
5. Upper left-hand (beneath "Contact" name), single space: In upper- and lowercase, type a headline that summarizes the story that follows, worded to grab the editor's interest and convince him or her to read the release.
6. Drop down several lines before beginning the lead paragraph(s). In this blank space, an editor can write copy desk markings, instructions, or the newspaper's headline. (Smaller papers may not rewrite if the release is well-written.)
7. If the story goes to newspapers outside your geographic area, precede the first words of the lead sentence with a dateline, in all caps, naming the city and state where the news originated. With today's means of instant communication the term "dateline" is a misnomer. Years back, when news took days to be transmitted, news stories

    included a date following the place of origin—hence the terminology.

8. If the copy extends to more than one page, indicate it with "—more—" centered at the bottom of the first page. (Do the same on subsequent pages when copy extends to other pages. However, news releases are more readily used when they are kept to one, one-and-a-half, or two pages to accommodate limited space problems.)

9. If copy extends to a second page, top the second page with a short version of the page 1 head, followed by the page number "2–2–2." Then drop down four lines before continuing the text. (Repeating a page number three times is traditional practice among reporters.)

10. Indicate the end of the copy with "# # #" centered two or four lines below the end of the text.

11. If days and dates are used within the copy, be sure that the day and date match—that Monday actually is February 5, not February 6.

12. Names must be full given names and include titles when appropriate. Be sure to check and recheck spellings of all names. (Misspellings of names are the easiest and fastest means to lose an editor's confidence that the information you send is reliable.) Write "CQ" over unusual spellings to show they are correctly spelled.

Although people's names are by far the most important to spell correctly, all words should be correctly spelled. And don't just count on your computer's spell checker to do it for you.

There's a poem *The New York Times* reported was circulating at The Coastal Corp. in Houston that "illustrates one way that computers can make people look dumb." The newspaper explains that spell checkers on computers are supposed to ensure that words are spelled correctly. But most computer programs don't ensure that the words are *used* correctly. The poem is an excellent reminder of things you should look for:

> I have a spelling checker.
> It came with my PC.
> It plainly marks four my revue,
> Mistake I cannot see.
> I've run this poem threw it,

I'm sure your please too no.
It's letter perfect in it's weigh,
My checker tolled me sew.

The news release that follows is from a Los Angeles–area attorney as an example of format. It is intended for release through wire services to news media throughout the country; therefore it carries a dateline (the city and state of origin). It is constructed in the inverted pyramid format so that it may be cut by editors when necessary to accommodate space limitations, without eliminating details most interesting to the average reader or listener.

Do's and Don'ts for Publicity Representatives

Do:

1. Evaluate your copy. Ask yourself: "To how many people is this story of interest?" If the potential readership is too limited, newspapers cannot afford to use it in the limited editorial space available each day.
2. Each community or suburban paper wants a local angle and local names. Try to give each newspaper a different lead, bringing the local angle into the lead; then follow with the general information.
3. Notify the editor immediately—by telephone if time is a factor—in case of a change of date or cancellation of an event.
4. Use either "For Immediate Release" or "Release at Your Convenience." Stay away from using definite release dates whenever possible. If a release date is set too close to the date of an event, it gives the editor too narrow a margin in which to find space for the story, and chances of its being used are reduced or eliminated.
5. Submit only clear, clean, double-spaced, typed copy. Releases in longhand, italics, or script-style type are absolutely taboo.
6. When a release includes more than a single page, use paper clips to fasten them. Never staple pages.

Don't:

1. Never call in your stories to the newspaper. Not only are newspeople too busy to take telephoned releases, the

WANDA GRASSE
Attorney at Law
1300 Fulton Avenue
Monterey Park, CA 91754
Tel. (818) 280–7651 - Fax. (818) 572–8560

Contact: Shirley Finlay

(213) 283–6712   *For Immediate Release*

Giant Class Action Suit Against Telephone Scam Artists Is Expected to Be More Effective Than Law Enforcement Efforts

LOS ANGELES, Calif.—California attorney Wanda Grasse filed a 40-page class action suit today in Los Angeles Superior Court against 257 separate individuals and entities engaged in unscrupulous telephone solicitation.

"Primary objective is to stop unscrupulous solicitors from preying on unsuspecting telephone subscribers by promising them something for nothing," says Ms. Grasse. The lawsuit seeks injunctive relief against companies that solicit sales by informing individuals that they will receive one of several prizes which must be claimed in person at the company's place of business.

Prizes generally include a new car, electrical appliances and trips. The victim seldom refuses to drive to the company to collect the prize, which is accompanied by a lengthy, high-pressure sales presentation. If the prospect does not purchase the product or service on the spot, another trip is generally awarded, which includes another sales presentation.

—more—

Lawsuit to curtail scam artist—2-2-2

"Some companies make it clear that the subscriber must purchase their product in order to receive the prize," a practice Grasse says is to avoid the taint of fraud. The caller does not state that the recipient has "won" a prize, but rather that the recipient has been "selected to receive" the prize. The victim is assured that one of five prizes will definitely be awarded, but only if he or she purchases the company's product.

Grasse emphasized that these practices, while objectionable and questionable, do not constitute actionable fraud. "The individuals who show up to collect their prizes are awarded trips," says Ms. Grasse. "Those who book travel arrangements through the telephone solicitors do get free hotel accommodations. None of them, however, get what they expected."

chances for error are greatly increased when the story is not presented in hard-copy form.

2. Don't play favorites among newspapers, editors, and columnists.
3. Don't doubleplant, sending the same story to two different people on the same newspaper.
4. Don't call to ask when your story was used or when it will be used.
5. Don't ask editors or reporters for clippings or extra copies of the paper or of pictures used. (Subscribe to a clipping service to collect your published stories.) Copies of photos may be available through the newspaper's photo department, for an extra charge. And the circulation department undoubtedly can provide extra copies of a particular day's edition, also for an extra charge.

Communication: An Ongoing Activity

Publicity is communication, and communication is not a one-shot activity. don't be disappointed if the information in a release isn't used. Keep trying.

The image of your company and its people is a composite of many impressions made over time. A publicity practitioner's job is to ensure that the impressions are positive and that they build respect, admiration, and esteem for the business.

Your communication with the public through publicity will create an appropriate atmosphere in your community so that your business goals are understood and accepted.

A publicity campaign should go on—and on. It's like advertising; the public's memory is so short that if you ever stop, people forget you almost immediately.

No matter the size of the business, keeping the name of it and the people associated with it before the public as often as possible in a positive manner through regular publicity releases wins prestige, dignity, and approval for the company and its people. When customers make purchase decisions they are deciding to buy two things: the product or service *and* the company. Therefore, a continuous flow of positive publicity about the company, its product and service, improvements, new location, research, finances, community support events, about its executives and personnel changes builds name recognition, acceptance, integrity, and image with the public in a way that nothing else can.

Publicity is a priceless extension of an advertising program. Employ it whenever and wherever possible.

18

From the Pros' Nest

*Tips, Techniques, Advice, and Counsel
from Prominent Advertising
and Marketing Professionals*

If you're like most heads of businesses—large and small—you'll welcome all the advice and help you can get. That's why we turned to recognized advertising authorities. In this final chapter nine prominent professionals in advertising and marketing share their expertise on important aspects of advertising.

APPORTIONING ADVERTISING DOLLARS contributes a philosophy that has been effective in determining how to use advertising effectively, p. 256.

SUCCESSFUL TELEMARKETING not only lists qualities a telemarketing representative must have with the questions to insure that telemarketing works, it also tells how to script the conversation, p. 257.

GET YOUR ADVERTISING NOTICED is an assessment of the criteria that must be met to effectively communicate a message, p. 259.

So, climb into the Pros' Nest and discover additional ways to tackle a task or a problem and get more bang for your advertising bucks—the pros' way.

Do You Need an Advertising Agency?

George Arnold
President/Chief Executive Officer
EvansGroup, Inc.
Dallas, Texas:

It all depends on the size of your business, the size of your advertising budget, and what you are trying to accomplish with your advertising.

For a little more than 125 years, advertising agencies have been assisting businesses in the United States. The theory of "agency" holds that it is less expensive (and therefore more efficient) to buy the services, part-time, of specialists such as artists, writers, marketers, and media strategists than to hire all these specialists yourself. Their combined costs are shared by a number of "clients"—businesses like yours. Agencies assemble teams of specialists and sell parts of their time to a variety of businesses. And, hopefully, everybody benefits from the arrangement.

Back to the question: If your business and your need for advertising to reach your target customers is great enough to need the services of more than one specialist, or if you need to run ads in multiple media, chances are good that you can benefit from a relationship with an agency. Few individuals are versatile enough to be really good at art, writing, media selection, and strategic marketing. It will cost you less to deal with a qualified agency than to staff your own business with three or four, or more, qualified specialists.

So how do you go about finding the right agency for your business? There are five key questions you need to have answered to increase your chances of making a wise selection, and it's a good idea to ask them in this order:

1. *Do they have one (or more) persons on their staff who understands my business?* It's not necessary that they be industry specific. For example, if you operate a chain of dry cleaning establishments, don't be preoccupied with whether the agency people have specific laundry and dry cleaning experience. It's much more important that they understand something, in depth, about small retail service businesses with multiple stores. If they can't show you relevant experience, keep on looking.

2. *Are they the right size for my budget?* Big agencies can't make money working with small businesses. So your account will likely end up either being neglected or being turned over to the "junior bird-people," those with little or no experience.

   The best rule of thumb is to ask how many clients they have who spend approximately in the range of your projected budget. If all their accounts are much bigger, beware. If yours will be the biggest account in the agency, that can be a plus for you, however.

3. *How good are they at creative problem solving?* Ask to see examples (case histories) of their work. If they're good, you can bet they're proud of it, and they'll be happy to oblige. Look for relevance to your business in those case histories, and then call the clients to confirm the agency's role and contribution to the success. One taboo: Never ask an agency to do "speculative" work for you. That's stealing from them. Agencies can't afford to give away what they do for a living any more than you can.

4. *How responsive are they?* Good agencies turn on a dime. They're quick and quick-witted. Phone calls should be returned within hours (not three days later), and they should clearly show an enthusiasm for helping you. It's a good idea to test agency responsiveness with a paid project before you hire them. Give them a problem to solve for you and pay them to solve it. Then see how quick (and good) they are.

5. *Do you like them?* Silly as it sounds, more agency relation-

ships come apart because clients don't like the people they're working with at the agency, and the agency doesn't like the client. If you believe you would enjoy having the people from the agency in your home three times a week, then the chemistry's right. After all, you spend as much time at your business as you do at home. If you don't really like them, don't hire them. Find somebody else.

One additional thought: Always be candid with your agency. Treat them like family—even partners. If you withhold important information from them, they can't do a good job for you.

George Arnold started in the advertising business more than twenty-five years ago as a copywriter.

Using Your Newspaper Effectively and Efficiently

Charles Gerardi
Assistant General Advertising Director
The Dallas Morning News
Dallas, Texas:

Newspapers have traditionally prided themselves on being a mass medium, with the ability to reach large audiences on a daily basis. But times are changing, and advertisers—with an ever-increasing array of media choices—now choose vehicles that offer the ability to target potential clients, thus getting the most out of every advertising dollar spent.

Newspapers have met this challenge. While still offering the mass appeal that attracts many national advertisers (Coca-Cola, AT&T, Sears), newspapers now extend numerous ways for local businesses to reach niche markets.

Not all newspaper readers will see every section every day, so careful selection of the proper section is crucial. For example, newspapers offer the ability to target a potential user of small business machines by using the Business section; a softball player in need of new equipment in the Sports section; or a fitness conscious individual searching for a new health club in the Health and Fitness section. No other medium allows the capability to target your message in a related editorial environment as newspapers can.

But thoughtful selection of the right section is not the only way a small business can utilize newspapers. Most newspapers have developed total market coverage or alternative delivery programs that allow advertisers to target both subscribers and nonsubscribers geographically with zip code–specific accuracy via the postal service. Many newspapers have also generated daily or weekly newspaper sections that are distributed only to certain zones. These sections offer the benefits of targeted geographic reach with significantly lower advertising costs.

Advancements in technology have opened other new horizons in newspapers as well. Several national packaged-goods manufacturers employ the daily newspaper to deliver product samples to subscribers. Paper towels, coffee, shampoo, and liquid soap packs are among the products that have arrived at consumers' doors via the newspaper. Fax and audiotext services also offer new inroads for newspaper advertisers in the future. Many advertisers have experienced the added value of newspaper-provided audiotext lines (Ski Hotline, Scoreline, Weather Talk, etc.) as a paid advertising vehicle or as added value for existing ad schedules. Can the days of customized desktop newspapers be far behind?

As technology continues to shape the future of communications in general, a newspaper is poised to meet the ever-changing demands of its customers.

Chuck Gerardi received a degree in advertising from Texas Tech University and has served in a variety of capacities in both classified and display advertising.

Watch Your Money

Gus Boyd
Boyd Marketing Communications
New York, New York:

Billings are an easy place to get cheated. Pay particular attention to them, and be sure the proper verifying documents accompany every statement.

All suppliers must furnish supplier invoices from *their* suppliers. Let's say an advertiser hires a photographer to take a specific photograph, on location or in a studio. Here is how the invoice might look:

Photography	$2,500
Model	750
Transportation	275
Prop rental	750
Film	275
Processing	650
Misc.	175
Total	$5,325

If you think about it for a minute, this accounting is a trap for the unwary. The only item that does not call for a supplier's invoice is the fee for the photographer, which was negotiated up-front. All other items, even the miscellaneous item, must be accompanied by the suppliers' invoices. Otherwise you are likely to be the victim of padded charges.

Simply put: All suppliers, including media, must furnish invoices from their suppliers for all money spent.

Gus Boyd has more than twenty years of experience with two of the world's largest marketing communications corporations, plus fifteen years of experience managing a direct response advertising agency.

Writing and Designing Ads

Liz McKinney-Johnson
McKinney Johnson Amato Marketing
Portland, Oregon:

1. *Think like your customer.* Never overestimate the importance of yourself or your business. The consumer has a myriad of choices for every product or service. Put yourself in his or her shoes.

2. *Focus on one or two strong points.* Don't try to put too much in one ad; the consumer will never be able to digest it all. Even if someone does plow through all your information, if you've already answered all the questions, what reason does this person have for calling you or coming in? Leave something to the imagination.

3. *White space is our friend.* Leave some space in your ad for the consumer's eye to rest. Give yourself some air between your ad and other ads on the same page. Most of all, give consumers a break. They're bombarded with messages all day long; they appreciate a well-designed and well-written ad as much as you do.

4. *Know your medium.* If your local paper has a lot of small ads, a bigger ad run less often will stand out. If everyone in the local paper loves the look of black ads with reversed type, try an ad with a dominance of white space. Do what it takes to be different within your own medium.

Liz McKinney-Johnson is a founding partner and creative director of her agency, a midsize shop that serves clients from Seattle to Miami.

Avoid a Rip-off

Raymond J. Champney
RJC International
Irving, Texas:

The simplest way to avoid becoming mugged by an advertising representative is to understand clearly your own business goals and customer profile.

If you are scheduling meetings with advertising people, have a checklist of your business goals and customer profile. Do *not* share this with sales representatives. Let them make their presentation on why their particular medium will benefit your business. Then ask specific questions from your checklist. If the individual cannot readily answer your specific questions in a manner that corresponds to your goals, end the meeting.

For example, an upper-medium-priced retail fashion store with a 70 percent to 30 percent female to male clientele, average age 32, is considering an advertising campaign. The goal is to create awareness, build traffic, and increase sales. The questions to be asked from your checklist are:

1. What is the size of the audience?
2. What is the ratio of female versus male readership, listening audience, or viewer profile?
3. Give an example of how the medium being considered has

created traffic or advertisers who have used this particular media in the past.

Remember that advertising is a business tool. To use it effectively, you must know in advance what you expect advertising to deliver for you. When sitting with sales representatives, do not let them sell you—make them tell you—how their particular advertising medium will help you to achieve your goals by asking them the questions you have prepared in advance.

Ray Champney has more than twenty-five years of experience with multinational, regional, and local businesses. He represents products and services ranging from worldwide consumer goods to a local billiard parlor.

Build a Brand Name

Marsha Lindsay
President/Chief Executive Officer
Lindsay, Stone & Briggs Advertising Inc.
Madison, Wisconsin:

My dad said to me, "Marsha—the Lindsay name and what it stands for are everything." Dad realized that customer perceptions are the only thing that competitors cannot steal or copy from you.

How do you harness perceptions to build more net worth? Here are four suggestions that will help you accomplish it.

1. *Dominate your market segment.* Recent research from Harvard Business School shows that brand dominance—that is, your ranking of 1, 2, or 3 in your category—is a better predictor of profitability than market share.

The same research showed that improved ranking was accomplished in part by increases in advertising. Increased advertising leads to increased brand preference, which increases sales, which drives revenue and leads to profitability.

Harvard also concluded that improving product quality triples the odds of market domination but only when supported by advertising. The lesson is: work for brand dominance with advertising.

First find a customer segment or geographic niche that you can dominate. Take Point Beer as an example. It can't dominate in the nation, or even in Wisconsin. But it can dominate in a five-county region in central Wisconsin. The deployment of ad dollars exclusively to that area reversed a decline and boosted sales 14 percent.

2. *Capture the attention of potential customers. The New York Times* says we're all exposed to 5,000 commercial messages a day. Of those we notice 11, and recall 7. How do you get attention in all that clutter when we're all hard pressed to recall even one ad we saw yesterday?

To get attention, you have to be bold. For example, imagine a newspaper ad. Picture a big bag of groceries. The headline: "Take your mother-in-law to the Chancery Restaurant, or lug the old bag home."

To get attention you need to take calculated, strategic risks in your headlines and visuals. Don't approve ads that feel safe. A safe ad is a bad ad. In fact, it's not an ad at all. If you're not prepared to get attention, you're not prepared to advertise.

There's an added benefit to employing attention-getting ads, too. They get noticed more, and you may not have to run them as much.

3. *Be likable.* Once you get someone's attention, you have to stay in their memory. Likability is a prime tenet of successful salesmanship. If people like you, they'll remember you.

By likability in your ads, I mean by your target audience. It doesn't matter if your spouse, your golf buddies, or even your sales force don't like your ads if they are not your target audience.

Likability is getting your customers to identify with you. If the ad is right, they will consider your product or service part of their own identity—necessary for the projection of their own self-image. (There's a reason that yuppies drive BMWs.)

4. *Be brief.* Whatever your message is, realize you have only a fraction of a second in which to say it. That's how long it takes a person to turn a page, press the remote control, drive by a billboard, or get distracted.

So even though it may be true about your product, you can't build dominance or likability by asking your ads to say you're "single-mindedly striving for excellence, speed, quality, value, convenience, a wide selection, and a whole lot more with a staff that's second to none."

Pick one thing. The simpler, shorter, snappier your message, the more impact it has.

Marsha Lindsay's agency, of which she is founder and chief executive, specializes in creative brand-building advertising for national and regional clients headquartered in the Midwest. The agency's creative work has won numerous national and international awards. She was named Wisconsin's Woman Entrepreneur of the Year in 1984.

Apportioning Advertising Dollars

F. Richard Wemmers, Jr.
Wemmers Communications, Inc.
Atlanta, Georgia:

"If I had only $1.00 to spend to tell prospects why they should buy my product or service, I would spend $.50 of it first to find out what my prospects do and don't know about me or my competition. Then I would spend the other $.50 relating my product's ability to meet their unfilled needs." This has been my basic philosophy of how to use advertising effectively for the past twenty-five years, and it has worked well for small and large businesses. From road graders to food products, I've followed this philosophy carefully, and the results have been very gratifying.

For instance, when there is a growing need for products to meet new environmental requirements, be the first to relate your product's assets to these requirements. Do it in a commanding way. Then the competition will have to work harder, and spend more, to show that they're as good as or better than you are. (Make sure your claims are accurate and can be documented.)

Focusing advertising messages on what your customers think they need or must have is eminently more successful than telling customers what you think they ought to need. Your customer's perception is reality! Whether it's right or wrong, true or false, is irrelevant.

Rick Wemmers has more than twenty-five years of advertising experience. Early in his career, he worked with the largest advertising agency in the world and became one of their youngest vice-presidents. He started his own full-service agency in 1978 and has enjoyed a successful business since. The agency's clients range from high tech to hotels.

Successful Telemarketing

Jerome S. Gladysz, President
Market Relations, Inc.
Fort Worth, Texas:

Telemarketing enables a business to reach out to prospects and customers rather than waiting passively for the customer to come to the business. Every time a prospect is called, there is an opportunity to close a sale or at least to add information to the customer database.

A good telemarketing representative is:

Curious. Curiosity enables a good caller to probe the mind-set of the potential customer to determine what the person's unique needs and wants are. Good callers have an honest curiosity that allows them to explore options conversationally and avoid confrontation.

Professional. A caller should have the proper training. Otherwise, the call degenerates into a series of "I'll get back to you" situations. Callers do not have to be technical experts in every facet of product or installation, but they should know how to handle frequent questions.

Persistent. The sign of a true telemarketing professional is one who asks one more question when 99 percent of the other sales reps would end the conversation. This is not being pushy but rather simply and honestly exploring how a deeper business relationship might be developed.

Responsive. Prospects must be made to feel important. Sellers do not exist in spite of the customer but *for* the customer.

There are six important questions to determine that a telemarketing campaign is focused on generating sales and building relationships with customers:

1. *What are the needs and wants of your chosen audience?* Develop a clear picture of what the purchaser expects in products, service, and support.
2. *What is the potential of the chosen audience?* It is not enough to know what they buy. It is important to know ev-

erything they could buy if they knew more about your product line.

3. *Do we have a user-friendly offer?* Take the reason for the call, and put it in a conversational format. Prove that the offer provides potential value to the customer.

4. *Have we anticipated conversational blocks?* There may be occasions when blocks to further dialogue may occur. Identify what they might be and how they could be addressed in a way that clarifies understanding rather than entrenching a viewpoint. This is a step or two beyond overcoming customer objections in that an obstacle to the sale has been finessed rather than argued out of the picture.

5. *Is there a receptive air for questions?* One objective of telemarketing is to discuss all the prospect's questions so that both parties can explore which purchasing option makes the most sense.

6. *Have we made it easy to respond?* Ask for the order, the next step, or whatever it takes to "get the train down the track."

Other considerations in managing telemarketing are these:

- *Measure, measure, measure.* The telemarketer needs to assess each conversation to determine if a follow-up call or elimination from the list is the best next step for that prospect.
- *Listen to feedback.* Feedback from your prospective customers can help you determine if your telemarketing tactics are working or need to be modified.
- *Pay constant attention to the telemarketer representative.* Hand holding isn't necessary, but no-fault coaching, encouraging words, redirection, debriefing, and opinion gathering will go a long way to ensure a professional program.

One of the key elements that distinguishes a productive telemarketing campaign from an ineffective one is scripting.

First spell out the specific goals of the telemarketing campaign. Analyze the target audience. Spell out their needs and desires and how the product [or service] can help them. Next, jot down a list of possible objections and how to respond. Determine which features would most appeal to the target audience as you craft the company image that will be projected.

Scripts can be divided into several distinct sections:

The introduction. Try to avoid using open-ended cordial questions that might initiate a negative response.

The probe. Incorporate questions to draw the person into the conversation and provide valuable information about the prospect's current situation.

The bridge. This is a transition between the warm-up and the close. A good technique is to paraphrase or restate what the person has said to create a feeling of being listened to.

The benefits. A maximum of three benefits explained in simple language is preferable. Anything more causes prospects' eyes to glaze over and ears to deaden.

The close. State what action will be taken if the prospect is hot.

The confirmation. Restate the steps that will be taken in order to crystallize the commitment.

The direct marketing tactics of telemarketing—and direct mail—are the most targeted of all the elements in the communication mix. They offer a method to leverage your database assets for communication with your most likely potential customers.

Jerry Gladysz is President of Market Relations, Inc. in Fort Worth, Texas. He represents business-to-business clients in a variety of industries including aviation, construction, coin operated amusements, machine tools, helicopters, and business forms. This essay is an excerpt of a white paper published by the Business Marketing Association in May 1993.

Get Your Advertising Noticed

Dick Maggiore, President
Innis Maggiore Group Inc.
Canton, Ohio:

Research shows that fully 90 percent of all advertising doesn't get noticed. It's not liked or even disliked. It simply doesn't reach the prospect's level of consciousness. So say something or show something in a different way, in a provocative way. But make sure it's relevant to your product or service.

There are three criteria that must be met to communicate a message:

1. Grab their attention. If you haven't broken through the clutter, you've paid for space, printing, or time, but you have yet to communicate to your target audience.
2. Be relevant. Talk the language of the audience and make sure to provide a tangible benefit or advantage. Otherwise you lose their interest.
3. The form of your communication must be memorable. Make them want to hum it, talk about it, laugh about it, anything. The assumption is that each communication is your only chance to get your story across. It's crucial that the message sticks with them.

Dick Maggiore is president of the advertising and public relations agency that was founded in 1973.

Jargon Decoder

An Advertising & Publicity Glossary

This glossary is provided not only as a reference for terminology used in this book but also to provide meanings for the jargon used by media representatives.

ABC   Audit Bureau of Circulation. An organization that verifies circulation figures for print publications.

AD/SAT   A proprietary system employing a satellite for facsimile transmission of advertising and other graphic materials to newspapers.

Ad Count   Total number of individual advertisements or commercials.

ADI   Area of Dominant Influence. An area in which a television station has a commandingly large share of the viewing audience.

Adjacencies   The specific time periods that precede and follow regular television or radio programming. Commercial break positions between programs available for local or spot advertisers. There is no network adjacency; only spot adjacencies are available.

Advertising Credit   In co-op, advertising money from the distributor, usually over and above retailer's regular accruals. Generally, money returned to retailer in form of "credit memo" to retailer's accounts payable.

Advertising Spot   What most people call a commercial. A short advertising message on a participating program or between other radio or television programs an

advertiser does not sponsor. Advertising spots may be:
a) *fixed,* broadcast at a time guaranteed by contract
b) *preemptible,* broadcast at a certain time unless bumped by an advertiser willing to pay a higher rate
c) *floating,* broadcast when the station decides (ROS/run of station)
Sometimes confused with SPOT ADVERTISING

Advertorial   A special type of advertising, unique and differentiated from regular advertising, which generates additional revenues and is intended to instruct or entertain the reader. It is part of a publication in which promotional and editorial material are jointly produced for the advertiser.

Agency Commission   The fee charged a client by an agency to select and oversee production work done by printing, recording, film companies or photographers. OR, the traditional 15 percent of a media buy allowed to agencies. For example, if an agency buys $1000 of commercial time, the agency pays the station $150 and bills the client $1000. If the client buys the time directly from the station, the charge is the full $1000.

Allotments   Poster showings consist of unilluminated posters and illuminated posters. The number of outdoor poster panels in a showing is referred to as the market allotment, which will vary by market size.

Alpha or Alphabetical Section or White Pages   Every business and residential telephone customer is entitled to a free listing in the alphabetical section (white pages).

Alphanumeric Keyboard   A keyboard that allows communication with a computer in letters and numbers.

Anchor Listing   A Yellow Pages reference line that directs the consumer to a display ad.

AP   Abbreviation for Associated Press, a news wire service.

Approach   The distance measured along the line of travel from the point where the outdoor advertising structure first becomes visible to the point where copy is no longer readable (having passed out of the line of sight).

Art   All illustration copy used in preparing a job for printing.

Arteries/Arterials   Used in Outdoor: the major streets of a city or town.

Assignment Desk   The people responsible for dispatching camera crews and reporters to cover a news event.

Audience   The number of people, reading, watching, or listening to a particular medium.

Audiotex Services   See Talking Yellow Pages.

Audited or Authenticated   The Traffic Audit Bureau (TAB) independently audits records and circulation data for outdoor posters and bulletins according to established procedures approved by the buyer and seller community.

Authorized Selling Representative An Authorized Selling Representative (ASR) assists national and regional advertisers in placing their Yellow Pages advertising.

Automatic Rebate In co-op, the amount of money agreed upon by manufacturer/vendor and retailer, usually given by credit memo, to retailer's accounts payable. In most cases, proof of media performance is required.

Availability A specific period of commercial time offered for sale by a station or network.

Average Quarter-Hour Share (AQH Share) The AQH persons expressed as a percentage of the total radio listening by the population being measured.

$$\frac{\text{AQH PERSONS TO A STATION}}{\text{AQH PERSONS TO ALL STATIONS} \times 100} = \text{AQH SHARE}$$

Average Quarter-Hour Rating (AQH Rating) The AQH persons expressed as a percentage of the population being measured.

$$\text{AQH PERSONS} - \text{POPULATION} \times 100 = \text{AQH RATING}$$

Average Quarter-Hour Audience (AQH Persons) The average number of persons listening to a particular (radio) station for at least five minutes in a quarter-hour within a specific daypart.

Average Time Spent Listening (TSL) The amount of time the average person listens to radio in the course of the average day or week. QUARTER-HOURS IN TIME PERIOD × AQH PERSONS ÷ CUME PERSONS = TSL

Backlighted Units Outdoor advertising structures which house illumination in a box to throw light through translucent advertising printed on plastic or heavy duty paper for higher visibility, especially at night.

Base Rate The lowest rate for advertising in print or broadcast media. This rate is for run of paper (ROP) or run of station (ROS); that is, media put your advertisement wherever they have space or air time. If you want some control over your advertisement's location or time or you require something special or extra, chances are you will have to pay more than the base rate.

Bicycling A method of sending commercials or programs between systems by mail or messenger.

Billboard An announcement, usually 10 seconds or less, at the beginning or end of a program that identifies the sponsor or advertisers. Also—a structure used for outdoor advertising.

Bird A colloquialism for any communications satellite.

Blanking A white paper border surrounding the poster copy area. It is applied between the poster and the panel molding. Under outdoor industry standards for 30-sheets, it is 6-½" to 11½" at the sides and 5" at the top and bottom.

Bleed An advertisement in which all or part of the graphic material runs to the edges of the page. There is usually a premium charged for a bleed ad.

Bleed Poster The use of blanking papers of the same color as the outdoor poster background, to bring the design area up to the molding.

Bleed Through A production difficulty created when the previous design used on an outdoor structure can be seen through the current message. This can occur because of the kind of paper used, the chemical reaction of certain pigments or because of excessive wetting from heavy rain.

Blind Ad An advertisement wherein the identity of the advertiser is concealed via use of a Box Number.

Blowup A photographic enlargement.

Boards A common term for poster panels and painted bulletins.

Body Type As distinguished from headline or advertising display type. Type commonly used for reading matter.

Bold Listing A unit of advertising in a directory in which the company name is printed in bold, capital letters.

Break A period when a broadcast is interrupted, such as when a commercial plays on the air . . . a commercial break.

Broadband Communications A frequently used synonym for cable television.

System It can describe any technology capable of delivering multiple channels and services.

Bulldog An early newspaper edition for delivery to distant areas.

Bulletins Outdoor bulletins measure 14 × 48 feet. Copy is reproduced by two methods: painting directly on the surface or posting paper with the advertising message preprinted.

Byline A name credit given the writer or reporter of a news or feature story.

Call Letters A broadcast station's name. Usually four letters starting with W, east of the Mississippi and starting with K, west of the Mississippi.

Camera Cue Light A red light on the front of a TV camera indicating it is the one in use.

Camera-Ready Copy which is ready for photography.

Campus Directory A telephone directory distributed to college campuses, geared to meet the needs of students, teachers, administrative staff, and local residents and businesses.

Cars Cable Television Relay Services. The microwave frequency bank used to relay television, FM radio, cablecasting and other signals to terminals for distribution over cable.

CG Character Generator. A device that electronically displays letters and numbers on the television screen.

Charting the Showing The process of scheduling proposed or actual display locations on a market's streets and highways. This process involves specific requests from the buyer that are planned to achieve maximum reach and frequency.

Circulation Circulation (potential viewers) is the foundation for determining the advertising value of outdoor. Outdoor circulation is based on traffic volume.
For newspapers it is the average number of newspaper or magazine copies distributed per issue, including subscriptions and newsstand sales.

Closing Date Also see "Deadline." The final date for contracting to run an advertisement in a newspaper or magazine; or, the final date for submitting material for an ad to appear in a certain issue.

Controlled Circulation For business papers this is usually called "qualified circulation." It is nonpaid. For suburban newspapers it means delivery of nonpaid copies to everyone in a specific area, regardless of whether they are subscribers or not.

Coat Out The process of covering a painted outdoor advertising message with white or grey paint before new copy is painted.

Code of Ethics The Outdoor Advertising Association of America (OAAA) has a voluntary set of principles pledging member plants to operate in the public interest.

Collating Posters Outdoor posters are made up of individual sheets. These sheets are organized or collated in the sequence needed so that the bill poster (the person doing the posting) will poster the advertising message properly.

Commercial Used technically to mean an advertising message broadcast during a program that the advertiser sponsors. Most of what people call commercials are, in broadcast parlance, advertising SPOTS.

Commercial Audience The commercial audience is operationally defined as those people who were physically present in the room with the TV set on at the time the commercial was on.

Commercial Signs Privately owned (usually on-site) advertising structures used on roofs, walls or other outdoor surfaces of business establishments or factories, for the purpose of identification or direction of that particular business.

Concentrating Advertising In this tactic, advertisers use their limited funds to buy a few large print advertisements, rather than many smaller ones; in broadcast they advertise in FLIGHTS. Some advertisers think they get more impact or look bigger this way and that, therefore, concentrating their advertising is more effective than trying to maintain continuity. Advertising may also be concentrated during periods of the year for seasonal products and promotions, such as special sales.

Condensed Type   A narrow or slender type face.

Consumer Directory   A Yellow Pages book that lists businesses and organizations whose products and services are aimed at meeting residential customers' specific needs.

Continuing   A method of scheduling advertising so that audiences have an opportunity to see ads at regular intervals. There are many patterns that can be used, including advertising once a day, once a week, once a month.

Continuous Tone   An image with a wide range of tones which is not made up of halftone dots. The image can be either negative or positive, in black-and-white or in color.

Contrast   Degree of lightness difference between tones; also called detail (as in highlight detail) or tonal separation.

Cooperative Advertising (Co-Op)   Also called Vendor Money. Funding available from manufacturers to either cover or share in the costs of advertising for their mutual benefit.

Copy   Printed text for a print ad, or a script for a radio or television commercial.

Copy Desk/Copy Editors   A table at which copyreaders work, often semicircular in shape. The city editor may sit in the slot at the center. Copy editors correct or edit copy written by reporters (or publicity copy) and write headlines for stories.

Cost Per Point (CPP)   A measure of radio's cost-effectiveness, the cost of delivering one gross rating point

$$\text{COST OF SCHEDULE} \div \text{GROSS IMPRESSIONS (000)} = \text{CPM}$$

Counting Station   A defined point on a street (arterial) where vehicles are recorded to determine outdoor billboard circulation. This method is used not only by the outdoor plant operator but also by federal, state and local traffic departments.

Coupon Advertising   Coupons bound into directories, offering discounts to consumers.

Coverage   A term used to define a medium's potential within either geography or demography. Usually expressed as a percent and is similar to percent reach (audience) or percent penetration (circulation).

   In print media, the number of copies (assumed to be greater than the circulation) physically received by people in the mail, from carriers, at newsstands, and as pass-alongs.

   In broadcast, it's an engineering measurement of how far and where a station's signal can be received. Coverage describes only potential. It doesn't tell how many people actually look into that publication or tune into that station.

In outdoor, the defined parameters of a market; usually refers to a county or counties, and the percent of this universe exposed to outdoor advertising structures purchased.

CPM (Cost Per Thousand) The CPM formula is the oldest means for comparing media rates. For print the cost per 1,000 units of circulation is calculated on the basis of the one-time rate for one black and white page, shown on the left. On the right is the formula for broadcast media:

$$\frac{\text{Rate per page} \times 1000}{\text{circulation}} = \text{CPM} \qquad \frac{\text{Cost of one unit of time} \times 1000}{\substack{\text{Number of households or individuals reached} \\ \text{during a time period or a given program}}}$$

"C" Print A glossy four-color print usually taken from a transparency. Often used as guide artwork for bulletin painters to follow for color and composition of illustrations. Four-color transparencies and prints also are used in other four-color ads but they are not called "C" prints.

Crawl A horizontal moving display of letters and/or numbers across a screen. Vertical crawls are called scrolls.

CU Close up. An announcer's face only, or a small item with a sig (signature/logo) card and price card.

Cue A sound or action noting the start or conclusion of a show. The signal to someone to say or to do something.

Cue Card A card placed out of camera range for someone to read from.

Cume Cumulative, unduplicated audience—the number of people reached over a period, usually a week.

Cume Persons The total number of different people who listen to a station for at least five minutes in a daypart. Also called Unduplicated Audience.

Cut A term used that calls for an instant camera change, from one camera to another.

Cut-In The insertion of a commercial, at the local level, into a network program.

Cut-Outs/Embellishments Letters, figures or mechanical devices that are attached to the face of a bulletin to provide a three-dimensional effect for greater attention value.

Daily Effective Circulation (DEC) Average number of persons exposed per day to a sign or group of signs.

Database A collection of data to support the requirements and requests for information of a specific group of users in performing specific tasks and functions. The difference between data and information can best be illustrated by imagining all the names and telephone numbers from a phone book written on different pieces of paper and thrown into a barrel. The barrel contains a huge amount of data, but unless it is organized (as in a phone book) its value as information is questionable.

Daypart A broadcast day is divided into parts: TV daytime, early fringe, prime access, prime time, late fringe, and late night. RADIO daytime, morning drive, afternoon drive, nighttime, weekends.

Deadline The last possible time for an ad in any format to be received by media to assure it's appearance.

Demographic A specific population characteristic such as age, income, sex, occupation, etc.

Descriptive Extra Line Extra line of copy in a Yellow Pages listing, designed to supply additional information in a larger size type.

Direct Mail Printed matter usually carrying a sales message or announcement designed to elicit a response from a carefully selected consumer or business market.

Display Ad A print ad that ranges in size from a full page, to partial pages or column-width ads measured in column inches. In Yellow Pages directories, display ads range from full pages to fractional pages and offer more information than a listing, plus design flexibility, visual impact and prominence.

Display Period The exposure time during which the individual outdoor advertising message is on display. Posters are normally contracted for monthly exposure; rotating bulletins usually display the same copy for a two to three month period; permanent bulletins' display period varies depending on individual contracts.

Dissolve A slow fade out of one camera as the other camera is slowly brought in. There are slow dissolves and fast dissolves.

Distribution The location of the individual advertising structures within a market, relative to exposure potential.

Dolly A command to move the camera in on the subject or away from it: "dolly in" or "dolly out" or "dolly back." (For side to side camera movement, see "pan.")

Drive Time The early morning and late afternoon/early evening hours when radio has its largest audiences and highest rates.

Dubbing Duplicating an original or master print of a commercial on videotape or audiotape, usually to distribute among television, cable or radio stations. A dub is often called a dupe.

Dummy A diagram or layout of a newspaper page, showing the placement of stories, headlines, pictures and ads.

ECU Extreme Close Up. Calls for filling the screen with the item. Used primarily for small objects such as watches, rings, small cans of food, or the tread design of a tire.

Edit To correct, revise, or rewrite copy to be used by media in any format.

Effective Circulation Potential viewers . . . the audience that has an opportunity to see an outdoor structure.

Effective Frequency The minimum level of frequency—number of exposures—determined to be effective in achieving the goals of an advertising campaign (e.g. awareness, recall, sales, etc.). This level will vary with individual products or services and the marketing objectives of the campaign.

Effective Reach The number of people reached by a schedule at the pre-determined level of effective frequency.

Efficiency The degree of value delivered by an audience relative to its space cost. Usually expressed in cost-per-thousand (CPM).

Eight Sheet A 5′ × 11′ outdoor poster panel generally placed for exposure to pedestrian as well as vehicular traffic. Frequently used in suburban shopping areas as well as point-of-purchase (POP) locales. Usually located in urban areas.

Exclusivity The contractual right to be the sole exhibitor of a program in a particular area during a particular time.

Exposure Represents the opportunity for a message to be seen and read, common to all media.

Extension The area of design made as a cut-out that extends beyond the basic rectangular space of an advertising structure. Added costs are normal practice for the use of extensions.

Face The style of the type, such as bold face or italic, Caslon or Bodoni. The surface of outdoor advertising structures on which the advertising message is posted or painted.

Facing Specifies the direction the outdoor poster may be seen to traffic flow. For example, a south-facing panel can be seen only by north-bound traffic.

Fade One camera is faded out before the other is faded in so that there is a moment of black on the screen.

Feature A distinctive article or story as distinguished from a news story. A feature is an in-depth treatment of a subject without the immediacy of a news story.

Fiber Optics Very thin, pliable tubes of glass or plastic used to carry wide bands of frequencies.

Fiber Optic Display An innovative use of electronic light-transmitting fibers to create changeable copy displays.

Fixed Location (1) A space position that remains constant from issue to issue; (2) A specific position requested by an advertiser.

Flagging A tear in paper used on an outdoor poster panel, causing the paper to hang loose and "flag" in the wind.

Flight An "in and out" broadcast advertising technique that allows advertisers to concentrate their advertising for impact. You simply advertise a lot for a period and then stop. You can rotate your advertisement among stations during the period of intense advertising to increase REACH, especially if you choose stations or programs that appeal to different audiences.

Flights can get you horizontal saturation if the spot is broadcast at the same time each day (thus to the same audience)or vertical saturation if it is broadcast at various times (thus reaching different audiences).

Flighting When commercials are scheduled to run at various times within a broad period rather than continually.

Focus Group A moderated discussion group formulated generally on a demographic basis to determine through panel questioning opinions of products, services or company image.

Font A complete assortment of letters, numbers, punctuation marks, etc. in one size and design.

Foreign Advertising Yellow Pages advertising placed in directories other than the advertiser's primary directory.

Four-Color Black, blue, yellow, and red used together to produce a full-color reproduction and used by almost all publications offering color advertising.

Freelance Artists, writers, photographers, producers, others who contract their services on a job-by-job basis.

Frequency The number of times the same audience—listeners, readers, or viewers—are reached (see or hear a particular advertisement). It is usually expressed as an average (such as 2.5 times or 6.4 times), since some people may see or hear an advertisement only once, others a dozen times.

Frequency in outdoor usually refers to the calendar month since this time period coincides with the standard contract practices.

Frequency Distribution A tabulation separating those reached by a schedule, according to their minimum levels of exposure; 2 or more times, 3 or more times, 4 or more times, etc.

Fringe Time The periods immediately before and after television prime time, 4:30 p.m. to 7:30 p.m. and after 11:00 p.m. until the next prime time period, in all time zones except Central, where they run an hour earlier.

Galley Proof A proof of text copy before being made into pages.

Geodemography A marketing science which combines demography with geography to create life style segmentation systems to define target audiences.

Geographics A reference to data about place—residence or work—including the type of location—urban, suburban, rural—and climate.

Gross Impressions (GIs)   The total number of exposures (not total audience) to a commercial schedule.

AQH PERSONS × NUMBER OF SPOTS = GROSS IMPRESSIONS.

GRPs   Gross Rating Points. Another way of comparing media vehicles and programs. The phrase is used more often for broadcast media, but the term has also been adopted by the outdoor industry.

Calculate this rating by multiplying the rating points (the percent of households, according to surveys, watching or listening to a program or station at a particular time—20 percent of a potential audience equals 20 rating points) by the number of times that program or station is heard or viewed during a given period (usually four weeks). The accuracy, of course, depends on the validity of the survey.

For example, a schedule that delivers 100 GRP's can be comprised of 5 primetime programs, each of which has a 20.0 rating (20.0 added 5 times equals 100 GRP's).

Halftone Printing Process   The most common means of printing pictures with a press. The various tones in a picture are represented by dots of different sizes; the darker the tone, the larger the dot size. The same number of dots per square inch is used throughout the picture, only the dot size is changed. Halftone dots are used in printing both black-and-white and color pictures.

Hand Count   When no official source traffic counts are available and/or obsolete, hand counts may be conducted by the plant operator.

Heading   Also called "In-column heading." Classifications in Yellow Pages directories that identify business groups.

Head-On   An outdoor advertising structure built so that all traffic approaches perpendicular to the face of the structure.

Illuminated   Outdoor advertising structures with electrical equipment installed for illumination of the message at night.

Imprints-Dealer   A strip on an outdoor board imprinted with the name, address and/or phone number of the local dealer handling the product being advertised.

Independent Publisher   A non-utility related company that publishes Yellow Pages directories.

Independents   Individually owned and operated cable television systems, not affiliated with an MSO.

Infomercials   A commercial that supplies information about a product, service or company, rather than strictly a sales message. They may be any length, from minutes to hours.

Insert   An advertisement printed by an advertiser and bound or stuffed loosely into a publication. It may also be a separate piece, usually of heavier stock.

Institutional Network A network operated in conjunction with a cable TV system, designed to satisfy the needs of businesses, schools, or government.

Intensity Outdoor poster showings are sold at different levels of advertising weight determined by the plant operator. The owner determines the most efficient way to buy the market at certain advertising weights. Common GRP showing sizes are #25, #50, #75, and #100. The seller designates what advertising weight is for sale.

Interconnect Connection of two or more cable systems by microwave, fiber, coaxial cable, or satellite, so that advertising or programming may be exchanged, shared or simultaneously viewed.

Italic The style of letters that slant, in distinction from upright, or roman, letters. Used for emphasis within text.

Keying Identification within an advertisement or coupon that permits responses to be tracked to a specific advertisement.

Lead Pronounced "leed." The first few sentences or the first paragraph of a news story, containing a summary or the introduction to the story. A straight news story follows the general newswriting rule of telling who, what, when, where, why, and sometimes how.

Line of Travel A line of traffic moving in one direction.

Lithography A popular printing method for producing large quantities of outdoor posters in full color.

Load Factor The average number of persons riding in each vehicle. The factor has been determined through national research as well as evaluation of government research and reports for highway capitalization.

Local Rate A reduced rate offered to local businesses by media, usually lower than for national advertisers. Local and retail rates may be the same, but sometimes separate and different rates are charged for the advertising retailers, banks and other financial institutions, theaters, and other local businesses.

Location List A list describing the location of all outdoor panels sold and delivered.

Logo Short for logotype. A distinctive design, perhaps a trademark, that is the company's or product's signature. On occasion, called a sig or sig cut.

LS Short for long shot. A wide-angle view that includes the subject, usually with a view around it.

Make Good A print ad or broadcast spot run by media to compensate for one that ran incorrectly.

Makeup The arrangement of stories, headlines, and pictures into columns in preparation for printing.

Mandatory Copy Copy that is required by law to appear in the advertising of certain products. This applies to all print media including outdoor. There are definite specifications as to size, positioning and rotation of such mandatory messages.

Masthead Part of a page printed in every issue of a newspaper or journal, presenting the name, ownership, management, subscription, and advertising rates, usually on the editorial page.

MCU or MS Short for medium close up or medium shot. Usually used interchangeably such as a bust shot of the announcer, then the top of a kitchen range, but not the range controls.

Media Performance A form of co-op which requires specific advertising media use. Must be documented with actual proof (tearsheet, affidavit) backed up by net media invoice. It is, perhaps, the most popular of the co-op plans being offered by vendor manufacturers and distributors. Also, because of requirements, represents the form of co-op most underused throughout the United States.

Medium/Media Terms used to describe magazines, newspapers, radio, Yellow Pages, television, etc., used to convey a news or advertising message to the public. Media is the plural of medium.

Microwave One method of interconnecting a cable system with a series of high frequency receiving antenna transmitters mounted on towers spaced up to 50 miles apart.

Milline Formula To compare the costs of advertising in different newspapers, it is customary to use the cost per line per million circulation, called the milline rate. Use the highest rate charged by each newspaper—not the rate you are contracting for—in the following formula:

$$\frac{\text{Line rate} \times 1,000,000}{\text{circulation}} = \text{milline rate}$$

The reason for multiplying by 1,000,000 is that the larger figures are easier to compare. If the rates you are comparing are quoted in column inches, this rate can be used in the formula instead of the line rate. Just be sure to use the same rate base—line or column-inch—for all the newspapers you are comparing.

Mobile Unit Television broadcast equipment used outside the studio.

Molding (Trim) The frame of wood, metal or plastic which surrounds the face of an outdoor advertising structure poster panel.

Monopole/Unipole Outdoor structures fabricated on a single steel pole or column.

MSO Multiple System Operator. A company that owns and operates more than one cable television system.

Multiple Facing An outdoor advertising location where there are two or more adjacent or stacked posters facing the same direction.

Narrowcasting Delivery of broadcast programming that addresses a specific need or highly focused audience.

Network A linkup of many stations by cable or microwave for simultaneous broadcast on all from a single originating point. The stations may be owned by or affiliated with the network.

Newsprint Paper made mostly from groundwood pulp and small amounts of chemical pulp; used for printing newspapers.

OAAA Outdoor Advertising Association of America.

Official Count The traffic count taken from official sources such as state or city Departments of Transportation.

Offset One of the major printing processes. Most of the process color printing in newspapers is done by offset lithography. Both water and ink are applied to the plate during lithographic printing; the water sticks to the non-image areas of the plate thereby keeping them free of ink. In offset lithography the ink image is first transferred or offset to a rubber-covered cylinder and then from the rubber surface to the paper. The plate never touches the paper.

On the Air The time when a program is being broadcast or recorded. Signified by signs in the studio and outside the studio doors.

On Location Video, still photographs or broadcast programming produced outside of a studio.

Open Rate Also known as base rate, one-time rate, transient, local, or retail. The highest rate charged in a medium, but subject to discounts as the volume of advertising increases. Discounts may be by percentages, but more often are shown as rates for different volume categories.

Outdoor Placement Agencies Companies or agencies which specialize in out-of-home media development, placement and checking/evaluation.

Outside Panel Poster located closest to the edge of the street, where two or more panels are positioned side-by-side.

Over-Printing Printing one color of ink on top of another, such as a black headline on a red tint block. This also is the method by which delicate skin tones, etc., are achieved in process color.

Overlay A paper strip, such as dealer imprint or a price, which is pasted on the face of an existing outdoor poster.

Package Plans, Rates Each broadcast station has its own combinations as inducement to advertisers. Some guarantee, for example, that a certain number of your advertising spots will be broadcast during specific times, yet you will be charged less than a fixed spot rate.

Page Makeup In stripping, assembly of all elements to make up a page. In computerized typesetting, the electronic assembly of page elements to compose a complete page with all elements in place on a video display terminal and on film or plate.

Pagination A sophisticated program which allows the system to be capable of automatic page makeup. Both the layout and makeup functions associated with the production of a newspaper page are done at one station electronically. The technology has reached the level where an entire page can be output at once, with paste-up stripping in halftones. A form of pagination is computer assisted makeup (CAM) where manual composition is still required.

Pan From the word "panorama." It means to move a camera sideways from one item to another using the same camera.

Panel Numbers Outdoor panels are given numbers to aid employees in the painting or posting of the advertising structure. These same numbers serve to pinpoint panels being purchased by a buyer.

Participating Programs Programs owned by stations, an advertiser on them is not identified as a sponsor and shares the program with other advertisers. These programs generally have good audiences and advertising spots on them can be economical buys.

Pasteup Prepared advertising copy and art for reproduction. All elements are in the proper position. Also called a mechanical or camera ready art.

Pay Cable Movies, sports and made-for-cable specials that are available to the cable subscriber for a charge in addition to the basic fee.

Penetration Another term for REACH. The percentage of total homes in a specific area that are reached by a specific medium. If a publication or station gets half a potential audience, it is said to have a penetration of 50 percent.

Ratio of the number of cable or pay-TV subscribers to the total number of households passed by the system.

Permanent Bulletin A painted outdoor display which remains in one location for the entire term of the single advertiser's contract.

Plant All of the outdoor advertising structures in a given city, town or area operated by an outdoor company, or plant operator.

Plant Capacity The total number of posters or bulletins in a plant.

Plant Operator A company or individual who operates and maintains out-of-home advertising structures.

Point Printer's unit of measurement, used principally for designating type sizes. There are 12 points to a pica; approximately 72 points to an inch.

Position The location of an advertisement on a page.

Poster Advertising messages posted on outdoor advertising structures.

Poster (30-Sheet) An outdoor advertisement with copy area measuring 9'7" by 21'7" wide.

Poster Panel An outdoor advertising structure on which 30-sheet posters are displayed.

Posterize A design developed in a manner or style characteristic of pictorial posters. All elements are eliminated except the ones which identify the product.

Posting Date The date on which the outdoor posters of a showing are scheduled for display. Most plants will have several posting dates during the month to even their work load and provide a variety of start dates to coincide with special advertising promotions.

Posting Listing The process of selecting the individual outdoor panels which will comprise a poster showing under contract.

Post-Ride A check of outdoor poster locations with advertising copy in place.

Pounce Pattern The method most frequently used for enlarging art and copy to fill an outdoor painted bulletin size. The design is projected onto large sheets of paper and traced in outline form. The outline is then perforated with an electric needle. The perforated sheets, known as pounce patterns, are held against the painting surface and dusted with charcoal dust, to reproduce the outline of the design on the surface to be painted.

Premium Rate The rate charged for something special or extra. The rate may be for color in print media, preferred positions (such as covers of magazines or pages up front in newspapers and magazines) or anything that requires special handling. The rate may be in addition to a base rate or it may be a separate, higher rate. For example, color may be an additional charge over a base black and white rate or may be charged as a separate and higher rate.

Pre-Pasting A technique for applying paste to the surface of outdoor posters in the plant rather than in the field.

Pre-Ride A check of available outdoor panels to determine specific locations to be included in a specific GRP showing.

Press Conference A meeting called by an organization or an individual to address the questions of the news media.

Press Release A news story submitted to the news media by a company to issue a statement or announce an event.

Press Run Total number of copies printed.

Prime Time When television has its largest audiences and highest advertising rates. In the Eastern, Mountain, and Pacific time zones it is from 7:30 p.m. to 11:00 p.m. In the Central zone it is from 6:30 p.m. to 10:00 p.m.

Professional Rate Newspaper classified advertising rate for regular users (real estate agencies or service firms, for example). It's lower than the transient rate charged occasional users.

Program Rate Quoted by the hour or shorter segment, it is the rate for sponsoring a program.

Proof of Performance Certification that advertising service has been delivered.

Psychographics Identified personality characteristics and attitudes that affect a person's life style and purchasing behavior.

Public Service Copy Copy of a civic or philanthropic nature posted in the interests of community welfare.

Quintile Analysis A set of summary statistical measures, dividing the universe into five ranges for the purpose of determining media exposure.

Rain-Lap Outdoor posters trimmed so that the upper sheets overlap the lower sheets, similar to the way shingles are laid on a roof. This lessens the possibility of flags due to rain seepage between the poster and the panel face.

Rated An advertising structure that has been evaluated for visibility, competition, direction of traffic, type of area and circulation.

Rates Charges for advertising time or space.

Reach Also known as cume, cumulative, unduplicated, or net audience. The number or percentage of people who have been exposed—seen or listened—to a specific publication or broadcasting station, usually measured during a number of issues or broadcasts. It is the net unduplicated audience. Reach is built up by FREQUENCY. Reach can be expressed as a Rating (percentage of the population being measured)

$$\text{PERSONS REACHED} \div \text{POPULATION} = \text{REACH RATING}$$

Reach/Frequency Formulas There are three factors in any reach/frequency formula: 1) Reach, 2) Frequence and 3) GRPs. Their relationship is expressed in these formulas, with any two factors predicting the third:

$$\text{REACH} \times \text{FREQUENCY} = \text{GRPs}$$
$$\text{GRPs} \div \text{FREQUENCY} = \text{REACH}$$
$$\text{GRPs} \div \text{REACH} = \text{FREQUENCY}$$

Example: If 100 GRPs are purchased to reach an audience with an average frequency of 4, the reach will be 25. Reach and frequency are radio's essential planning parameters.

Renewal Paper Extra posters sent to plant operators to replace those that may be damaged during display period. Usually 10–20% of total order.

Reverse Reverse resembles a negative of a picture. What was black becomes white or vice versa. Reverse usually refers to type.

Riding the Showing A physical inspection of the outdoor panels which comprise an advertising buy . . . either pre-buy or post-buy.

ROP Run of paper. The newspaper inserts your ad wherever it decides. Newspaper base rates are quoted ROP.

ROS Run of Stations/Schedule. A broadcast commercial for which a definite time is not specified.

Rotating Bulletin The movement of an advertisers outdoor message from one location to another at stated intervals to achieve more balanced coverage of a market.

Run In transit advertising, a card in every vehicle of the transportation system being used. Rates are quoted as a run or fraction of a run.

San Serif Type A type style without fine cross strokes on the end of the letters. It is often used for display ads, headlines and captions.

Scatter Plan A broadcast media advertising plan in which spots are run during a variety of broadcast programs. It provides diversification of audiences.

Screen Used to simulate various shades of color through use of dots, lines or textured patterns.

Screen-Printing A method of printing for small to moderate quantity runs which employs stencil rather than metal plates.

Sections Removable pieces of an outdoor bulletin, permitting rotation of the unit to another location.

Segmenting (an audience) Aiming a publication or especially broadcast programming (particularly in radio and cable) at a particular part of the population, selected by age, income, buying habits, or other demographic factors. In theory this permits the publication or station to deliver a specific group of highly desired, identifiable prospects to advertisers to help them get the maximum effect for their money by advertising only to an audience segment that can (and desires to) use their types of products or services.

Serif The short cross-lines at the ends of the main strokes of many letters in some type faces.

Setback The distance measured from the line of travel to the center of the outdoor advertising structure.

Shop-at-Home Programs that allow subscribers to view products and/or order them by cable television, including catalogues, shopping shows, etc.

Shopper What shopping guides are called. Consisting almost entirely of ads, they have nonpaid controlled circulation and are distributed in specific geographic areas to give complete coverage. Most are weeklies.

Short Rate What you pay if you fail to fulfill an advertising contract. You advertise less than you planned during the period of the contract and, thus, do not earn the rate you contracted for. You will be billed for the difference between what you have already paid and what you still owe at a higher rate for the advertising you actually ran.

Showing In the outdoor advertising industry this refers to the coverage of a market, not the number of posters. A 100 showing is complete coverage of a market; a 50 showing is half of it, and so on. In some communities 10 posters might be a 100 showing, while in much smaller places one poster could be a 100 showing.

In TRANSIT advertising, the number of cards included in a unit of sale. Size of showing determines the market reach/frequency.

Snipe A line of boldface type, sometimes on a strip at the bottom of an outdoor poster, usually a dealer imprint. National boards sometimes use snipes for local identification.

Spec A prepared "speculative" or "suggested" rough sketch of a layout incorporating copy, illustrations and design, used to promote the prospect's products and services.

Special Features In broadcasting, the news, weather and traffic reports, sports reviews, market summaries, and the like. Sponsoring them can be effective as an advertising technique, since they often have large audiences.

Split Screen A split (television) screen is achieved as a wipe that stops halfway and gives the appearance of two images side by side. It permits simultaneous presentations of two separate situations, as with both sides of a telephone conversation.

Spot Color When two or more colors are used in an ad but never touch each other.

Spot News News of immediate and vital interest.

Spotted Map A map of a market with dots to show the placement of outdoor panels or bulletins for a general or specific buy.

Stacked Panels Outdoor advertising structures with the facings built one above the other. Also called deck panels.

Stock Poster A standard design covering a specific category of business which may be purchased and used by advertisers in that category merely by adding their trade name to the stock poster design.

Straight News Story Also called hard news. A story that deals only with the objective details of an event or occasion.

TAB Traffic Audit Bureau for Media Measurement is the official bureau of circulation verification of the out-of-home advertising industry. It is a nonprofit organization and it audits as an independent third party. TAB establishes the standards for the measurement of the circulation quoted by plants and by doing so assures buyers that they get the exposure they pay for.

Tabloid A newspaper about half standard size, usually 14 inches by 10 to 12 inches wide. Tabloids are unfolded rather than folded in half as is the standard-sized newspaper.

Take Ones Attachments to transit advertising car cards whereby riders may take a coupon or a return request form. The Take Ones are contained in an attached envelope or in pad form. There usually is an additional charge to cover maintenance.

Talking Yellow Pages Talking Yellow Pages are available in some areas and consist of two services. One is a voice information service, where users call a local phone number and enter a four-digit code to access current information on sports, horoscopes, news, soaps, etc. The second service allows consumers to call an exclusive access code found in the company's Yellow Pages ad and to hear the advertiser's recorded message.

Target Audience The desired or intended audience for advertising as determined by the advertiser. Usually defined in terms of specific demographic purchase or ownership characteristics.

Tear Sheet A sheet torn from a publication to provide specific documented performance of ads run in newspapers. An entire full-page tearsheet must be submitted with co-op claims.

Teletext A one-way system of storing and displaying printed and graphic material on the home television screen.

Touch Color When two or more colors are used in a Yellow Pages ad and the colors come together and actually touch.

Trade Publication A publication edited specifically to reach members of a specific occupational group. Such publications contain articles and advertisements directed to the group's interests and make an excellent advertising vehicle when they relate in some way to your market.

Trademark A legally registered symbol or mark that represents a particular brand product or service.

Traffic Audit An authentication of circulation of outdoor media as applied to the advertising structures. Data are collected either by official (government) count or by hand count. In all cases, counts are verified by TAB.

Type Style Variations of the thickness, thinness, slant, etc., for a unit of type.

Universal Directory Advertising Codes Universal Directory Advertising Codes (UDACs) are abbreviations used to represent the various sizes of items available in a directory.

Utility Publisher Company that publishes Yellow Pages directories for a telephone company. This includes the 7 Regional Bell Operating Companies (RBOCs) that were created by the breakup of AT&T.

Vehicle A member of a medium: an individual newspaper, magazine, radio station, etc.

Voice-Over The voice of an actor or announcer who is heard but not seen in the commercial.

Volume Rate Also called a bulk rate, a volume rate may be either for total space or time used or for total dollars expended during a contract period, usually 12 months. As more advertising is done, unit costs decrease, such as per newspaper line, magazine page, or radio and television minutes or seconds.

Wave A single mailing, or a group of interviews conducted at about the same time. A survey may consist of several waves.

Wave Posting Concentration of outdoor poster showings in a succession of areas within the market. Usually coincides with special promotions in each of these areas by the advertiser.

Widow In composition, a single word in a line by itself, ending a paragraph; frowned upon in good typography.

Wipes A camera term used to call for a certain kind of transition, whereby one screen image is wiped off camera by the next one, either vertically or horizontally.

Zapping The changing of television channels by the viewer during commercial breaks either to find other programming or to avoid commercials, often resulting in an erosion in commercial ratings.

Zoned Edition An edition of a city newspaper for a specific geographic area, which may be within the city or in a group of suburban communities. It can be purchased for less than full-run dates. A zone edition is for both news and advertising. It may consist of localized pages, a separate section, or a tabloid insert. It may be published every day or only on certain days, but almost always on Sunday. Big city newspapers often use zone editions to meet competition from suburban newspapers both for readers and advertisers.

Many of the definitions are reproduced with permission from information supplied by the American Association of Newspapers, The Institute of Outdoor Advertising ("Outdoor 101"), National Cable Television Association ("A Cable Television Primer"), Radio Advertising Bureau ("1992 Radio Marketing Guide and Fact Book for Advertisers"), the Small Business Administration, and the Yellow Pages Publishers Association ("Yellow Pages Industry Facts Booklet).

Index